THE
PRACTICE
of
STILLNESS

THE

PRACTICE

of

STILLNESS

MINDFUL LIVING
for LATTER-DAY SAINTS

JACOB Z. HESS WITH CARRIE L. SKARDA

DESERET
BOOK

Image Credits:
Pages xii–1, 2, 10, 12, 14, 16, 20–21, 24, 26, 30, 32, 34, 36, 38, 44, 54, 58, 60, 62, 66, 76, 84, 92, 94, 96, 98, 100, 104, 106, 108, 110, 112, 116, 118, 122, 124, 126: Liliia/Adobe Stock; page 4: Gala_Didebashvili/Adobe Stock; pages 6, 8, 18, 64, 74, 90–91, 102: Aleksandr Matveev/Adobe Stock; page 22: mojie/Adobe Stock; pages 28, 46: shurkin_son/Adobe Stock; page 40: Ron Dale/Adobe Stock; page 42: Ghen/Adobe Stock; page 48: songglod/Adobe Stock; page 50: lukulo/Adobe Stock; pages 52, 56–57: reconceptus/Adobe Stock; pages 68, 120: madiwaso/Adobe Stock; page 70: ozzichka/Adobe Stock; page 72: Silmairel/Adobe Stock; page 78: helgafo/Adobe Stock; page 80: Artnizu/Adobe Stock; page 82: keystoker/Adobe Stock; page 86: JMattsonJohnson/Adobe Stock; page 88: fledermausstudio/Adobe Stock; page 114: pattozher/Adobe Stock; background: Alex/Adobe Stock

© 2024 Jacob Z. Hess and Carrie L. Skarda

Visit us at deseretbook.com

Library of Congress Cataloging-in-Publication Data

(CIP data on file)
ISBN 978-1-63993-358-7

Printed in China
RR Donnelley, Dongguan, China

10 9 8 7 6 5 4 3 2 1

CONTENTS

INTRODUCTION

In a world with so much going on, why would anyone want to spend more time in stillness and silence?

Because that's what Jesus did. The New Testament records nine different times the Lord retreated to find greater stillness—a habit that Luke states he did "often" (Luke 5:16, NKJV).

Even so, many Christians still assume that deeper stillness and silence must be sought far away from their own tradition. Over the last decade, many believers have become interested in what it could mean to more deeply connect with stillness practices in their own heritage of faith. Channeling Nephi, Latter-day Saints might say, "If the Lamb of God, he being holy, should have need to be still and alone with God, O then, how much more need have we to experience this ourselves!" (see 2 Nephi 31:5).

This is more challenging than it looks. That's because fast-paced schedules have a kind of momentum that can drag us along and rush even that which matters most. Gospel living itself can start to feel like yet more tasks to "get done" in an efficient manner: "Finishing a prayer" . . . "Getting a chapter read" . . . "Doing a visit" . . . "Doing a temple session" . . . doing, doing, doing.

But make no mistake: the possibilities for mindfulness, stillness, and contemplation are everywhere in The Church of Jesus Christ. This devotional journal acts as a guided tour to the abundance of Latter-day Saint faith practices that offer regular chances to pause, turn toward a loving God, and receive His tender comfort and guidance.

Elder David A. Bednar taught in April 2024 about a "higher and holier dimension of stillness" that "entails much more than simply not talking or not moving." For those seeking to live as "covenant people of the Lord," the apostle repeatedly points toward something this "spiritual stillness of the soul" can make available: namely, a clearer awareness of our relationship to God as our cherished Father and Jesus Christ as our one Savior.[1]

These sixty entries can be followed consecutively or in whatever order you feel drawn to first. Each one begins with a brief exploration of a mindful approach to that aspect of gospel living, followed by some questions to spark personal reflection about your own life. We close each entry with a focused, practical invitation that will encourage you to lay aside the book and try one small experiment to deepen your own experience with contemplative Christianity.

Whether you are single or married, a long-time member or a recent convert, or someone looking in from the outside with curiosity, we hope this practical guide will help you get a deeper sense of just how many opportunities there are in the life of a Latter-day Saint to stop, be still, and seek to know the living God for ourselves.

MINDFULNESS OF THE INTERNAL WORLD

GROUNDING IN THE
BREATH OF LIFE

> "When Jesus asks you and me to 'repent,' He is
> inviting us to change our mind, our knowledge,
> our spirit—even the way we breathe."
> RUSSELL M. NELSON[1]

The "breath of life" (Genesis 2:7) is a gift which God "giveth to all" (Acts 17:25). Yet breathing is something many of us take for granted and pay little attention to over the course of a day.

With the next breath you take, see what it's like to experience it as a gift from the One who is also "preserving you from day to day, by lending you breath, that ye may live and move and do according to your own will, and even supporting you from one moment to another" (Mosiah 2:21).

PONDER. Many feel a greater calm or peace by bringing attention to the physical sensations of breathing—in the nostrils, chest, belly, etc. What is it like for you when you bring attention to your breath? If you feel some discomfort from doing so, why do you think that is? Are you willing to make this awareness of breath something you practice now and then and see how your experience changes over time?

_____

_____

_____

_____

_____

PRACTICE. Next time you pray, first spend a few minutes resting your attention on the rise and fall of breathing. When your mind wanders off, gently bring it back to the sensations, emotions, or words as an anchor. Remember, you are not *thinking* about the breath here—instead, do your best to *directly experience* the breathing.

Note that for some abuse survivors, focusing on the breath can bring up anxiety or discomfort. Instead, consider keeping your eyes open and having a soft gaze on a chosen point of focus, while slowly repeating a calming word.

SYNCHRONIZING
THE MIND
AND BODY

"Have you ever contemplated the wonders of yourself, the eyes with which you see, the ears with which you hear, the voice with which you speak? . . . What a remarkable thing you are."

GORDON B. HINCKLEY[2]

It's common for many of us in today's digital world to "live in our heads." The hamster wheel of repeated thoughts can be exhausting, especially if we don't know how to step away from what scientists call "rumination," a kind of negative mental loop that can spiral and drag us down.

This is why practices that help us reconnect with the body can be helpful—drawing our minds, bodies, and spirits back into the unity they were created to enjoy. It's this union which also constitutes life itself—with a "fulness of joy" dependent on our bodies and spirits being "inseparably connected" (Doctrine and Covenants 93:33).

PONDER. What signs help you see that you're disconnected from your body and living in your head? Have you ever been able to step away from rumination by actively engaging in something physical? If not, would you be willing to try?

_____

_____

_____

_____

_____

_____

_____

PRACTICE. Take a few minutes to let your attention rest on the different sensations throughout your body, either first thing in the morning or last thing at night. Start from the top of your head and go down to the bottom of your feet, taking time to notice the range of sensations—from the texture of the fabric underneath you to the temperature of the air around you, as well as anything else you notice throughout the body. This can be done when you're lying down or when you are moving in a yoga practice, which can help synchronize the body and mind.

TAPPING INTO THE CLEANSING POWER OF FASTING

> "Is not this the fast that I have chosen?
> to loose the bands of wickedness, to undo
> the heavy burdens, and to let the oppressed
> go free, and that ye break every yoke?"
>
> ISAIAH 58:6

It's hard for many to imagine fasting as a practice of light or joy instead of a source of headaches, fatigue, and irritability. Even Jesus seems well aware of how natural it is to experience a "sad countenance" in times without food (Matthew 6:16). Yet the same Lord reassures us this challenging practice can lead to our joy being "full"—even to the point of equating "fasting and prayer" with "rejoicing and prayer" (Doctrine and Covenants 59:13–14).

Like deep cleaning a room, fasting can help clear out our bodies to make space to receive greater light and power from God. The temporary emptiness also reminds us of our reliance on God and each other for our daily bread—representing a kind of prayer offered with our entire bodies.

PONDER. What emotions did you experience the last time you fasted? If you avoid fasting because of the discomfort it can evoke, what would it be like to hold those challenging feelings in compassionate awareness—allowing this to be a chance to practice equanimity and nonreaction in the face of unpleasant sensations?

_____

_____

_____

_____

_____

PRACTICE. Before your next fast, set the stage for a new experience by vocalizing in prayer your hopes for the day. Allow the various sensations, feelings, and thoughts of your fast to be there, with a gentle and welcoming attitude for all of them. When discomfort arises, observe it without getting too caught up in it. When sweetness, peace, or joy arise, notice them with gratitude.

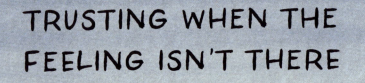

TRUSTING WHEN THE
FEELING ISN'T THERE

> *"Because thou hast seen me, thou hast believed:*
> *blessed are they that have not seen,*
> *and yet have believed."*
>
> JOHN 20:29

It can be confusing to hear another share about feeling God's love, joy, or peace when we don't feel the same. Some might ask, "Why not me?" Just as not seeing the Lord necessitates greater faith, struggling to feel the joy, peace, and love of His presence also asks us to show more trust in Him.

Knowing this can help us appreciate the diversity of experiences and gifts in the body of Christ.

Take heart as well in knowing that your capacity to feel can grow and expand in this life, with all who trust God one day sure to experience joy, peace, and love that "eye hath not seen, nor ear heard, neither have entered into the heart of man" (1 Corinthians 2:9).

PONDER. How much capacity would you say you have right now to feel peace, joy, and love in your day-to-day relationships with friends and family—and how does that current sensitivity level influence your ability to feel close and connect with God? Have you ever felt challenged by hearing stories from others who perhaps experience emotions more intensely than you do?

_____

_____

_____

_____

PRACTICE. Make a short inventory of past and present influences on your capacity to experience emotion, ordering them based on what you believe to be most impactful. Next, appreciating that your capacity to feel emotion is evolving and developing, lay out some details of a plan that will help deepen your emotional sensitivity to peace, joy, and love in the months and years ahead. This plan could include adjustments to how you manage stress and care for your health, or a new resolve to work through past trauma. Listen for nudges from the Spirit as to what more you can do to further awaken your capacity to experience feelings at a deeper level.

FOLLOWING
THE PEACE

> "Thou wilt keep him in perfect peace,
> whose mind is stayed on thee."
>
> ISAIAH 26:3

When we grapple with competing priorities and possible choices, it's reassuring to remember how much intimacy the Lord invites in our day-to-day lives. "Look unto me in every thought; doubt not, fear not," said the Lord (Doctrine and Covenants 6:36), with Alma encouraging his son to "counsel with the Lord in all thy doings" (Alma 37:37).

Before you consider the logic, reasons, or feelings regarding a course of action, take a moment to get grounded in the peace that the Lord offers. From this place, what do you notice about the options in front of you? See if the peace is pointing in one direction or another. While it's possible to feel interested or even passionate about the wrong course of action, peace (or lack of peace)—deep in our gut—is a sign we can trust.

PONDER. What does the sensation of peace feel like in your body? How can you tell when your mind is in a peaceful state? Have you ever struggled to feel peace about something you otherwise felt excited to pursue?

_____
_____
_____
_____
_____
_____
_____
_____

PRACTICE. Consider a major question or decision facing you in the near future. Before grappling with the options, take some time to settle into a state of peacefulness in body and mind. From this place, turn your attention toward one potential direction and then another, comparing the sense of ease and harmony within you. Is there a particular direction you feel the peace pointing you now? If there is still no clarity, return your attention to the peace itself. Maintaining this focus, notice if new questions, options, or guidance you hadn't considered before emerge.

PLACING YOUR HEART
IN GOD'S HANDS

> *"They . . . did wax stronger and stronger in their
> humility, and firmer and firmer in the faith of Christ,
> unto the filling their souls with joy and consolation,
> yea, even to the purifying and the sanctification of
> their hearts, which sanctification cometh because
> of their yielding their hearts unto God."*
>
> HELAMAN 3:35

It's normal for people to pray in hopes the divine will align with their desires. But throughout scripture, we see beautiful examples of prayer focused on aligning personal hopes with God's wishes, rather than the other way around.

Inevitably, this can involve a "wrestle" before God as we work to bring our desires in harmony with divinity (Enos 1:2). At a time when words like *obedience* and *submission* can invoke suspicion in some, that hopefully changes when the One inviting our yielding is perfectly loving and wise. In that case, the act of yielding to God is empowering—even if it feels uncomfortable or impossible in the moment.

PONDER. Is there something in your life right now that feels right—what God wants—but that you have been resisting? What would it be like to bring that difference into an open conversation with a loving Father? In what ways do your prayers generally reflect an affirmation and assertion of your own will, rather than a pursuit of higher desires and dreams?

_____

_____

_____

_____

PRACTICE. If you're unsure what to speak in prayer, remember Paul's encouragement that the Spirit can show us what to say (see Romans 8:26). Listen for that guidance in your next prayer and "labor for an inward stillness," where your own thoughts and emotions cease to dominate, and as one writer says, "God alone speaks in us, and we wait in singleness of heart, that we may know His will, and in the silence of our spirits that we may do His will, and do that only."[3]

OBSERVING AGITATION
FROM A PLACE OF PEACE

"I will not leave you comfortless: I will come to you."

JOHN 14:18

When anxiety and other distress arise, it's understandable that we seek out anything to make our discomfort go away—including whatever relief "the world giveth" (John 14:27). Yet many still long for the deeper comfort Jesus promised to His followers: "Learn of me, and listen to my words; walk in the meekness of my Spirit, and you shall have peace in me" (Doctrine and Covenants 19:23).

Rather than trying to resist, fight, and control your emotional weather patterns, you can learn to make space around inner turbulence and observe it from a deeper place of spiritual calm. However impossible that may seem, this is a learnable skill that can be practiced by you too.[4]

PONDER. When agitation and fear arise, do you ever notice yourself getting anxious about your anxiety? However understandable that is, in what ways might this kind of tense reaction keep anxiety around longer? Can you feel—or at least imagine—what it would be like to experience this same feeling of anxiety from a place of deep and profound calm, like you're watching it from the other side of a plexiglass window?

_____

_____

_____

_____

_____

PRACTICE. Next time a flare-up of anxiety comes, experiment with making gentle space for it and cradling the feeling tenderly, like you would a crying, distraught baby. Instead of resisting, see what it's like to allow your feelings to be exactly as you find them—watching, waiting, and resting in your awareness of anxiety, which is not anxious. From that place, you have choices in how to respond. Is this discomfort signaling anything meaningful and raising something to your attention? Do you need to make an adjustment of some kind? Is there something you feel prompted to explore or share about this feeling in prayer?

NAVIGATING INNER NOISE

> "When they heard this voice, [they] beheld that it
> was not a voice of thunder, neither was it a voice of a
> great tumultuous noise, but behold, it was a still voice
> of perfect mildness, as if it had been a whisper."
>
> HELAMAN 5:30

Some mistakenly assume the goal of mindfulness is to enter a state of perpetual internal calm, rather than to be compassionately present to *whatever* arises in the field of awareness. Some become disheartened or confused when quieting the external world at times unveils the noisiness of the internal one.

This noise can include harsh internal voices that aren't as noticeable until we become still. It can be easy to react to these negative internal voices by shrugging in shameful agreement, trying to drown them out, or even arguing with them.

Elijah models an inspired alternative as he sits observantly through noise and distraction, recognizing: "The Lord was not in the wind: and after the wind an earthquake; but the Lord was not in the earthquake: And after the earthquake a fire; but the Lord was not in the fire." Finally, after the fire, he was able to welcome "a still small voice" (1 Kings 19:11–12).

PONDER. What could it mean in your own life to observe occasions of tumultuous "mind weather" with the same nonreactive calm as Elijah? How can observing negative thoughts and voices, without judging or arguing with them, help you better hear the voice of the Lord and the wisdom of your own spirit?

_____

_____

_____

_____

PRACTICE. Like Elijah, do your best to avoid being reactive to the increase of noise that may initially present itself as you pay more attention to your inner world. Observe the changing thoughts, feelings, and sensations inside much like you would look upon shifting weather patterns overhead. Instead of tensing up, tune in to the quiet wisdom that often reveals itself in small, more subtle ways.

NOT BELIEVING
EVERYTHING
YOU THINK

> "Blessed be the name of my God, for his Spirit
> hath not altogether withdrawn from me, or else
> where is thy glory, for it is darkness unto me?
> And I can judge between thee and God."

MOSES 1:15

Everyone can have thoughts or feelings that seem strange, dark, and troubling. Rather than embracing everything that comes up inside as "reality" or "who we are," it's helpful to approach mental and emotional content with gentle curiosity, asking ourselves: Which of these thoughts and feelings are inspired reflections of who I really am and want to be—and which are not?

Gentleness can lead troubling thoughts and feelings to have less hold over us than trying to resist and push them away. As we learn to discern what is aligned with God's will for our future—and what is not—we can make wise choices that bring greater happiness and peace. The Lord can help each of us discern which parts of our experience we should embrace and which we should let go of and allow to heal.

PONDER. Are you believing any thoughts that would be wise to scrutinize further? Are there feelings coming up that God might be glad for you to observe and explore with His help? When you notice thoughts, feelings, or sensations that seem at odds with your highest values, what would it be like to approach them with compassion and curiosity, rather than immediately fighting them or embracing them?

_____

_____

_____

_____

PRACTICE. When your mind generates thoughts that don't benefit you or rehashes outgrown stories of who you used to be, consider gently redirecting your mind with the prompt, "No, remember, we're not following that old story anymore." You can also imagine troubling thoughts or feelings like a river passing by, letting them drift by as you sit on the bank, watching them calmly. Try these gentle approaches not in an effort to chase away old mental or emotional content, but to ground yourself in truer, present realities.

MINDFULNESS
WITH GOD

SPENDING TIME
ALONE WITH GOD

> *"I retired to the woods . . . on the morning of a beautiful, clear day. . . . Having looked around me, and finding myself alone, I kneeled down and began to offer up the desires of my heart to God."*
>
> JOSEPH SMITH—HISTORY 1:14–15

As simple as heartfelt prayer looks on the surface, there's usually a lot more going on. Even after seeking out a quiet place of solitude, Joseph had to work through some intense opposition designed to thwart this personal communion.

That young prophet is not the only one whose chance to communicate and connect with God has been threatened by surprising resistance. There will be turbulence we each undoubtedly have to navigate to arrive at our own rich interaction with God. Instead of delaying prayer until such obstacles are overcome, consider bringing those hurdles directly to the Father in prayer.

PONDER. How often do you have a chance to spend time alone with God? When you try, what internal or surrounding resistance do you sometimes face? How can you respond well to that kind of turbulence when it comes up?

_____

_____

_____

_____

_____

_____

_____

_____

PRACTICE. Next time you have an opportunity to be alone with God, try bringing your attention to your thoughts and feelings first—pausing to give yourself time to notice what's happening in your mind and heart. When you feel ready, direct your attention toward God, searching for the words to offer. Take time to listen to whatever impressions, feelings, and thoughts arise during this sacred time of communion.

STILL ENOUGH TO
HEAR HIS VOICE

> "As well might man stretch forth his puny arm
> to stop the Missouri river in its decreed course,
> or to turn it up stream, as to hinder the Almighty
> from pouring down knowledge from heaven upon
> the heads of the Latter-day Saints."

DOCTRINE AND COVENANTS 121:33

Discerning the difference between our own thoughts and the voice of God is something we can get better at. Joseph Smith taught that we could "grow into" the capacity for revelation and encouraged the Saints to learn to "notice the first intimation" of the Spirit's arrival with "pure intelligence flowing" into them and perhaps "sudden strokes of ideas."[1]

Pay attention to the range of physical sensations, feelings, and thoughts that could be the Spirit uniquely manifesting Himself to you. His voice might stretch and challenge us. But even then, a tangible peace can often accompany the yielding of our minds and hearts to that guidance.

PONDER. When was the last time you felt or heard God's voice in your heart or mind? What are the ways you have been able to recognize His voice in the past? And how might you better identify and listen to it in the days ahead?

_____
_____
_____
_____
_____
_____

PRACTICE. This week, try living the way Alma encouraged, letting "all thy doings be unto the Lord, and whithersoever thou goest let it be in the Lord; yea, let all thy thoughts be directed unto the Lord; yea, let the affections of thy heart be placed upon the Lord forever" (Alma 37:36). Consider each feeling, thought, and activity as another chance for intimacy with the Lord. We really don't have to do this all alone!

TEACHING YOURSELF
TO READ AGAIN

> "My soul delighteth in the things of the Lord;
> and my heart pondereth continually upon the
> things which I have seen and heard."

> 2 NEPHI 4:16

It's impossible to ponder and delight in something that you struggle to give sustained attention. And amidst today's endless digital distractions, reading anything of substance has become increasingly difficult for many. The mental discipline of focusing—and refocusing—on the words of a single page has become necessary for many to relearn.

In this way, we can rediscover what "feasting upon the word of Christ" (2 Nephi 31:20) truly means—something the young Nephi may have learned from the prophet of his youth, Jeremiah, who wrote, "Thy words were found, and I did eat them; and thy word was unto me the joy and rejoicing of mine heart" (Jeremiah 15:16).

PONDER. What conditions would help you settle and prepare internally for a meaningful reading experience? What would it really take to experience your time with the words of God like a true feast?

_____
_____
_____
_____
_____
_____
_____
_____
_____
_____

PRACTICE. Take a few minutes to prepare mentally and emotionally before partaking of the words of Christ. As you begin reading, notice any thoughts, emotions, and sensations in the body. Experiment with taking just one verse, word, or sentence, and letting that morsel be relished or savored for a moment before moving on. If and when you notice your mind wander, get curious about where it has gone and gently bring it back—unless, that is, you find some inspiration in its departure.

SABBATH AS
RESTFUL RETREAT

> *"The sabbath was made for man,
> and not man for the sabbath."*
>
> MARK 2:27

While even short periods of stillness can be emotionally beneficial, longer periods of quiet can be uniquely impactful. This is why meditators often seek out extended retreats that can last for days.

Christians have an opportunity for deeper retreat every weekend. "Keeping the Sabbath day holy is a refuge from the storms of this life," taught Elder Quentin L. Cook.[2] Instead of just a day, consider this a sacred practice—the practice of Sabbath, where we come together to lay aside the hurried rush of normal life, and take up an entire day for greater stillness, connection, and communion.

PONDER. When was the last time you found deeper rest on the Sabbath—something more than just an afternoon nap, where your heart came away feeling restored and replenished? What specific adjustments to the day's design would create more opportunities for mental rest, emotional space, and spiritual communion?

_____

_____

_____

_____

_____

_____

_____

_____

PRACTICE. As your next Sunday approaches, try approaching the day like you would a genuine retreat. Similar to the "spa menus" at luxurious resorts where you pre-select various rejuvenating activities, make a list or brainstorm with others a custom-designed day that would make your Sabbath retreat more of a "delight" (Isaiah 58:13). That could include going on a walk, dropping by someone who needs a visit, reading and talking with loved ones, singing together, or escaping to a cozy spot in your home to read scriptures, pray, or journal.

THE RENEWAL OF SACRAMENT

> "Meditation is one of the . . . most sacred doors through which we pass into the presence of the Lord. . . . The sacrament is one of the best opportunities we have for such meditation."
>
> PRESIDENT DAVID O. McKAY[3]

Anything we repeat often tends to fall into the background—becoming part of our lives, but not an object of conscious thought. With intention, however, we can turn a repeated action into a poignant celebration, much like we do for many holidays.

The sacrament has the potential of becoming a sweet commemoration in our life each week, as we are intentional beforehand and take the opportunity to kneel before God in preparation. Whatever challenges, struggles, and regrets we may feel, this is a moment we can literally become new, again and again.

PONDER. When was the last time you felt renewed and fresh inside spiritually? If it's been a while, what would it take to prepare yourself in the weeks ahead to receive that sacramental blessing of rebirth again and again?

_____

_____

_____

_____

_____

_____

_____

_____

_____

PRACTICE. Looking ahead to your next opportunity to take the sacrament, take conscious steps to prepare yourself by speaking with the Lord about anything weighing on your heart and mind. If you feel unsure or stuck, consider connecting with your bishop, who has keys to help you feel and see what the Lord wants. Do whatever it takes to experience that newness of mind and heart once again.

LIFTING HEARTS
TOGETHER TO GOD

"I did look unto my God, and I did praise him all the day long; and I did not murmur against the Lord because of mine afflictions."

1 NEPHI 18:16

The act of lifting our heart to God in praise and worship can shift the energy inside us more quickly than almost anything: "Praise to the Lord! Oh, let all that is in me adore Him!"[4]

Our many hymns, prayers, ordinances, and talks are more than just words or actions—representing opportunities to commune with God and have our souls nurtured and restored. Yet there are moments for all of us when joining together with others for worship stretches us emotionally. Instead of avoiding church or judging yourself harshly for not having a better experience, consider approaching your current experience with greater gentleness and curiosity. This allows learning and growth to unfold that would be lost if you simply checked out.

PONDER. When was the last time you felt the Spirit during a worship service? What adjustments to your own worship experience could further open your heart and mind to be more receptive to hearing Him?

_____

_____

_____

_____

_____

_____

PRACTICE. Do you notice your mind wandering at church? Instead of treating that like a problem, consider it a normal part of the practice of mindful worship. Notice where the mind has gone, then gently and firmly bring it back: to the words of the speaker, to the sound of the music, and to the emblem of the sacrament in your hand. Listen for nuggets of inspiration and consolation along the way. As you work with the wandering mind, trust that your stillness, focus, and communion will deepen over time.

MAKING CONFERENCE
A RETREAT

> *"Whether by mine own voice or by the voice of my servants, it is the same."*
> DOCTRINE AND COVENANTS 1:38

So many weary hearts yearn for some kind of relief or replenishment. In modern society, that typically means anticipating an upcoming holiday or planning a special vacation escape. Great effort can go into designing getaways that maximize refreshment and enjoyment.

Much like every community has special holidays, Latter-day Saints look forward to general conference weekend. With a little more advance thought, this can become a weekend retreat different from any other. Rather than viewing these days as simply more meetings, the experience of *conferencing* can be a rich practice in itself—setting aside space and time to gather in a consecrated state of mind and heart.

PONDER. What would it take to experience the entire weekend of general conference as a special extended retreat? What kinds of adjustments would you need to make in your life, schedule, and home for that to happen?

_____

_____

_____

_____

_____

_____

_____

_____

PRACTICE. On an evening before conference weekend arrives, plan a "general conference pep rally" that gathers family or friends for an hour to get excited about what's coming. Create some specific boundaries around your time that weekend to allow for more space than usual—even if it requires some special arrangements with family and work obligations. Notice the difference it makes in your internal experience of the conference to create the mental and emotional space you need to receive what is being offered.

THE TEMPLE AS SANCTUARY

"Enter this door as if the floor within were gold;
And every wall of jewels all of wealth untold;
As if a choir in robes of fire were singing here;
Nor shout nor rush but hush . . . for God is here."

FROM *WORDS OF LIFE*[5]

Elder Dieter F. Uchtdorf has called temples "sacred spaces where one can feel especially close to heaven and rejoice in the influence of the Holy Ghost."[6] Yet even the temple can be approached in our lives as another task to get done when we focus on *doing* a session . . . *doing* a name . . . *doing* a baptism.

What if our experience in the temple could become a welcome opportunity to *get away* from all the hyper-efficiency and experience what some cultures call "non-doing"[7]—retreating to a sanctuary of stillness where we can allow our minds to rest and our hearts to be in His presence?

PONDER. What feelings or sensations come up for you as you enter the temple and participate in its ordinances? Since the temple is a rich and textured experience designed to teach us over a lifetime, some elements will likely not be immediately understood. What would it be like to show self-compassion as you reflect on the full range of your experiences there and be okay sitting with mystery and not-knowing?

_____

_____

_____

PRACTICE. On the way to the temple for your next visit, consider turning off your phone and radio, seeing how it feels to drive in silence. Once you have a chance to sit inside the temple, take a moment to settle into the present moment by tuning into the body—feeling your feet on the floor, the chair beneath you, and your hands in your lap.

When your mind wanders during an ordinance, notice where it's gone and gently redirect your attention back to the instruction, the image, the physical sensation of sitting—or even the rising and falling of the breath itself. There are times, of course, when the wandering may be inspired—in which case, allow your attention to follow wherever you're being led until you receive what God has for you to see, feel, or hear.

SAVORING

SACRED

PROMISES

> *"Lift up thy heart and rejoice, and cleave unto the covenants which thou hast made."*
>
> DOCTRINE AND COVENANTS 25:13

Day-to-day life for many of us can revolve around our own thoughts and feelings, as if we are following a teaching to "live by every thought that proceeds out of your head." But as Jesus affirmed in his ministry, true believers are to live not by their own bread or feelings or thoughts, but "by every word that proceedeth out of the mouth of God" (Matthew 4:4).

This profound shift in perspective is scaffolded in sacred promises between Saints and their God: "I will take you as my people, and I will be your God" (Exodus 6:7, NRSV). Among other things, this means we are "not [our] own" (1 Corinthians 6:19) *or* on our own, providing an anchor outside of the swirl of our evolving experience. As one man going through heavy trials remarked, "Some days I do the right thing because I feel it—and other days I do it because I promised."

PONDER. Would you say you have learned to "cleave unto" your covenants, making them the hinge-point of the rest of your life? Imagine holding in one hand a question or difficulty you're facing right now and covenants you have made with God in the other. What do you experience as you sit with both?

_____

_____

_____

_____

_____

PRACTICE. While the moment of making a covenant is special for the newness of life it signals, that new life can take some practice. For each of us, there are times we drift from sacred promises in our mind, heart, and lifestyle. This can include a thought or feeling contrary to His will or the formation of a habit that is leading us further from the covenant path. When noticing such drift, appreciate your covenants as anchor points to which you can return over and over, again and again. Each time you do so, you deepen your attachment to God, reduce the drifting distance, and receive more and more the special kind of love and peace President Russell M. Nelson has taught the Lord offers us on the covenant path.[8]

FINDING REST
IN THE LORD

"When thou liest down at night lie down unto the Lord, that he may watch over you in your sleep."

ALMA 37:37

Although there are many causes of poor sleep, we can all take steps to improve our rest. For instance, the Lord has counseled, "Retire to thy bed early, that ye may not be weary," a shift that can require surprising amounts of practice, persistence, and patience (Doctrine and Covenants 88:124).

Living in a world that prioritizes stimulation and being busy, we can easily miss or misinterpret the subtle signals from our bodies and minds that we need rest. Consider consecrating your nights unto the Lord—placing them in His hands as an important part of your discipleship. This can set the stage for similar emotional reprieve in the day that follows, allowing you to find more of that "perfect peace" offered to those whose minds are "stayed on" and sustained by Him (Isaiah 26:3).

PONDER. Given the demands on you at this phase of your life, what types of rest are accessible and genuinely replenishing to you? What would it be like to consciously surrender your fatigue and burdens to God and ask Him to watch over your daily periods of rest?

_____
_____
_____
_____
_____
_____
_____
_____

PRACTICE. Instead of carrying the weight of the world on your own, make it a practice to speak openly to your Father in prayer, with the Lord by your side, and the Holy Spirit guiding your words and feelings (see Doctrine & Covenants 84:88). Regularly place your burdens on Them as you seek a greater sense of peace and comfort. If it's helpful, you may want to write down the feelings and expressions you feel prompted to share, and whatever you experience in response.

STARTING THE DAY
WITH THE LORD

"And in the morning, rising up a great while before day, he went out, and departed into a solitary place, and there prayed."

MARK 1:35

While mornings can be a difficult time for many to feel connected with God, there are ways to reclaim the power of our day's beginning. The Lord invites us, "Arise early, that your bodies and your minds may be invigorated" (Doctrine and Covenants 88:124).

The challenge of mornings goes well beyond mere physical fatigue. "The very moment you wake up each morning," C. S. Lewis taught, is where "the real problem of the Christian life comes," when "all your wishes and hopes for the day rush at you like wild animals. And the first job each morning consists simply in shoving them all back; in listening to that other voice, taking that other point of view, letting that other larger, stronger, quieter life come flowing in. And so on, all day."[9]

PONDER. What are mornings like for you? Are there adjustments you can make—physically, nutritionally, or schedule-wise—to tap into the power of mornings more regularly?

_____

_____

_____

_____

_____

_____

_____

_____

PRACTICE. To make your mornings more meaningful, carve out some consistent time when you can be alone with God—even if you have to push back on pressing demands. In that space, plan for a genuinely sweet time of sharing, exploring, and learning—letting "the affections of [your] heart be placed upon the Lord," much like you would spend good time with anyone else you love. As part of this, make time to worship, praise, and ponder what has been done for you and what can yet come to pass, "letting [your] heart be full of thanks unto God" (Alma 37:36–37).

LIVING WITH CHILDLIKE
WONDER AND CURIOSITY

> *"Oh, there is so much more that your*
> *Father in Heaven wants you to know."*
> PRESIDENT RUSSELL M. NELSON[10]

In painting a mental picture of the life He was trying to lead them toward, the Lord made the shocking statement to early followers that they should aspire to "become as little children" (Matthew 18:3). An angel likewise teaches King Benjamin in the Book of Mormon that the Lord's people are to become "as a child, submissive, meek, humble, patient, full of love, willing to submit to all things which the Lord seeth fit to inflict upon [them]" (Mosiah 3:19).

Children in their innocence have eyes of wonder during experiences that many adults have ceased to see with any interest. But it's possible for even grown-ups to learn again how to approach each moment with a beginner's mind: being open to new discoveries, rather than acting like an expert who already knows what to expect.

PONDER. Is there anything in your life that is important and meaningful, but which you've stopped seeing as beautiful because it happens so regularly? What would you love to bring fresh curiosity and wonder to again?

_____

_____

_____

_____

_____

_____

_____

_____

PRACTICE. See what it's like to approach daily activities over the next week with a childlike curiosity and wonder. Try this with important experiences like time with a family member, a sacred ordinance, or reading inspired text, approaching each as if you were doing it for the very first time. But also try this with more routine activities like eating, walking, or doing chores: feeling the ground underneath you, along with the full spectrum of sensations from smell, taste, and touch to the wide palette of colors.

RECORDING GOD'S
HAND IN YOUR LIFE

"Treasure up the things which ye have seen and heard."
ETHER 3:21

Sacred scripture is full of reminders about the value of making "a record of [your] proceedings" (1 Nephi 1:1), with the Lord Himself encouraging His followers to "write the things which ye have seen and heard" (3 Nephi 27:23).

In addition to helping us recognize and remember the ways in which God is working in our lives, journals can spark the flow of even more revelation. After encouraging Saints to write in a special place "the important things you learn from the Spirit," Elder Richard G. Scott promised that "as you write down precious impressions, often more will come."[11]

PONDER. How often do you write down what the Lord is communicating or doing in your life? When was the last time you had the experience of writing something down and having that prompt more insight and inspiration?

_____

_____

_____

_____

_____

_____

_____

_____

_____

PRACTICE. Identify a place that can be your own "small plates" where you too can "write the things of [your] soul" (2 Nephi 4:15) and that which is of most worth in your life. Don't worry about whether your insights are grand or complete; instead use the journal as a working scratch pad, helping you lean deeper into the process of receiving and deciphering God's unfolding will in your life—while learning for yourself how to "[delight] in the things of the Lord" and "[ponder] continually upon the things which [you] have seen and heard" (2 Nephi 4:16).

CELEBRATING GOD'S
GOODNESS IN YOUR LIFE

"If ye loved me, ye would rejoice."

JOHN 14:28

The Lord wants us to relish, treasure, and celebrate our sacred experiences, much like He experienced when interacting with His own early followers, telling them, "My joy is great . . . because of you . . . ; yea, and even the Father rejoiceth, and also all the holy angels, because of you" (3 Nephi 27:30).

Elder Ulisses Soares contrasted "the sensation of emotion, awe, or amazement common to all who wholeheartedly center their lives on the Savior" with the complacency and indifference that can settle on us all.[12] Like believers who did "rejoice and glory" anciently in anticipation of His coming (Ether 9:22), we can likewise "rejoice with exceedingly great joy" in our lives right now, "even as though he had already come among" us (Mosiah 3:13).

PONDER. How do you praise, celebrate, and rejoice in the Lord in your personal worship? In what ways do these affections help you feel closer and more connected to Christ?

_____

_____

_____

_____

_____

_____

_____

_____

_____

_____

PRACTICE. We've also been encouraged to rejoice "in the truth" (1 Corinthians 13:6) and "in every good thing" (Deuteronomy 26:11). Write down or talk with someone about all the things in your life that you genuinely get excited about and relish. Evaluate if those align with what you most deeply *want* to be celebrating—and what you believe God wants you to treasure most right now in your life.

SAVORING THE
LITTLE MOMENTS

> "This people has refused the waters
> of Shiloah that flow gently."
>
> ISAIAH 8:6 (NRSV)

It's most often the dramatic news that gets attention and the sensational videos that get shared. Accordingly, we sometimes expect our experience with God to be equally dramatic and intense—something that really sweeps us off our feet.

Little wonder, then, that we sometimes miss the simple ways God may be acting in our lives, as well as the subtle pleasures of life: the taste of food, the colors of a sunset, the smile of a child, the touch of an embrace, or quiet time reading.

PONDER. When was the last time you noticed the mixture of colors in a sunset or sunrise? What other subtle pleasures could you be missing in your life and relationships with loved ones, including God? Can you identify any dramatic influences that absorb your attention and make it difficult to notice the wide array of other beautiful things in life?

_____

_____

_____

_____

_____

_____

_____

_____

_____

_____

_____

PRACTICE. Over the next few days, watch out for small moments and subtle experiences that you may otherwise miss. Keep an eye out for unremarkable aspects of a normal day at home, school, work, or church that deserve a little more savoring, treasuring, and relishing. Make note of what you discover.

FINDING JOY
IN OTHERS' JOY

> *"Charity envieth not; . . . seeketh not her own,*
> *is not easily provoked, thinketh no evil; rejoiceth*
> *not in iniquity, but rejoiceth in the truth."*
>
> 1 CORINTHIANS 13:4–6

As we grow in our capacity for deeper Christlike love, we inevitably encounter some resistance within. That can include envy of the blessings that have come to another. We may also notice times when our life and inner dialogue become increasingly self-focused, and the happiness of others is far from our heart and mind.

Like other aspects of charity, this capacity for sincere gladness when others experience joy is something we can nurture and develop.

PONDER. When was the last time you felt joy because of the joy someone else was experiencing? What was that feeling like in your body, heart, and mind?

_____

_____

_____

_____

_____

_____

_____

_____

_____

_____

PRACTICE. Bring awareness to your current capacity for rejoicing in the joy of others. Notice—without judgment—what thoughts and feelings emerge when you hear of the good fortune of someone else. Since charity is a gift from our Heavenly Father received through sincere prayer and offered "with all the energy of heart" (Moroni 7:48), come to that loving Father in prayerful appeal and counsel, sharing your feelings and thoughts. Earnestly ask for the capacity to feel the pure love of the Savior for others and for yourself. Then pray for others by name, pausing to notice how you feel.

A JOYFUL PRACTICE OF
DAILY REPENTANCE

> "Nothing is more liberating, more ennobling, or more crucial to our individual progression than is a regular, daily focus on repentance."
>
> RUSSELL M. NELSON[13]

The core of any meditation is noting when the mind has wandered off—then bringing it back over and over. In much the same way, repentance is all about staying attentive when *any* part of us has wandered off—and bringing it back over and over.

Elder Dieter F. Uchtdorf spoke of "small and simple acts of realignment" as helping draw us back when we depart from God's hopes for our lives. Rather than viewing them as exceptional moments, we've been encouraged to see these course corrections as part of an ongoing, daily time of reflection and introspection, "where we can walk with the Lord and be instructed, edified, and purified," as we relish this "opportunity for recalibration."[14]

PONDER. Have you been able to experience the joy prophets promise in approaching repentance as a daily restoration and recalibration? If not, what would it take to begin to experience that for yourself?

_____
_____
_____
_____
_____
_____
_____

PRACTICE. Make some adjustments that allow you to experience repentance as a regular practice of intimate, restorative moments that bring us back to God. This can be especially challenging for those who feel shame and regret and often berate themselves because of past or current struggles. Pray for strength to let go of self-talk that distances you from your Father's loving, enabling power. Fix your mind on God as an adoring Father who sees His children like any loving parent does and is eager to help them learn and grow.

MINDFULNESS IN RELATIONSHIPS

THE PRACTICE OF PRESENCE

> *"Caring for the poor and the needy is less about giving stuff away and more about filling the hunger for human contact. . . . You yourself are one of the best gifts that you can give to other people in need."*
>
> SHARON EUBANK[1]

Even when we really do want to be there for people, we are surrounded by so much stimulation in modern living that it can leave us in a state writer Linda Stone calls "continuous partial attention,"[2] reflecting a constant scattering of our focus. We've all probably experienced what it feels like to both receive and give distracted attention. The contrast with an experience of total and complete attention is profound. Do you know what that feels like? That kind of undivided attention is becoming increasingly rare. But it's something we can happily work toward and practice in our relationships.

PONDER. When was the last time you experienced whole, undivided attention from someone in your life—or offered that to someone else? In your experience, what does being fully present feel like compared to the "continuous partial attention" that so many of us are prone to experiencing? In what ways can you cultivate this deeper kind of presence in your own relationships?

_____

_____

_____

_____

_____

_____

PRACTICE. Watch for opportunities to practice this full-heart attention in your different relationships. When you notice your attention or interest wandering, consciously bring it back—to the face in front of you, the needs in front of you, and the precious human being you are with *right now.* Consider this another kind of rich mindfulness practice: bringing yourself back to the precious people in your life.

RECEIVING LOVE
FROM OTHERS

"For what doth it profit a man if a gift is bestowed upon him, and he receive not the gift? Behold, he rejoices not in that which is given unto him, neither rejoices in him who is the giver of the gift."

DOCTRINE AND COVENANTS 88:33

When the fisherman Simon Peter refused the Savior's offer to wash his feet, he probably saw himself as doing something noble. He could wash his own feet, after all, and was perhaps sparing the Lord the indignity with his declaration. But the Savior's gentle correction—"If I wash thee not, thou hast no part with me"—teaches us all something important (John 13:8).

It's not just giving that draws us close to others. "Every gift that is offered to us—especially a gift that comes from the heart," President Dieter F. Uchtdorf said at a Christmas devotional, "is an opportunity to build or strengthen a bond of love."[3] Whether through a physical gift, an act of service, or through words and gestures, opportunities to *receive* love are also a chance to draw closer with those around us. Don't miss those opportunities.

PONDER. Have you ever felt uncomfortable receiving a gesture of love, like Peter? What past experiences have you had that have shaped your ability and desire to receive the love of others?

_____

_____

_____

_____

_____

_____

PRACTICE. Make a list of people in your life you've been able to receive love from in the past. Why do you think their love has been something you've been able to accept? Are there others you've struggled to receive love from when they've wanted to offer it to you? Make a second list of people in your life you'd like to connect with more by receiving love more openly, while extending your own love further.

SHARING A MEAL
WITH FRIENDS
OR FAMILY

> *"They broke bread at home and ate their*
> *food with glad and generous hearts."*
>
> ACTS 2:46 (NRSV)

In a fast-paced society, the act of gathering with loved ones for a meal is a radical act of stopping and uniting around a common time and place. Research on family meals, for instance, has shown consistent impacts on a range of healthy outcomes for children.[4]

Far more than partaking of the food alone, the company, conversation, and love shared with family, friends, and neighbors can be nourishing and rich in many ways. As we relish the full sensory experience of sounds, sights, smells, and feelings, a mindful meal can become a rich practice of communion in itself.

PONDER. How often do you have a chance to gather with loved ones and unite in a common meal? When you do, how rushed or relaxed does it feel? What more could be done to encourage everyone to rest in each other's presence a little more?

_____

_____

_____

_____

_____

_____

_____

_____

_____

_____

PRACTICE. Next time you gather with family, friends, or neighbors to eat, notice all the smells, tastes, and sounds of your experience. Suggest to the group that you enjoy practicing the "art of dining"[5] together—potentially even preparing the meal and cleaning up afterward as a part of deepening your time together.

CREATING
SANCTUARY
AT HOME

"We hope and pray that each member's home will become a true sanctuary of faith, where the Spirit of the Lord may dwell. Despite contention all around us, one's home can become a heavenly place, where study, prayer, and faith can be merged with love."

RUSSELL M. NELSON[6]

Whether we live alone or with others, Elder David A. Bednar reminded us that this work of "making our homes sanctuaries" is "essential in these latter days"—important both "for our spiritual strength and protection today" and "even more vital in the future."[7]

Turning your home into a nourishing sanctuary from the world can include anything that you believe would make your home a place of peace and healing, learning and growth. These changes can take intentional planning and design, leading to inspired adjustments, with President Nelson encouraging that we work "carefully to transform" and "remodel" our homes into "center[s] of gospel learning." This home-centered, Church-supported approach, he promised, would increase our emotional connection with God and "unleash the power of families," while decreasing "the influence of the adversary in your life and in your home."[8]

PONDER. How much like a sanctuary and refuge does your current dwelling feel? What adjustments could create an atmosphere of even more peace and joy at home for you?

_____

_____

_____

_____

_____

_____

PRACTICE. Brainstorm a list of possible steps to spiritually remodel your home. Think through your daily schedule, and the priorities reflected in your house's overall emotional and physical atmosphere, including the images on the walls and the smell in the air. Then pick one thing to adjust this week.

NOURISHING AND CHERISHING RELATIONSHIPS

> *"We must cherish one another, watch over one another, comfort one another, and gain instruction that we may all sit down in heaven together."*
>
> LUCY MACK SMITH[9]

Scripture records that "the soul of Jonathan was knit with the soul of David" and that he "loved him as his own soul" (1 Samuel 18:1). The Book of Mormon likewise pleads with believers to have their "hearts knit together in unity and in love one towards another" and to avoid contention (Mosiah 18:21).

This deepening of relationships doesn't happen without conscious and intentional cultivation. For a married couple, that may mean regularly setting aside time for continuing courtship. For families, it might mean pushing back on other demands so they can protect and prioritize regular time together. Healthy friendship needs this too.

PONDER. How often are you able to make time to nurture relationships around you? When opportunities arise—at a family gathering, a friend's invitation to lunch, a graduation celebration, or in your ministering—how present and "all in" are you?

_____

_____

_____

_____

_____

_____

_____

PRACTICE. Jot down the names of a few people who are—or have been—important to you, but who you've been out of contact with. Take time this week to knock on a door, make a call, or send a text or email to check in on one of these friends. Also consider making adjustments to your schedule that could open up more regular opportunities for connection—such as reserving a few minutes immediately following your morning worship to reach out to whomever comes to mind.

STUDYING THE GOSPEL WITH FRIENDS OR FAMILY

"Appoint among yourselves a teacher, and let not all be spokesmen at once; but let one speak at a time and let all listen unto his sayings, that when all have spoken that all may be edified of all, and that every man may have an equal privilege."

DOCTRINE AND COVENANTS 88:122

In contrast to some other educational settings, the Lord encourages us to create an open atmosphere where the Spirit can teach us all. Sometimes we are the teacher, and sometimes we are the learner, with everyone getting a turn at some point—be that in Sunday School, Relief Society, elders quorum, youth and children's classes, or in our individual homes.

Compared with solo study, studying together as a group, couple, family, or class can be more challenging—as multiple perspectives and personalities merge in a pursuit of further light and knowledge. Approaching these shared study sessions as opportunities to practice nonjudgmental awareness may help us benefit and learn from those who have different perspectives than we do.

PONDER. What do you notice going on in your heart and mind when you study the gospel with others? Are there any unique challenges to shared study for you—ways this kind of class, group, or family study stretches you?

_____

_____

_____

_____

_____

PRACTICE. The next chance you have to study the gospel with others at home or church, pay attention to where your mind goes. When your attention wanders, experiment with bringing it back to the discussion gently and firmly. If there are moments you notice tension within, see if you can consciously shift your heart back to a place of softness, as you practice holding the whole experience—questions, comments, instructions, feelings, thoughts—from a place of compassion and curiosity.

PRAYING WITH
FRIENDS OR FAMILY

> *"And when they had prayed, the place was shaken where they were assembled together; and they were all filled with the Holy Ghost. . . . And the multitude of them that believed were of one heart and of one soul."*
>
> ACTS 4:31–32

We pray so often that it's easy to miss what a group prayer does for us in a family or congregation—beginning with the countercultural act of simply stopping and experiencing stillness together. But it's more than that. Collective prayer invites hearts and minds to come together and unite around a single expression of love, purpose, praise, gratitude, and entreaty before the living God—all of which has special significance in an age of widening fragmentation and estrangement.

During a shared prayer, a single individual does their best to give voice to the heart and mind of the entire family, group, or congregation—as well as to the will of God. During that short span of time, those words become a common anchor to which people's attention can gather and return when it wanders. As hearts and minds reach for the Lord together, a new spirit can be infused into the whole.

PONDER. When you gather with others to pray, what do you notice happening in your own mind and heart? When you notice your attention wandering away from the words of the prayer, what do you do in that moment?

_____
_____
_____
_____
_____

PRACTICE. If you notice your mind wandering during prayer, you are not alone. This is what minds do—they ebb and flow like the ocean. The next time you pray with others, notice when this is happening and consciously escort your attention back to the words being shared. Repeating the words of the prayer in your mind is another way to deepen your personal connection to the prayer being spoken.

PRAYING THROUGH MUSIC

> *"My soul delighteth in the song of the heart; yea,*
> *the song of the righteous is a prayer unto me."*
>
> DOCTRINE AND COVENANTS 25:12

Congregational singing is such a common part of Christian worship service that it's easy to ignore it in the background. But from a mindfulness perspective, it's striking to consider what's happening when an entire room of people draws not only their attention, but their voices to a common auditory and visual anchor, combining the words, music, and rhythm.

All this becomes an unfolding focal point we're invited to rest in and unite upon, much like a group prayer. Even when attention naturally wanders, the singing practice invites people back over and over, like a melodious meditation.

PONDER. How often do you find your attention wandering during congregational hymns, and how do you respond when it does? What kinds of physical sensations and emotions do you also notice during the singing?

_____

_____

_____

_____

_____

_____

_____

PRACTICE. Approach the next hymn you sing as a collective musical meditation, appreciating how the song draws your hearts and minds together as a congregation. Ponder the meaning of the words coming out of your mouth. Perhaps even close your eyes during portions of the song when you remember the words. When you notice your mind wandering, look to the text and melody of the song as a meditative anchor, leading your attention back over and over (while accepting this as a normal part of the rich practice of singing together).

TEACHING CHILDREN STILLNESS

"Jesus once was a little child, a little child like me; And he was pure and meek and mild, as a little child should be."

JESUS ONCE WAS A LITTLE CHILD[10]

Many parents today invest considerable resources to teach their children how to focus and be more mindful. Latter-day Saint youth have a chance to learn the "skill of still" every weekend in their Primary and youth meetings at church.

The home provides many other opportunities to teach children how to settle their minds, direct their attention, and regulate their emotions. All this helps young souls learn to be present to the words they are hearing, the faces they are seeing, the feelings they are experiencing, and especially that "still voice of perfect mildness" (Helaman 5:30). Instead of prompting children over and over to "pay attention" or "be reverent," we all have a part to play as a family of faith—parents and grandparents, neighbors and ward members—to teach and show young people *how* to pay attention and be still.

PONDER. How well do you model the practice of reverent stillness to young people in your circle of influence? In what other creative ways can you help children or others around you appreciate how practices of prayer, scripture, and sabbath can prepare them to hear and know God?

_____

_____

_____

_____

_____

PRACTICE. In the hustle and bustle of life, even adults have a hard time stopping on a dime. Next time you gather in prayer, especially if young people are involved, don't expect everyone to immediately settle. Instead, try building in a short period of silence or conversation that allows minds to quiet. Consider going around the circle and sharing something you've each felt grateful for today prior to starting the prayer—or inviting children to count five breaths before you begin.

STRENGTHENING RELATIONSHIPS
BEYOND THE VEIL

> "And he shall turn the heart of the
> fathers to the children, and the heart
> of the children to their fathers."
>
> MALACHI 4:6

Groundless, aimless, and without meaning: this is how many people today feel. What could it mean for them to reconnect to their roots and heritage? Research on the tangible benefits of knowing family stories from the past[11] aligns with Latter-day Saint conviction about the value of strengthening relationships across generations on both sides of the veil.

Alma asks us, "Have you sufficiently retained in remembrance the captivity of your fathers? Yea, and have you sufficiently retained in remembrance his mercy and long-suffering towards them?" (Alma 5:6). With so many fictional dramas drawing our attention, the fact is many of us have little attention to explore the real-life adventures of our ancestors.

PONDER. How much heart and mind do you give on a regular basis to connecting with the simple heroes of your own heritage? What adjustments could you make to draw out your heart more authentically and consistently to your own fathers and mothers who came before—exploring their words, lives, and legacies?

_____

_____

_____

_____

_____

_____

PRACTICE. In the FamilySearch website, look for your "Calendar of Ancestral Moments" by going to this link: https://www.familysearch.org/campaign/calendar. See if you can find a birthday coming up soon. Even if you don't have many documented ancestors, look for any information you do have. Choose an ancestor, see if you can find out some of their story, and think about celebrating their birthday by singing to them with other family members. Consider setting aside an hour each Sunday when you can practice different ways to draw hearts to your fathers and mothers of old.

CULTIVATING
ZION BELONGING

> "Behold, doth he cry unto any, saying:
> Depart from me? . . . Hath the Lord commanded
> any that they should not partake of his goodness?
> Behold I say unto you, Nay; but all men are privileged
> the one like unto the other, and none are forbidden."
>
> 2 NEPHI 26:25, 28

Despite how expansive Jesus's invitation is, we can sometimes wonder if we belong among His followers. Paul encouraged the Saints to see themselves as "all baptized into one body" and "made to drink into one Spirit," so much so that when "one member suffer, all the members suffer with it" (1 Corinthians 12:13, 26).

Elder D. Todd Christofferson has encouraged us to "love and treat each other the best we can," and seek to withhold judgment as we bring everyone to "the great feast of the Lord."[12] While reminding us that "each of us has a special place in God's heart," President Russell M. Nelson taught of the unique connective belonging covenants provide as they lead us to a "much closer" relationship with the Lord.[13]

PONDER. Who at church is easy for you to care for, and who do you perhaps have to stretch to love? What divine qualities need to grow within you for you to more graciously welcome those who sometimes challenge you or make you a little uncomfortable?

_____
_____
_____
_____
_____

PRACTICE. Elder D. Todd Christofferson highlighted the following affirmation as a centerpiece for what he called "a personal expression of belonging in your own life." As you repeat this, consider how well the words describe your own sense of connection in the Church: "Jesus Christ died for me; He thought me worthy of His blood. He loves me and can make all the difference in my life. As I repent, His grace will transform me. I am one with Him in the gospel covenant; I belong in His Church and kingdom; and I belong in His cause to bring redemption to all of God's children."[14]

UNDERSTANDING MORE BY
COUNSELING TOGETHER

> *"Many of the brethren have used the expression that 'revelation is scattered among us.' And it's really true. The Church is governed by councils, and that's how we grow, that's how we make progress."*
>
> JEAN BINGHAM[15]

Rather than having one leader dictate and discern alone, we've been taught to aspire for a better way as fellow disciples. "In our meetings, we do not just sit around and wait for [the prophet] to tell us what to do," President M. Russell Ballard taught. "We counsel openly with each other, and we listen to each other with profound respect for the abilities and experiences [everyone] brings." The apostle went on to emphasize the power of bringing together two different kinds of truth seeking: "listening to each other and listening to the Spirit!"[16]

"No one is trying to figure out, 'Well, what's the agenda here? What's the hidden message?'" Elder David Bednar also shared.[17] "The only objective is to try to discern and apply the Lord's will and His timing." In that process, Jesus reassures all seeking to follow Him that He won't be far away: "Where two or three are gathered together in my name, there am I in the midst of them" (Matthew 18:20).

PONDER. Have you felt inspiration arise in your own opportunities to counsel, be that in leadership positions or in family relationships? If not, what adjustments can you make so that these deliberations become more revelatory, edifying, and unifying?

_____

_____

_____

_____

PRACTICE. Next time you join a discussion, notice how well you're able to give your full attention to the person speaking, compared with when your mind is caught up in your own thoughts. In a distracting moment, consciously guide your attention back to the speaker. Look for other ways to contribute to an environment where everyone feels heard and respected, including being mindful of your language and tone of voice.

MINISTERING
AS HE WOULD

> *"They did watch over their people, and did nourish them with things pertaining to righteousness."*
>
> MOSIAH 23:18

President Jeffrey R. Holland described President Russell M. Nelson's call for a "holier approach to caring for and ministering to others"[18] a "heaven-sent" opportunity to "mature" in "rising above any mechanical, function-without-feeling routine." In this way, he taught, we can better demonstrate "pure religion" (James 1:27) by following the Lord's counsel to "love one another; as I have loved you" (John 13:34).[19]

We can all improve at listening to nudges to "bind up the brokenhearted" (Isaiah 61:1) and "lift up the hands which hang down" (Doctrine and Covenants 81:5), whether by a simple text, email, call, or personal visit. Only the Lord knows exactly what people need and what gifts and talents we can uniquely offer others—which is something He's willing to guide us to know if we're open to it.

PONDER. Who in your life is facing something challenging, and who could use some extra support right now? Do you have enough space in your life to receive promptings and inspiration about someone who may be struggling, including people who are hesitant to share out loud that they really need help?

_____

_____

_____

_____

_____

PRACTICE. Mr. Fred Rogers had a practice of arising early and praying over a list of names individually. Based on what he felt that morning, he would reach out to certain people that day.[20] Experiment this week with praying over the names of certain people. Then, make time to reach out to those who may need to hear from you—listening for promptings of who that might be and what you could say or ask. Even something simple can touch hearts, like "I was just thinking about you and wanted to know how you're doing." Consider making an evolving, dedicated list of people that you want to remember and pray over in your own morning worship time.

SUFFERING WITH
THE SUFFERER

> *"Remember them that are in bonds, as bound with them; and them which suffer adversity, as being yourselves also in the body."*
>
> HEBREWS 13:3

It's not always easy to know how to be with someone who is suffering. We may feel nervous or uncomfortable and want to distract the person from their pain. When Jesus became "exceeding sorrowful, even unto death" in his own greatest suffering, He asked His own closest friends to wait and "watch" with Him (Matthew 26:38). They couldn't take away His pain, but this is something they *could* do: staying awake and staying close.

This acute suffering Jesus experienced also led Him to be "filled with mercy" that He "may know according to the flesh how to succor his people according to their infirmities" (Alma 7:12). Our own painful experiences give us greater ability to suffer with others too, which is part of the root meaning of the word *compassion*.[21]

PONDER. How often would you say that you are suffering *with* those around you who are hurting and legitimately "mourning with those that mourn"? (Mosiah 18:9). Do people who are hurting find your words and presence comforting? What do you think can sometimes make it difficult for you to suffer with others?

_____

_____

_____

_____

_____

_____

PRACTICE. Like it was for Jesus's disciples, it's not always easy for us to stay aware of and awake to what loved ones are facing. Make a list of the people in your life who are suffering the most—including, perhaps, some people you know less well. Then spend some time contemplating what it would mean to *join them* in their suffering to a greater degree. How would your life look and feel then, and how would you perhaps act differently?

NURTURING OTHERS' SPIRITUAL GROWTH

> *"You know that the rulers of the Gentiles lord it over them, and their great ones are tyrants over them. It will not be so among you; but whoever wishes to be great among you must be your servant."*
>
> MATTHEW 20:25–26 (NRSV)

The Lord asks those called to lead to be the "servant of all" (Mark 9:35) and to "watch over the church always, and be with and strengthen them" (Doctrine and Covenants 20:53). This is harder than it looks. Joseph Smith cautioned that "it is the nature and disposition of almost all men, as soon as they get a little authority, as they suppose, they will immediately begin to exercise unrighteous dominion" (Doctrine and Covenants 121:39).

Saints are encouraged to overcome this common disposition, especially since those who lead in the Church are "commissioned to stand in the place and stead of [their] Master" in ministering to fellow men and women, as Elder Bruce R. McConkie taught.[22]

PONDER. Take a moment to imagine standing in the Lord's place as you minister to brothers and sisters in your ward and to your family and friends. What adjustments in your heart and mind could help you receive more of the Savior's personal love and power, as you seek to represent Him well to the people around you?

_____

_____

_____

_____

_____

_____

_____

PRACTICE. Next time you have a chance to direct or lead in a calling, notice what thoughts come into your mind and what feelings come into your heart. Instead of just saying the first words that come to mind, try reaching for something higher and holier—acting as a living conduit of the Lord's own patience, kindness, and love.

SHARING WHAT GOD
WANTS YOU TO SAY

> *"For it shall be given you in the very hour, yea, in the very moment, what ye shall say."*
>
> DOCTRINE AND COVENANTS 100:6

Compared with the few years it takes children to learn how to speak, it can take much longer to learn how to speak the words God puts into your heart. Thankfully, opportunities to practice are everywhere in the restored gospel, with Latter-day Saints seeking the right words to share in talks, lessons, testimonies, and priesthood blessings, as well as in ministering visits to those in need. Even more frequently, we can seek God's guidance in the words we offer in prayer.

All this runs against our natural human tendency to say whatever we think and anything that comes to mind. By contrast, trying to speak in the Lord's name provides a rich opportunity to partner with heaven in aspiring for something far better—to put into words, as best we can, what the Lord would have us share.

PONDER. How often do you try to voice what God wants you to say in prayer? The last time you shared something as a teacher or minister, did you seek inspiration to share what God wanted you to say? What kinds of challenges or habits get in your way of doing this more and acting as a vessel for the Spirit?

_____

_____

_____

_____

_____

_____

PRACTICE. Next time you have a chance to minister or teach, spend some extra time seeking to discern God's will for your visit or lesson rather than merely sharing something you think could be interesting. You might try sitting in silence to better observe your thoughts and feelings as you explore matters with God. Approach prayer as a daily chance to not only compare your preferences with God's but also to actively seek to bring them together in a newfound unity.

MINDFULNESS IN CHALLENGE AND CELEBRATION

LIVING PEACEABLY
AMID CONFLICT

"When you are offering your gift at the altar, if you remember that your brother or sister has something against you, leave your gift there before the altar and go; first be reconciled to your brother or sister, and then come and offer your gift."

MATTHEW 5:23–24 (NRSV)

Conflict is a normal part of life, even between thoughtful and good-hearted people. Being accepting and patient with that fact is a counterintuitive first step to living "peaceably with all" (Romans 12:18). Otherwise, it's easy to get angry with anger and impatient with others' impatience.

Followers of Christ can instead learn to bring softness of heart to hardness—the kind that disarms and deescalates with curiosity and kindness. The motivation for such forbearance and forgiveness can be hard to find. Yet "even as Christ forgave you," Paul says, "so also do ye"—thus letting "the peace of God rule in your hearts" (Colossians 3:13, 15).

PONDER. Have you been able to navigate conflict with people in your home, work, or congregation in a peaceful and generous way? If not, can you see any adjustments on your part that could pave the way for better experiences in this regard?

_____

_____

_____

_____

_____

_____

PRACTICE. Next time a conflict arises in one of your relationships, notice what's going on inside. How does your heart feel toward this person? Pray for the Lord to help you soften your heart and give you more of His capacity to respond peaceably. Then listen for words and ideas that can help bring renewed tranquility to the situation. Stay willing to be proactive in your reconciliation like the Lord encouraged by putting ideas in writing or verbalizing them when the moment is right.

LOVING WHEN YOU
DON'T FEEL LOVING

> "If you love those who love you, . . . if you do good to those who do good to you, what credit is that to you?"
>
> LUKE 6:32–33 (NRSV)

It is easy to interpret the *feeling* of love as synonymous with love itself. But Jesus's life and teachings point to something more: the chance to consciously exercise and nurture love when the feeling is not there. It's not just with "enemies" we may struggle to feel love—but also in family relationships, marriages, and friendships.

That moment when feelings of romantic love settle, for instance, may be the perfect time to practice even deeper love—seeing this as an opportunity to give to another out of pure desire for their well-being, rather than from an expectation of personal reward.[1] This is how God loves us, demonstrated by the fact that "while we were yet sinners, Christ died for us" (Romans 5:8). If we wait until we feel love or deem someone "loveable" before showing and demonstrating love, we're not loving as God loves.

PONDER. As you bring to mind to mind someone in your life whom you struggle to love, what thoughts and feelings arise about how they act or fail to act? After acknowledging these thoughts and feelings, shift your attention from pursuing "being loved" to "being loving," regardless of the other's behavior. How does focusing on being loving feel different in your body?

_____

_____

_____

_____

_____

PRACTICE. For some, Christlike love is experienced in the body as a sensation of light and spaciousness. Bring to mind again a relationship that does not organically evoke love, imagining both of you surrounded by the Lord's light and love. How do the natural feelings between you shift as you are immersed in this kind of pure love? If resistance or hard feelings arise, allow those to be a part of the practice, letting those be something you lovingly observe too.

HOLDING QUESTIONS
WITH HUMILITY

> "Many therefore of his disciples, when they had heard this, said, This is an hard saying; who can hear it? . . . From that time many of his disciples went back, and walked no more with him."
>
> JOHN 6:60, 66

Unanswered gospel questions and "hard sayings" can provoke a range of reactions. On one end of the spectrum, some lean so far into certainty that they almost deny serious questions or doubt should ever exist. On the other end of the spectrum, people can elevate and valorize questions so much that they abandon their faith.

Peter responds differently. He doesn't say, "This makes total sense; those others are crazy for leaving." But neither does he abandon Christ in the face of difficult doctrine. Instead, this humble follower recenters on what he does know. Despite not fully understanding, he attests, "Thou art the Christ, the Son of the living God" (Matthew 16:16).

For Latter-day Saints, approaching such a period of questioning with similar recentering means we're better able to tolerate feelings of confusion or frustration that may arise, while anticipating further light and knowledge to come. At the same time, we can offer compassionate space for those sharing our pew who approach their faith with more—or less—certitude.

PONDER. Where do you tend to fall on the spectrum between glorifying certainty and glorifying doubt? How can you bring more gentleness, humility, and grace to unresolved questions in your life? What more can you do to approach important questions with reassuring confidence and hope, as you anticipate that God will continue to guide you?

_____

_____

_____

PRACTICE. Catch yourself when you find judgmental thoughts arising toward those who are on the opposite end of the certainty spectrum from you and do your best to re-anchor yourself in compassion. Practice bringing that spacious, nonjudgmental, and kind attitude to those sharing the pew with you. When you're ready, expand your practice and invite some of these neighbors over for dinner!

RESTING IN YOUR
DEEPEST IDENTITY

> "Make no mistake about it: Your potential is divine. With your diligent seeking, God will give you glimpses of who you may become."
>
> RUSSELL M. NELSON[2]

Questions of identity have fascinated and challenged the human family throughout history. Amidst the confusion of our day, a living prophet of God has spoken plainly on the matter, saying, "I believe that if the Lord were speaking to you directly, the first thing He would make sure you understand is your true identity."

"My dear friends, you are literally spirit children of God," President Nelson continued, cautioning that any identifier that replaces or distracts from the most important understandings of who we are will "ultimately let you down."[3]

PONDER. Has any other label in your life or that of a loved one displaced or taken priority over the three identifiers President Nelson encouraged us to remember: "child of God," "child of the covenant," and "disciple of Jesus Christ"?[4] If so, how can you develop more personal attachment to these deeper divine identities?

_____

_____

_____

_____

_____

_____

PRACTICE. President David O. McKay once taught, "It is a good thing to sit down and commune with yourself" and "to come to an understanding with yourself" in a way that helps settle your deeper commitments to God and those around you.[5] In a quiet moment today, try sitting down to commune with yourself, while reflecting on the statement "I am a child of God" or "I am a disciple of Christ." Gently observe what thoughts, feelings, or images emerge for you as you center your attention on these truths. Notice what distracts you from them as well.

LETTING GO OF
SOMETHING GOOD FOR
SOMETHING BETTER

> "All among them who know their hearts are
> honest, and are broken, and their spirits contrite,
> and are willing to observe their covenants by
> sacrifice—yea, every sacrifice which I, the Lord,
> shall command—they are accepted of me."
>
> DOCTRINE AND COVENANTS 97:8

When something good or pleasant comes into life, it's natural to want to hold onto it. One way discipleship pulls us beyond that which is merely natural is by inviting us to occasionally lay aside what may seem good for something ultimately better.

We lay aside food for a certain period as part of a fast so we can receive spiritual cleansing and the chance to offer physical relief to someone in need. We lay aside a portion of money for tithes and offerings as a reflection of our love for God and a way to show our trust in the infinite resources available through the "windows of heaven" (Malachi 3:10). We also lay aside portions of our time—the Holy Sabbath, morning worship time—with confidence God will multiply these sacrifices and draw us closer, providing peace that cannot be gained in any other way.

PONDER. How much is sacrifice part of your daily life as a disciple? What kinds of sacrifices stretch you most? Are there other unique sacrifices, like the social media fast President Nelson once encouraged,[6] you could consider trying?

_____

_____

_____

_____

_____

PRACTICE. Next time you lay aside or let go of something—be that food, money, or time—notice what's going on inside. Watch the thoughts, feelings, and sensations that arise, while appreciating the spectrum of experiences often involved in sacrificing what God asks as a way to grow our love for Him.

FEELING BUT NOT FOLLOWING

> *"He suffered temptations but gave no heed unto them."*
> DOCTRINE AND COVENANTS 20:22

Emotion of any kind can feel strong enough at times that it can be difficult to do anything other than follow what we're feeling. Yet prophets remind us we are agents to "act" for ourselves and not simply be "acted upon" (2 Nephi 2:14). Stephen Covey described being personally impacted by three unattributed lines he came across: "Between stimulus and response, there is a space. In that space lies our freedom and our power to choose our response. In our response lies our growth and our happiness."[7]

It's possible to learn new ways of responding to sorrow, fear, or anger without letting these emotions overwhelm, control, or drive us. At an extremely troubling moment, Mormon wrote to his son Moroni, "May not the things which I have written grieve thee, to weigh thee down unto death; but may Christ lift thee up, and may his sufferings and death, and the showing his body unto our fathers, and his mercy and long-suffering, and the hope of his glory and of eternal life, rest in your mind forever" (Moroni 9:25).

PONDER. How do you typically respond when you feel a strong emotion like sorrow, fear, craving, or anger? What is it like to feel a strong emotion without immediately responding to the impulse to act? How can you cultivate the habit of creating space between a certain stimulus and your response to it, in a way that allows more conscious choices in your life?

_____

_____

_____

_____

_____

PRACTICE. Watch this week for a moment when you feel an urge to react impulsively to an intense emotion. Instead, try to pause. Notice the sensations in your body, including the places of tension or heightened energy, the impact of the emotion on your breathing and thoughts, and how long the intensity stays at a peak. Consider journaling about what you learned.

LEADING AND EDUCATING
YOUR HEART

> *"The education . . . of our desires is one of*
> *far-reaching importance to our happiness in life."*
>
> JOSEPH F. SMITH[8]

"You've gotta want it!" life coaches cheerfully chant. But what if your heart doesn't rally to a noble call or you don't feel the desire for something God invites? While it can be easy to let our current feelings be the final word, John teaches, "If our heart condemn us, God is greater than our heart" (1 John 3:20).

An important part of the gospel's hope is the "new heart" that can be given us (see Ezekiel 36:26). However much we'd all prefer an instantaneous and dramatic heart upgrade, this can take time as we work with God to move our desires in a better direction. "Only by educating and training our desires," Elder Neal A. Maxwell has said, "can they become our allies instead of our enemies!"[9] When your desires feel at odds with God's will and your own long-term happiness, take heart and stay hopeful that you can lead them—with divine help—in a better direction over time.

PONDER. Are any of your desires currently at odds with God's will as revealed in scriptures and through living prophets? In what ways have you sought to work with those desires and lead them in a better direction? In what other ways can you do that in the future?

_____

_____

_____

_____

_____

PRACTICE. Much like you can notice the wandering mind and bring it back to an anchor in meditation practice, you can do the same with a wandering heart—noticing when it has drifted and consciously, intentionally, bringing it back to where you believe God wants your heart to be. In moments when your own desires drift away from covenantal promises, exercise this deeper *desire for your desires*—and consciously lead your heart back to where you most want it to be. Make this a life practice that you build into the regular course of your day-to-day.

ONE DAY AT A TIME

> "If ye will turn to the Lord with full purpose of heart,
> and put your trust in him, and serve him with all
> diligence of mind, if ye do this, he will, according to
> his own will and pleasure, deliver you out of bondage."
>
> MOSIAH 7:33

Many kinds of compulsive habits drain and distract people today, though some are more socially acceptable than others. Those seeking greater freedom often yearn for some dramatic moment that allows them to be rid of the addictive pattern for good.

Sometimes this happens. But more often, the process of leaving behind addiction can require a longer journey with the Savior to renovate the heart, mind, and eventually one's entire life.

PONDER. Is there anything in your life that you would classify as a compulsive or addictive behavior (where you can't seem to stop, even though you keep trying)? On a scale of 0 to 10, how motivated are you to find freedom from this pattern? Are there any deeper pains or problems that may be contributing to this compulsive pattern?

_____

_____

_____

_____

_____

_____

_____

PRACTICE. Next time you engage in this compulsive-addictive pattern, instead of shifting toward self-condemnation, try letting yourself notice the feelings in your body, mind, and heart in the minutes and hours afterwards. Allow whatever you observe to teach you something about the addictive habit itself. Then, appreciate that the *very next moment* can be new thanks to Jesus Christ, who came to make "all things new" (Revelation 21:5). Instead of seeking *freedom* alone, do whatever you can to seek Jesus Himself: the One who can deliver this precious gift back into your hands, especially as you keep turning back to Him over and over, moment by moment.

KEEP GETTING UP

> *"We are troubled on every side, yet not distressed;*
> *we are perplexed, but not in despair; persecuted,*
> *but not forsaken; cast down, but not destroyed."*
>
> 2 CORINTHIANS 4:8–9

In great movies, the heroes fall down over and over as they face overwhelming forces they can barely endure. Yet in the very moment they're ready to give up, they always manage to dig deep enough to get up again. Even when they get knocked down again, they find a way to keep moving forward until they eventually discover how to break free.

You can be like that too. "Though he fall," the Psalmist says, "he shall not be utterly cast down: for the Lord upholdeth him with his hand" (Psalm 37:24). What if we approached the setbacks in our life with the same stubborn resilience as our heroes, buoyed by our confidence in the Lord? Each fall could then become a chance to learn and grow a little more, preparing for the next right step.

PONDER. Is there any area of your life where you keep feeling knocked down? What if you approached this struggle with the resilience of a movie hero?

_____

_____

_____

_____

_____

_____

PRACTICE. The next time you have a setback in something important to you, pause and listen. Whose voice do you hear at this moment? Is the voice harsh and critical, or gentle and affirming? Are the truths it's speaking shaming or encouraging? As you listen for the voice of the Lord, approach these challenging moments with fresh eyes. Keep learning. Keep growing. Keep hoping. Keep connecting. And keep getting up! You'll get there. You have infinite worth. And your future is full of beautiful possibilities.

THE PROTECTION
OF WATCHFULNESS

> *"Watch yourselves, and your thoughts,*
> *and your words, and your deeds."*
>
> MOSIAH 4:30

Jesus encouraged His followers to "watch and pray always"—a wise warning regarding the relentless designs of the adversary (see 3 Nephi 18:18; Luke 21:36). This contrasts with the increasingly popular message that any sort of fear is always a bad and unhealthy thing. The Lord here suggests that there is a rightful place for healthy vigilance and watchfulness in our lives.

Of course, the Lord is equally clear that fear is not to permeate or overwhelm our lives, encouraging His followers to "fear not" (Doctrine and Covenants 6:34) and to "be not afraid" (Luke 12:4). We may appreciate watchfulness not as fearfulness, then, but rather as a valuable practice of wise and cautious attentiveness—"keeping an eye" on various elements of our lives. Research has found that when people learn to catch early signs of a depressive episode or addictive craving, it can measurably reduce their power[10]—and give people a better chance to escape.

PONDER. Do you currently have a practice of personal "watchfulness" in monitoring thoughts, words, and actions in your life? If not, what could it mean for you to take seriously the repeated counsel throughout scripture to stay "awake" in various parts of your life to possible dangers and needed adjustments? (2 Nephi 1:23; 4:28).

_____

_____

_____

_____

_____

PRACTICE. Allow yourself to experiment with healthy vigilance, caution, and watchfulness in your life. What areas of your life—and your family's life—are vulnerable to the intrusion and encroachments of the adversary? Identify ways you can "astonish" forces of darkness by taking preemptive and preventive steps in preparing your own "places of security" (Alma 49:5).

SITTING WITH DISCOMFORT

> *"They did submit cheerfully and with patience to all the will of the Lord."*
>
> MOSIAH 24:15

When discomfort comes up, the most normal and natural reaction we have is to push it away and do something to avoid the feeling. Sometimes that may be just what we need, but when this becomes how we respond to any and all discomfort, it becomes a real problem. Discomfort can often teach us something valuable, for instance, guiding us away from certain decisions. If we cut off that signal, we could miss the message.

A different kind of discomfort can arise that stops us from pursuing something good. Discerning the difference between the two may require, at a minimum, learning how to sit with the discomfort and watch it. No matter where it comes from, then, it can be smart to do something other than pushing the discomfort away. Watching and observing it compassionately will help you discern what to do next.

PONDER. Have you ever felt discomfort that guided you away from a decision you may have otherwise made? What have you learned about telling the difference between that and the discomfort that can oppose something good?

_____

_____

_____

_____

_____

_____

_____

_____

PRACTICE. Next time you feel an uncomfortable sensation, instead of acting immediately to make it go away, experiment with this instead: just watch it, observing and sitting with it until it changes (because it always does). Patiently and gently watch, wait, and listen. This doesn't mean the discomfort will quickly go away. But as it shifts and evolves over time, trust that you'll know what to do next.

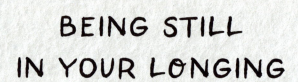

BEING STILL
IN YOUR LONGING

> *"Let us cheerfully do all things that lie in our power; and then may we stand still, with the utmost assurance, to see the salvation of God, and for his arm to be revealed."*
>
> DOCTRINE AND COVENANTS 123:17

Even after we've done all we can do, our impulse in a time of great need is often to do *even more*. But the Lord invites us to try something more challenging: *to stop* and to be still—waiting on His mighty arm, fully confident in what He can do for us.

Standing still sometimes evokes questions we avoid by being in perpetual motion: "Is the Lord going to be here for me? Can I really trust Him?" President Emily Belle Freeman testified that "the Lord will show up and stand by you, and He will bless you where you are standing. He will meet you where you are, but He won't leave you there. He will bring you to a better place, a place of happiness and joy."[11]

PONDER. When it comes to personal dreams that currently remain unfulfilled, how do you currently hold them in your heart? Is there any area of your life right now where you have already done what lies in your power, and now it's time to be still, "with the utmost assurance" to see the arm of the Lord revealed?

_____

_____

_____

_____

_____

_____

PRACTICE. Placing a deep heartache in God's hands can be a powerful comfort. Signal that intent in prayer and in your own sacred journal record. Yet even after an encouraging moment like this, it can be natural to notice some ebbing in your trust and resolve. Remember that placing our hearts in God's hands as a trusting practice we can do every day (see Mosiah 4:11). Again and again.

SORROWING BEFORE THE LORD

> "Enoch . . . had bitterness of soul, and wept
> . . . and said unto the heavens: I will refuse to
> be comforted; but the Lord said unto Enoch:
> Lift up your heart, and be glad; and look."
>
> MOSES 7:44

Sorrow and grief come to all of us, in different ways and times—linked especially to hopes, dreams, and people who matter most. Yet it can be tempting to see any kind of sorrow as a problem that we need to escape and push away. That can make any lessons and meaning in our experience easy to miss.

As best you can, make space for your sorrow and observe it from a place of compassion. Even with all He knew, "Jesus wept" when encountering loss (John 11:35), and was described by Isaiah as a "man of sorrows, and acquainted with grief" (Isaiah 53:3).

That makes Him uniquely able to walk with us in our sorrow, teaching us, consoling us, and providing customized relief and "succor" (Alma 7:12) that no one else can. You don't need to grieve alone.

PONDER. What sources of sorrow, grief, or loss (not just of a person, but of an opportunity or dream) are you currently experiencing in your life? How well have you been able to hold this emotional pain with compassion—acknowledging your grief in a nonjudgmental, accepting way?

_____

_____

_____

_____

PRACTICE. Even if a "hole in your heart" doesn't completely get filled, you can learn to cover everything in love and "make your heart bigger than the hole."[12] As you acknowledge different contributors to grief and sorrow you may be experiencing, consider visualizing what it would look like to surround any of these sacred holes of loss in your own heart with protective layers of love.

BEGINNING TO HEAL
FROM PAST HURT

> *"And God shall wipe away all tears from their eyes;
> and there shall be no more death, neither sorrow,
> nor crying, neither shall there be any more pain."*
>
> REVELATION 21:4

When Jesus's early disciples were "tossed with waves" in the middle of the sea, they rowed as hard as they could, yet went nowhere (Matthew 14:24). We can feel similarly stuck in past pains. We want to forgive, heal, and move on, but how? It's interesting how Christ quickly offers His presence to these early disciples as comfort, but He does not, initially, calm the storm. Rather, He affirms Peter's proposal to walk straight into it.

Christ offers us the same immediate comfort while beckoning, "Come directly into the pain, into the suffering, and into the storm. Come to Me. And when you get distracted, as even faithful Peter did, refocus on Me. I've got you."

PONDER. Is there anything painful in your own past which seems to keep coming up in your life today? How open do you feel to the Lord leading you through a process of healing that is as deep as your current pain? If you're not open to it, what might change and expand that possibility for you?

_____

_____

_____

PRACTICE. Rather than continuing to paddle as you have been, or asking for the storm to stop, consider focusing on Christ and asking Him what His step is for you. It may look like reading a particular book, going for a walk with someone you've been avoiding, signing up for a therapy appointment, or trusting someone else to hear your story. Taking that step may feel as scary and counterintuitive as walking on water, but we can take comfort in knowing Christ is in the storm with us. He has saved drowning souls before from the worst storms imaginable, and He knows how to do it for you too. One step at a time.

RELISHING
HOLY WEEK

> "On Easter Sunday we celebrate the most long-awaited and glorious event in the history of the world . . . the day that changed everything."
>
> DIETER F. UCHTDORF[13]

In the Old City of Jerusalem, tucked between narrow alleys lined with colorful merchant shops, are nondescript ceramic plaques tacked to ancient stone walls known as "stations of the cross." Although not the Lord's actual historical route, pilgrims since the 1700s have followed these touchstone markers to commemorate the Via Dolorosa—"The Way of Suffering"—the path Jesus likely followed on the way to His Crucifixion.

Walking this path is a full sensory experience, punctuated by moments of deep spiritual reflection—kind of like how life can be on other days. In a talk referencing this path through the Old City of Jerusalem, President Jeffrey R. Holland said, "One of the great consolations of this Easter season is that because Jesus walked such a long, lonely path utterly alone, we do not have to do so. His solitary journey brought great company for our little version of that path."[14]

PONDER. Not all of us can make it to the Old City, but we can all mindfully reflect on what Christ endured that Holy Week. What moments from His final week are important to you? As you review them in your mind, pause at these "stations" and imagine being in that moment with Christ. What emerges for you in this visualization?

_____

_____

_____

_____

_____

PRACTICE. Entering a historic cathedral, a church, or holy grounds like the Sacred Grove can generate a profound sense of awe. That inspiring sensation is amplified when you share the experience with other spiritual seekers. Something about being there together feels unifying and humbling. Imagine bringing that feeling of awe, unity, and humility to your Easter sacrament meeting.

SEEING HIS HAND
IN ALL THINGS

"Gratitude ... opens our minds to a universe permeated with the richness of a living God."

BONNIE D. PARKIN[15]

Of all the messages President Nelson could have shared in the middle of the pandemic, he chose to focus on "the healing power of gratitude."[16] Instead of only being grateful for that which brings us joy, comfort, and love, we are encouraged to give thanks in "every thing" (1 Thessalonians 5:18) and to "[receive] all things with thankfulness" (Doctrine and Covenants 78:19).

Like so much of what the Lord invites us to do, this can feel counterintuitive at first—even impossible. How are we supposed to feel gratitude in difficult times? This is perhaps only possible when the Lord helps us see our life with new eyes. Then, we can say with the Psalmist, "Let us come before his presence with thanksgiving, and make a joyful noise unto him" (Psalm 95:2).

Rather than a gratitude that is fickle and intermittent, this is a practice that can endure and make us more celestial. As Paul put it, "Cease not to give thanks" (Ephesians 1:16).

PONDER. Have you ever felt genuinely grateful for an experience that stretched and challenged you? How different would your life be if you experienced gratitude as more of a ceaseless practice—in everything and for all things?

_____

_____

_____

_____

_____

_____

_____

PRACTICE. Take a few moments at the beginning or end of each day to write down three to five things you appreciate. Making this a daily practice will help expand your awareness and hone your focus, helping you recognize God's hand in areas of your life you might have overlooked. Even in especially difficult times, keep up this practice, trying to find something to be grateful for, no matter how small.

A CONTEMPLATIVE
CHRISTMAS

> "Take time this Christmas season to sit for a few
> quiet moments and let the Savior's Spirit warm you.
> . . . Sit quietly with that little baby and come away
> spiritually strengthened . . . Let that moment be one
> of rest and refreshing and reassurance and renewal."
>
> D. TODD CHRISTOFFERSON[17]

Bishop Desmond Tutu, the Anglican archbishop in South Africa, once described how his relationship with God changed as he grew older. Rather than approaching heaven with endless petitions in "a kind of shopping list," he explained that he had learned to "grow in just being there with God. Like when you sit in front of a fire in winter, you are just there in front of the fire, and you don't have to be smart or anything. The fire warms you."

Referring to these remarks, Elder D. Todd Christofferson said, "I think that is a lovely metaphor—just sit with the Lord and let Him warm you like a fire in winter."

PONDER. Have you been able to sit quietly for a few moments this holiday season before the Christ child in a way that brings renewed hope and peace? If not, when could you find space and time to try that?

_____

_____

_____

_____

_____

_____

_____

_____

_____

_____

PRACTICE. In your next prayer, lay aside any list of petitions you may be accustomed to raising, and instead try just "being there," like you would in front of a fire in winter. How does that feel, compared with other experiences of prayer?

BEGINNING
AGAIN

> *"A thrill of hope, the weary world rejoices,*
> *for yonder breaks a new and glorious morn!"*
>
> "O HOLY NIGHT"[18]

When the apostle John saw God sitting on His throne, he heard, "Behold, I make all things new" (Revelation 21:5). Tomorrow doesn't have to be the same as today. That's one of the most encouraging promises of the gospel.

No matter where we are—and no matter where we have been—the Lord offers us a new mind (see Romans 12:2), a "new heart," (Ezekiel 36:26), and "newness of life" (Romans 6:4). If that kind of a mighty change sounds hard to fathom, maybe try appreciating the newness of the breath you are breathing right now—which is unlike any other breath you've ever taken.

It's possible to learn to approach future moments in our lives the same way: each one fresh, different, and brand new.

PONDER. How does it feel to approach this day, even this moment of your life, as brand new, and "fresh with no mistakes"?[19] Do you believe your own life can change in fundamental ways?

_____

_____

_____

_____

_____

_____

_____

_____

PRACTICE. All this sounds nice enough: new breath, new moment, new day, new year. But after you take a deep breath and move forward, the same struggles, fears, and pains experienced before can sometimes come rushing back. What then? None of the above changes. It all still applies. No matter what happens, the next moment can also be brand new. This can be true of every moment because of Jesus, who offers us a fresh start. Right now. As often as we need.

NOTES

INTRODUCTION

1. David A. Bednar, "Be Still, and Know That I Am God," *Liahona*, May 2024.

MINDFULNESS OF THE INTERNAL WORLD

1. Russell M. Nelson, "We Can Do Better and Be Better," *Liahona*, May 2019.
2. Gordon B. Hinckley, "The Body Is Sacred," *Ensign* or *Liahona*, November 2006.
3. Henry Wadsworth Longfellow, *The New England Tragedies* (Boston: Tickner and Fields, 1868), 21.
4. Judson Brewer, *Unwinding Anxiety: New Science Shows How to Break the Cycles of Worry and Fear to Heal Your Mind* (New York: Avery, Penguin Random House LLC, 2021).

MINDFULNESS WITH GOD

1. "Discourse, between circa 26 June and circa 2 July 1839, as Reported by Wilford Woodruff," Documents, volume 6, josephsmithpapers.org.
2. Quentin L. Cook, "Shipshape and Bristol Fashion: Be Temple Worthy—in Good Times and Bad Times," *Ensign* or *Liahona*, November 2015.
3. David O. McKay, in Conference Report, April 1946, 113–114.
4. "Praise to the Lord, the Almighty," *Hymns*, no. 19.
5. As quoted by Spencer W. Kimball in "The Things of Eternity," *Ensign*, January 1977, originally in Charles L. Wallis, ed., *Words of Life* (New York: Harper & Row, 1966), 45.
6. Dieter F. Uchtdorf, "After Christ parted from His disciples," Facebook, 15 June 2023.
7. Andrew James Pike, *Intention and Non-Doing in Therapeutic Bodywork* (Philadelphia: Singing Dragon, 2021).
8. See Russell M. Nelson, "Overcome the World and Find Rest," *Liahona*, November 2022; and Russell M. Nelson, "The Everlasting Covenant," *Liahona*, October 2022.
9. C. S. Lewis, *Mere Christianity* (New York: HarperCollins, 2001), 198–199.
10. Russell M. Nelson, "Revelation for the Church, Revelation for Our Lives," *Ensign* or *Liahona*, May 2018.
11. Richard G. Scott, "How to Learn by the Spirit," *New Era*, September 2014.
12. Ulisses Soares, "In Awe of Christ and His Gospel," *Liahona*, May 2022.

13. Russell M. Nelson, "We Can Do Better and Be Better," *Ensign* or *Liahona*, May 2019.

14. Dieter F. Uchtdorf, "Daily Restoration," *Liahona*, November 2021.

MINDFULNESS IN RELATIONSHIPS

1. Sharon Eubank, "Turning Enemies into Friends" (Brigham Young University forum, January 23, 2018), speeches.byu.edu.

2. Linda Stone, "Continuous Partial Attention—Not the Same as Multi-Tasking," *Bloomberg*, 23 July 2008, https://www.bloomberg.com/news/articles/2008-07-23/continuous-partial-attention -not-the-same-as-multi-tasking.

3. Dieter F. Uchtdorf, "The Good and Grateful Receiver," 2012 Christmas Devotional.

4. Megan E. Harrison et al., "Systematic Review of the Effects of Family Meal Frequency on Psychosocial Outcomes in Youth," *Canadian Family Physician*, vol. 61 (2), February 2015.

5. Sara Paston-Williams, *The Art of Dining: A History of Cooking & Eating* (New York: National Trust Books, HarperCollins, 2012).

6. Russell M. Nelson, "Closing Remarks," *Ensign* or *Liahona*, May 2019.

7. David A. Bednar, "Prepared to Obtain Every Needful Thing," *Ensign* or *Liahona*, May 2019.

8. Russell M. Nelson, "Becoming Exemplary Latter-day Saints," *Ensign* or *Liahona*, November 2018.

9. Lucy Mack Smith, Relief Society Minutes, March 24, 1842, Archives of The Church of Jesus Christ of Latter-day Saints, 18–19.

10. "Jesus Once Was a Little Child," *Children's Songbook*, 55.

11. See Jacob Hess, "Family history as a public health intervention?," *Deseret News*, 4 March 2024, https://www.deseret.com/faith/2024/03/04/can-family-history-help-youth/.

12. D. Todd Christofferson, "The Doctrine of Belonging," *Liahona*, November 2022.

13. Russell M. Nelson, "The Everlasting Covenant," *Liahona*, November 2022.

14. D. Todd Christofferson, "The Doctrine of Belonging," *Liahona*, November 2022.

15. Sarah Jane Weaver, "Video: Revelation is 'scattered among us,' President Bingham says," *Church News*, 11 August 2021.

16. M. Russell Ballard, "Counseling with Our Councils," *Ensign*, May 1994.

17. Sydney Walker, "Video: What it means to Elder Bednar to 'counsel in council,'" *Church News*, 17 November 2021.

18. Russell M. Nelson, "Ministering," *Ensign* or *Liahona*, May 2018.

19. Jeffrey R. Holland, "Be With and Strengthen Them," *Ensign* or *Liahona*, May 2018.

20. Tim Madigan, *I'm Proud of You: Life Lessons from My Friend Fred Rogers* (Sheridan: Gotham, 2007).

21. "Compassion," Oxford English Dictionary, https://www.oed.com/dictionary/compassion_n?tl =true&tab=etymology.

22. Bruce R. McConkie, "Only an Elder," *New Era*, January 2003.

MINDFULNESS IN CHALLENGE AND CELEBRATION

1. M. Scott Peck, *The Road Less Traveled: A New Psychology of Love, Traditional Values and Spiritual Growth* (New York: Touchstone, 2003).
2. Mary Richards, "President Nelson posts about labels and true identity," *Church News*, 20 July 2022.
3. Russell M. Nelson, "Choices for Eternity," Worldwide Devotional for Young Adults, 15 May 2022.
4. Russell M. Nelson, "Choices for Eternity."
5. David O. McKay, "Consciousness of God: Supreme Goal of Life," *Improvement Era*, June 1967, 80.
6. Russell M. Nelson, "Your 7-Day Social Media Fast," *New Era*, March 2019.
7. Stephen Covey, foreword in Alex Pattakos, *Prisoners of Our Thoughts: Viktor Frankl's Principles for Discovering Meaning in Life and Work* (Oakland, CA: Berrett-Koehler Publishers, 2010).
8. *Teachings of Presidents of the Church: Joseph F. Smith* (1998), 301.
9. Neil A. Maxwell, "According to the Desire of [Our] Hearts," *Ensign*, November 1996.
10. See Willem Kuyken et al., "Efficacy of mindfulness-based cognitive therapy in prevention of depressive relapse: An individual patient data meta-analysis from randomized trials," *JAMA Psychiatry*, vol. 73 (6), 2016, 565–574. See also Eduardo Ramadas et al., "Effectiveness of Mindfulness-Based Relapse Prevention in Individuals with Substance Use Disorders: A Systematic Review," *Behavioral Sciences*, vol. 11(10), 29 September 2021, 133.
11. Emily Belle Freeman, as reported by Mary Richards, "President Freeman and Sister Dennis testify of Jesus Christ through West Africa ministry," *Church News*, 22 November 2023.
12. "Sandy Hook Parents Francine and David Wheeler | SuperSoul Sunday | Oprah Winfrey Network," OWN, 20 November 2013, https://www.youtube.com/watch?v=4tsg4NqHYvY.
13. Dieter F. Uchtdorf, "The Gift of Grace," *Ensign* or *Liahona*, May 2015.
14. Jeffrey R. Holland, "None Were with Him," *Ensign* or *Liahona*, May 2009.
15. Bonnie D. Parkin, "Gratitude: A Path to Happiness," *Ensign* or *Liahona*, May 2007.
16. Russell M. Nelson, "President Russell M. Nelson on the Healing Power of Gratitude," November 2020, https://www.churchofjesuschrist.org/media/video/2020-11-1100-president -russell-m-nelson-on-the-healing-power-of-gratitude?lang=eng.
17. D. Todd Christofferson, "Be at Peace," *Liahona*, December 2015.
18. Traditional carol.
19. Kevin Sullivan, *Anne of Green Gables*; Ottawa, Canada: Anne of Green Gables Productions, 1985.

ACKNOWLEDGMENTS

A special thanks to Debi Barley, for inspired and meaningful contributions to early drafts of the book. And to Rachel Reist for thoughtful feedback and inspiring several other entries. We also express our appreciation to Alison Palmer and Kristen Evans for shaping and improving our manuscript through remarkably helpful editing. Appreciations to my sweet baby girls, Emma and Olivia, for modeling grace in affliction. And to their brothers William, Sam, Joseph, and Joshua, for patience with their father's continuing practice of mindful living. And especially for Monique, who witnesses close-up the many ways I fall short, but loves me anyway.

—JACOB

Thanks to the many whose desire for deeper stillness, connection, and compassion inspired this book. To my book brother, Jacob Hess, and the incredible team at Deseret Book: Thank you for your vision and tenacity in turning ideas and words into a beautiful, tangible reality. And to my partners in full-catastrophe living—Kevin, Savanna, and Michael. There's no one else I'd want to be in this practice with.

—CARRIE

INTRODUCTION

I am thrilled to celebrate my term as Cupertino Poet Laureate by gathering into one place so many of the diverse voices from our greater community. When I first conceived of this project, I imagined a small collection of poems from a dozen or so local poets and writers.

Instead, our anthology consists of three hundred and fifty pages from over eighty contributors. It's clear I had underestimated the need felt by Bay Area writers to not only express themselves creatively but also find a home for this expression! I'm so happy to provide that space here.

The idea for this anthology was born years ago, before I became Cupertino's fifth Poet Laureate. I was in a workshop facilitated by Ann Muto, Cupertino's fourth Poet Laureate, and as I sat listening to brave writers share early versions of their poems, I wanted to bottle up all the poems to take home and read again and again. Becoming a poet laureate wasn't on my to-do list at the time, but the idea of collecting voices stuck.

When I was selected to serve, I knew that instead of a contest, which pits creators against each other, I wanted to celebrate the community's creativity and my time as Cupertino Poet Laureate by bringing my community's voices together. The result? A beautiful community anthology that will carry our voices into the future.

The works in this book are separated into sections of poetry and prose and ordered alphabetically by contributor last name. Our contributors range in age from elementary school students to writers in their ninth decade; from people penning their first piece to celebrated writers with a long list of publications; from writers native to Cupertino to transplants from a world away. The poems and prose pieces each person sent in tell their stories, their experiences – both imagined and real – and their emotional landscapes in authentic, unique voices.

This anthology is a collection of some of the most captivating voices I've read because they are the voices of my friends and neighbors. The voices of the people who work at tech giants and the voices of teachers in the schools down the street. The voices of the children struggling to become, and the voices of their grandparents learning to let go. The voices of people who live here and the voices of people who have passed through.

In short, this anthology is the voice of Cupertino.

Some of the poems and writings within these pages began when an idea at a Cupertino Poet Laureate event generated a stream of creativity. During my term, I had the privilege and joy of igniting the creative spark for the attendees of my many programs. Their courage in trying new things and sharing their first drafts in workshop ignited my own creative fires.

When I teach creativity workshops, I like to engage in the activities and challenges alongside the participants. Sometimes this isn't feasible. But when it is, I dive in feet first because there is something about the creative energy of a group that affects the creative process and product.

The initial draft of the following poem started in a workshop. I let it marinate for a while before taking up the pen again. I am honored to share it with you here:

I'M NOT ONE OF THE GREATS

I'm not one of the greats.

Poems don't spill
from me fully formed
to draw on the heartstrings
at the seat of your soul.

They don't even drip,
drop by inky drop,
onto the page to meld
into the outline
of something beautiful.

I wasn't touched
by the Muse
or gifted by God
with the words
of the angels.

Instead I must sink to my knees
and dig with trembling fingers
deep into the dirt, yanking out rocks
and stones to create a space
for the hard-shelled seed
that holds only the ghost
of something more.

I must water it with my tears
and feed it with the blood of my truth.
Guard it from the greedy hands of doubt
when the shoot breaks through
and coax its plain, common stem
with whispered promises that carry
warm cotton candy scents
and the sting of kerosene from yesteryears.

CELEBRATE CREATIVITY

I stand close to watch the bees
and butterflies that land in fleeting frenzies
on its rainbow petals as they unfurl
to reveal the future's burning sun —
just once before they drop.

No, I'm not one of the greats.
Nor do I wish to be.

I'm content to share a sliver,
a tiny piece of my existence,
with words melded and formed
with the strength of a blacksmith
molding iron in the forge. Then watch
as they flutter out into the world,
like snowflakes scattered on the wind
that land for just a moment
on the tip of someone else's tongue.

I'm not one of the greats.

But poetry has made me,
as it makes anyone who finds
the courage to commit a glimpse
of their perfectly imperfect psyches
to paper, extraordinary.

I chose to share this poem in the anthology because I feel the message speaks to *all* of us. Whether we're writers or not, we are all creators. It is not an easy task to take an unformed thought, a memory of emotion, a taste of your imperfections and fear, and set them free in the world. By having the courage to act, you are, my friend, extraordinary.

It has been my honor to serve this community of extraordinary people as Cupertino Poet Laureate. I look forward to continuing my mission of celebrating the imagination in each of us by helping others explore and express their creativity. I hope you'll join me.

With warmth and gratitude,

Kaecey

Keiko,
Stay creative!
xo Kaecey

Kaecey McCormick
Cupertino Poet Laureate, 2018-2020
www.kaeceymccormick.com

CUPERTINO
POET LAUREATE
Celebrate Creativity

POETRY CONTRIBUTORS

Advay Anand
James Andrews
Donna Austin
Jyoti Bachani
Floi Baker
Gloria Bares *Gloria Bares*
Edith Barr *Edith Barr*
Débora Benacot
Milan Bhardwaj
Jade Bradbury
Jennifer Swanton Brown
Lynn Carole Brown
Kedaton Campbell
Melody Chen
Dara
David Denny
Carolyn Donnell
Jeanne Farrington
Karen Franzenburg
Constance Guidotti
Vicki Harvey
Jack Hasling
Marian Hirsch
Mirna Hirschl
John Hogle
Larry Hollist
Anita Holzberg
Kelvin Hu
Jannah Hussaini
Nhi Huynh
Deeya Jain
Veena Karthik
Eva Kashkooli
Dania Khan
Sandra Khoury
Joyce Kiefer
Hilary King
Phyllis Klein
Sundeep Kohli
Lita Kurth
Gene F. Lee
Nathan Lee

Deborah LeFalle
Caroline Lindley
Paul Liu
Pushpa MacFarlane *Pushpa MacFarlane*
Sinead McCaffery
Maggie McCormick
Lesa Medley
Rodrigo Muralles
Ann Muto
Charlotte Pannell
Jane Park
Robert Pesich
Nils Peterson
Stephanie Pressman
Charleene Puder
Polina Runova
Maya Sabatino
Lisa Scott-Ponce
Samhita Srivatsan
Christina Stubler
Aabha Vadapalli
Amrutha Vaidyam
Arike van de Water
Peter Verbica
Vivek Verma
Kathleen Virmani
Arya Vishin
Kristin Weller
Amanda Williamsen
Flo Oy Wong
Jing Jing Yang
Amelie Yun

PROSE CONTRIBUTORS

Floi Baker
Melody Chen
Katerine Escobar
Kelly A. Harrison
Trisha Iyer
Deborah LeFalle
Alexandra McCormick
Hunter McDivitt
Kiara Palominos
Nils Peterson
Julia Satterthwaite
Florence Srmek Schorow
Amelie Yun

POETRY

ADVAY ANAND

TRANSITORY IMAGES

It never fails to strike when least anticipated,
As a Leviathan being rounding its circuits,
Taking with it immeasurable amounts of virtue
The temporal beast that devours that which is transient
And impermanent; That is how a glorious past is destroyed,
Utterly scattered and shattered; Never to regain any form
But there always exists nature
That does not conform to the rules of time,
And will live to be enjoyed by posterity
It is futile to assume that creation can outlast
The eternity of the natural world
And our place within it is proportional to an atom
Among the stars.

In Friedrich's *Abbey In The Oakwood*, for instance, how the forlorn structure decays
Among the oaks, lifeless, in disrepair, a woeful silhouette
Located amidst the desolate graveyard, and such is the sad state
Of man's creation; A line of monks waits to enter the abbey,
Carrying with them a coffin, while an ominous mist silently screams
Of death, disaster, distress; But above it all the moon allows its gleam
To unfurl itself and light up the heavens, and there it stays
For generations; immune to the challenges of time.

JAMES ANDREWS

THE WINDOW WASHER

The rain has stopped,
and we are drinking *kopi* inside the Seasons cafe in
Johor Bahru.
Done with our errands, we consider
the birthday party dessert:
pandan cake, Nonya *kueh*, kiwi tarts?

Outside
there is a man washing windows.

My eyes follow him across the glass
as he
      reaches up
           sweeps the sponge
                steps to the right.

Each reach, sweep, step
a ballet
learned in the rainforest,
where men dance, bird-like, in lanternlight
and *orang-utans* swing among ironwood trees.

Through the glass
a rainbow
      arcs
         over oil palms.

Tonight
it will be pandan cake, and
I
will dance.

FLYING KITES

Old men flying kites,
wind fluttering ribbon tails.
When will the rain come?

THERE IS NEVER SNOW

There is never snow
on this side of the mountain.
Only sunflowers!

DONNA AUSTIN

CUPERTINO IS UNIQUE AND LIKE NO OTHER CITY

Cupertino is unique and like no other city
    A precious mix of special,
        talented,
            educated, industrious,
                culturally vibrant people
Cupertino's history is one of exploration and innovation!
    Our priorities
        are education, research,
          hard work
            protecting our environment
      and lifelong learning!
Making room for our librarians, teachers, dentists, caretakers, lawyers, mechanics,
engineers, gardeners, plumbers, fire fighters, police officers, janitors, health care
providers, housecleaners and others from all walks of life is our biggest challenge!

Making room for sharing that 'American Dream!
    Balance,
      Creativity,
        And Caring, are the key!
           Together we can find the way!

JYOTI BACHANI

A MODERN FAIRYTALE

With time stolen
From their busy lives
Safely private
In a public place
The simmering passion
Of their gentle kisses
Warmly melted the hour
Creating the singularity
Each second of which
Contained an eternity
Of all the fairytales
In which the prince
Makes the princess
Live happily ever after.

Now if life intrudes
All she needs to do
Is dive into the memory
Of that moment's glory
To feel the
Smiling sunshine
Light up her spirit
Touch the beauty
Of infinite love
Rekindled instantly from
Once upon a time.

FROM DIRT TO DUST

I want to be
Swaddled in a soft duvet
Curled up in fetal pose
With my back covered up
With your body's weight
And me held strongly
And firmly till I feel
Secure to unfold

And lie on my back
Sprawled out
Open arms
No covers
With my head in your lap
And your hands
Pressing down on
my forehead and scalp
Till my shoulders drop
Down to the floor

So I am free to
Welcome you
Beside me
hold you gently
And melt & rock
Until we are still

And you rise up
To sit beside me
Gazing into my eyes
And move my feet
To butterfly my legs
I close my eyes
To hear better

As you describe
The beautiful flower
Georgia O'Keefe saw
That bloomed with
your desire once
Soft and strong
That bears pain
Gives pleasures
Yields nectar
Gets treated like dirt

See it with love
That it so deserves
Say you are sorry
For the wrongs
Of this world
And rest your head
On my soft belly

So I can run
My fingers through
Your hair
And maybe pull
Your ears for
Being so cheeky
And we laugh
Hysterically because
I'm still very ticklish

This is what I wish
But instead
I'll go sit by a tree
Feel it's bark
Scratch my back
Breathe the air
And if I'm lucky
Get a caress
From a gentle breeze
Which will whisper
In my ear
You are dust
Come fly with me
And I will be free.

A QUANTUM GARDEN

There is a secret garden
In my heart
Where my mind goes
To take a walk
Amongst the sounds
Sights and unsure caresses
Of memories past
That won't fade
Because their beauty
Is nurtured by a
Quantum entanglement
With Schrodinger's Cat
And spooky action at a distance
That will only collapse
To reality when measured

Do I dare take stock,
Or simply continue to walk?

Jyoti Bachen

SLOW FLOW

It's dawn
The world is still calm
I'm half awake and well rested
I reach out and find you near
I snuggle up to spoon
My breath matches yours
You pat my hand
There is peace
In the universe

The world can end now

But the world never ends
We learn to bury our dreams
Pull our self together
And carry on
Enslaved to its dictates
Sacrificing to perpetuate it
Unable to permit
The slow flow
That sustains us.

FLOI BAKER

CALI

September 1, 2008

On this very date one year ago,
 there would be only twelve days left
before you would be sucked into the
vacuum of the unknown…
No longer shackled by the manacle that
kept you prisoner to the disease.
I kept asking "Why?" "Why?" "Why?!"
Maybe I shouldn't have brought you here.
Going over and over it in my mind.
Questioning myself,
"If only…..?" "If only!"

Soon you would be gone.
I could feel you purring in those final moments,
as I held your soft cat body against me…
purring through your last breath.
Looking to me…
An untrusting street cat…now with total
 trust in me…your gift to me.
 "I can't bear this!" "I can't!"
But I had to… for you…because you had to.
I could never be as brave as you were.

 The technician was crying
 as she patted you on the head,
     and said softly,
 "Good-bye sweet cat."
 I asked, "Is she gone?"
The doctor said, "Keep talking to her."
I tried hard to be calm, for your sake.
I tried…but I was no longer an adult.
My sweat and my tears became one.
And you…in my arms, trusting me…
     were gone.
      Gone!
And now…you are free.
But how I have missed you! Sleeping on
my pillow, and the funny way you drank
water. Not like any of the other cats!
I remember how the fur on your back

would twitch with tremendous pleasure
when I sang your song to you.
Everyone here knows their own
little song, and you knew yours!

No more sitting in the window sill
  to watch your kittens playing
in the yard. Ten years old now,
I remember the day they were born…
And how many times you moved them
    so they would be safe from
      the curious on the street!
  When I had to take them to the clinic
        for a brief stay,
the doctor who took care of them
named them the "Popcorn Cats."
When I asked him why, he said,
"Because they're always jumping
    and hissing and spitting."

Cricket, the runt of the litter,
  now Miss Independence,
with the gold tip on her tail
to match the exact same spot where
  you had a white one.
Flirt still acts out to get his way, just
  like a kid! And it works!
Ribbon, as usual, sits on the blue
  upside down flower pot…
her vantage point to jump from
when trying to attack some of
    the cats on the
other side of the window.
And Little Cali is just like you…
so shy, with your mannerisms exactly!
The very heart and soul of you!

    When they're inside,
      I no longer ask them,
    "Where's the big dog,"
  in that certain tone of voice that
      totally got their attention…
  Sucking in my breath, I'd hesitate, then...
"Where's the big dog?!" He so amused them
as he lay on the cool floor near them.
  I'm sure they thought he was a giant!
No longer do I ask them that, because

the last time I did, I had to tell them…
    "The big dog is in heaven
      with your Momma."
  They were all sitting together,
    so quiet, so attentive,
Listening, listening, looking ever so serious.
      But I tell them,
"Your Momma is still watching over you…
  and will always love you."
 You were such a good mother, Cali!

  I have the poignant memory
of the time we were in the lobby
  after one of your last visits
    to the doctor.
I was holding the carrier with you in it,
  when a lady there looked inside,
    and exclaimed,
"Oh, you have a Calico Cat!"
    I told her,
"She's white with Calico patches."
Again, she exclaimed, enthusiastically,
  "She's beautiful!"
  I said, "Thank you,"
  trying to sound positive.
But at that particular moment,
  it startled my very being,
  which cried out, inside myself
"And such beauty cannot die!"

  As I lit the golden candle…
  And watched its golden flame…
I prayed a fervent prayer for you,
  And whispered your name,
    CALI!

TO WINTERSONG

For All Februarys Since 1992
Dedicated to God

This is my Gethsemane
Where I come
When I am broken,
To gather new strength.
Where the moon is beautiful
   over this place,
I wrestle with the angels.

For too long I couldn't come
 To where my longing is.
But at last I stood…my soul naked,
Beneath sheltering branches,
Where nature's cross is carved
 in rude wood,
And the Tiger Lily is resurrected
 at my feet.

In this place, the sacred chair
Is a reminder of the pain,
 the thirst.
Where we sought the warmth of the sun
 for comfort.
Now, with heavy heart
 and trembling hand,
I slowly reach to touch it.
To ask a blessing upon it.

Wild wind shakes the branches
 Above me,
Blowing my hair freely
To mingle with the branches
      And the leaves.

   In anguish,
With my tears spilling over,
You forgave me everything.

MEMORIES

In a dusty attic in an old cedar chest,
    I found…

An ivory comb that kept
    her hair in place.

A lock of golden hair
    tied with a bit of lace.

A tarnished silver heart
    holds the faint image of her face.

Satin slippers
    that danced into dusk…

A crumbling red rose
    once beautiful when given to her,
    with a promise and a kiss.

Voices fading into twilight years

The echo of laughter
    Frozen in a memory.

Timeless images and silent tears.

DAUGHTER OF THE MOON

I am a daughter of the moon. I dance on those nights when it casts its silver to the earth. I stand with my face naked, looking long and long, as it drifts in the sky, wafted by clouds. A mist covers it and touches my face, and we are one. I am a daughter of the moon.

NOVEMBER MOON

It's been years, but
it seems like just yesterday
  that the unforgettable
November storm happened.
The weather had been moody
  all day.
One could feel an energy in
  the air....
like,,, you're waiting on the threshold
  of something mysterious that's
  about to happen.

I was at home with my
  beloved dog, Mai Tai
    when it all began...
    early evening.
The raw energizing force
 of the wind... and the
spattering of rain drops.
 I wanted to be out in it!
To feel it ... to be a part of it ...
  to be closer to it.
 So I carried my dog
 to the deck, where we
stayed until it started
 raining in earnest!
Nature was getting wild!
    And I loved it!
 I felt connected to it.
    Belonged to it!

When we came back into
  the house,
I kept the door open
 because there was a
 spectacular view of
the moon from there,
and I wanted to share the
 moment with my dog.
 So we sat on the floor
    together,
watching from the doorway.

The moon was beginning its rise...
huge and full, one of the brightest

I had ever ever seen…
back lighting the clouds in
the most lustrous silver,
as shafts of the radiance
were sifted down through
    silvery rain.
Absolutely spellbinding!
And I… was under the spell
of that "wild November moon!"

While I watched with my dog,
the moon became surrounded
 by clouds that were
    so filled…
and spilling over with light
    shining so gloriously,
it seemed they must have
    been divinely lit!

 Then like the ever changing
  colors and patterns
  of a kaleidoscope,
   that wild moon
 became nearly covered
with glass-like blue clouds.
  Electrifying!
But with just a twist and a turn,
 those would become wispy
    smoke clouds,
   and vaporous,
obscuring the moon's face.
And then quite suddenly,
 would lift away like a curtain
    being drawn,
 to reveal a wind-swept sky
and it's starry companions.
 It all changed so quickly,
  and much too soon the
    outline of it
  was barely visible.

I could not …. just could not believe
I had actually seen all that … and felt
  that I was a part of it ….
    but most of all,
  to have shared it
with my beloved dog!

It would be her last November with me.

And now I knew why the weather
had been so moody and mysterious
          that day!
   We were on the threshold…
          the very edge
of the most magical storm that
   brought the silver rain
          and the
   never to be forgotten
   wild and wondrous
     November moon!

RAVEN

Here in the Valley, it's a common sight to see crows.
Raucous obnoxious birds, they are everywhere;
In the trees, caw caw cawing,
sitting atop telephone poles, and on the wires,
in the streets looking for food,
or flap flap flapping through the air.
But you oh raven, fine feathered fellow
so full of yourself,
you were no such ordinary crow!
    Oh, no no no!
Black, shiny, and silken,
Smart, and oh so bold!

It was my good fortune to arrive at
Peet's Coffee Shop, El Paseo,
one afternoon, just in time to see you,
arrogant bird, larger than life,
parading among a patio audience there.
Taking your time…
Cocking your head slowly
    from side to side…
cluck-clucking with pride,
knowing you were the show!

  Captivating was your presence,
  as purple iridescent beads rolled
  off your glossy back in the sunlight,
bouncing one after the other
with each audacious step you took.
While your audience on both sides of the aisle,
leaned away in their chairs,
unsure, as you sauntered through…
though no doubt in awe of you,
so ominous was your dark mystique!

As you strolled past me,
I caught that mysterious glint in your eye,
perhaps holding secrets of days gone by.
I wondered…. could you be an ancestor
of that Raven from long ago…
The one who visited our famous Mr. Poe?
In pondering it, this I did know…

If you should perch upon my door,
I'd be the one to say,
    "Nevermore!"
And nevermore!

GLORIA BARES

IN THE REDWOOD GROVE

I see her coming toward me on the path in the park,
      an aged Asian woman,
      her round, wrinkled face expressionless,
      shoulders and back bent forward.
      She concentrates on moving in small steps,
      trusting her cane to keep her balance.

A young man waits a short distance from me.
      "Hello," I say, "Isn't the park beautiful
      in this afternoon light?".
      "Yes. Mom and I come here for our daily walk," he replies
      in soft tones of practiced reticence.

I walk ahead to her, extending my hand.
      Hers lingers warm in mine,
      fingers gently exploring,
      massaging, as if she learns about me through Braille.

She lifts her head.
      A warm smile energizes her face,
      greeting me like a long-ago friend.
      Eyes the color of brown sugar
      circle my face for several minutes.
      I wonder what deep wells of wisdom lie
      behind these searching eyes?

We walk together, hand in hand, very slowly,
      down the path to where her son stands patiently.
      "My mother doesn't speak any English," he says.
    "It didn't matter," I reply.

EDITH BARR

ONE BLOCK, FOUR SEASONS

daily walk unveils
scents, sounds, sights – such richness
one block – four seasons

seven yellow leaves
nature's sweet caress - on the
artificial grass

rise before the sun
returning after sunset
days framed in darkness

too busy for spring
joys unseen, then - from my shoe
a crushed blossom falls

long days, warm evenings
dawn walks are crisp and bracing
summer turns to fall

WALKING AROUND THE BLOCK

Walking around the block
Always the same path
Every day different and the same
Feel the connection

Always the same path
See the flower bud, blossom, fade
Feel the connection
The mourning dove calls from her nest

See the flower bud, blossom, fade
Where is the moon? Can I see the sun?
The mourning dove calls from her nest
Across the field I see the skyline

Where is the moon? Can I see the sun?
The smell of moist earth and grass
Across the field I see the skyline
Redwoods next to palm trees

The smell of moist earth and grass
Blessed by the miracle of rain
Redwoods next to palm trees
The journey ends at the beginning

Blessed by the miracle of rain
Every day different and the same
The journey ends at the beginning
Walking around the block

26 June 2019

OAK TREE

The tree branches skyward and groundward
Swaying in a breeze that shakes branches and leaves
The leaf's veins running out from the stem
The sharp points on the leaf's edge

Swaying in a breeze that shakes branches and leaves
The feel of the branches under my hands, my feet
Dancing with the sweet slow rhythm of life

The leaf's veins running out from the stem
The sharp scent of the leaf's sap
Bitter – the taste of green

The sharp points on the leaf's edge
Cutting into the flesh of my hand
Dropping to the soil – our blood mixes – tree sisters

31 July 2019

DOG & BEE

A dual-voice poem

Compact and yellow with

Spots

Stripes

of black

creeping

flying

in search of

safety

pollen

I am searching for

I always know

a way home

Leaves & branches stretching
overhead block the view

Leaves & flowers spread out below

Four paws tremble on the earth

Four wings vibrate in the air

Bright eyes searching

Five eyes searching

I don't know

I can see

Where I am.

HAIKU COLLECTION

sourced oceans apart
our parents lives flow through
my sister and me

***

autumn equinox
balances in northern lands
New Zealand's spring wakes

***

indoors filled with light
laughter, warmth seems everywhere
turning look outward

***

sorting old papers
hopes and fears intermingled
lungs filled with dust

DÉBORA BENACOT

UNTITLED
TRANSLATION BY MARGARET YOUNG

Días de crecer como el bamboo	Days of growing like bamboo
y noches con espinas en el lomo	and nights with thorns in my back
tu ausencia es este trapo sucio	your absence is this dirty rag
con que repaso los recuerdos	I used to rub my memories
uno a uno	one by one
hasta que brillen	until they gleam
absurda paradoja	absurd paradox
que sea tan opaco	how opaque it is
el vidrio por el cual	this glass through which
osas mirarme.	you dare to look at me.

CANDYWOMAN

Si digo mi nombre	If I say my name
en voz alta	out loud
tres veces	three times
frente a un espejo	in front of a mirror
casi seguro	I will
aparezco.	almost certainly
	appear.

CONSUELO DE TONTOS / FOOL'S CONSOLATION

Un poema no cambia el mundo	A poem does not change the world
ni anuda el hambre	or knot hunger
ni aplaca guerras	or placate wars
y sin embargo	and yet
en el lugar y momento indicados	at the right place and time
tal vez pueda ser	perhaps it might be
una tregua de palabras	a words truce
embrague de los mundos	clutch of the worlds
cierta especie de alimento.	some kind of nourishment.

EVENTUALLY

It's been a long day/life/nightmare

you are a heart that waits
the traffic lights
to keep its blood moving

you are a pair of blurry eyes
with broken windshield wipers

and you wonder
who unleashed the pain/rain/sadness
what liquid architecture has been growing
around our fears
is there a home to come back to
why are we all in this hurry

eventually, you'll learn

stop asking the wrong questions.

Inspired by the painting "Evening Rain" by William Dunn for the Spoken Art Project: Visual Art through the Lens of Poetry, 2018

MILAN BHARDWAJ

BREAD OF LIFE

Earth: a mass, dead inert,
Over millennia by sun
Baked into nutrients rich
For life to sprout which
It sustains and supports.
Light - this process' heart
That turns matter into bread
Rising with life's bubbles.

Mortal: senses, spirit apart,
Over time by Grace
Softened into spirit's cast,
Sprouting a consciousness vast
Offered to divinity as food first.
Light- this process' heart
That turns life into bread
Rising to incorporate spirit's spaces.

REARVIEW MIRROR

On passage through Life's roads,
Sometimes see ahead:
Snarl severe with traffic's pace slowed.
Delay with railway crossing gates closed.
The storm's gift of a blocked tree's load
Or repair and roadworks' closed roads.
Minor hitches, petty glitches incommode,
That leave me mildly upset and annoyed.

But at times with anxious heart's overload
In accidents entangled; mishaps embroiled,
Seeing other's lives and limbs destroyed.
Plans, trips, excursions spoiled and foiled.
Vehicle soul-soiled, from scenes recoiled;
Seen looming mountains menacing wild,
Faced sheer precipitous cliff-faces side,
With fears, worry, dismay, dread inside.

In darkness navigated, of light deprived.
Also in misfortune's furnace been broiled.
And faced times with energy's fuel devoid.
Seen road ahead to be a dark abyss void.
Towed vehicle with its baggage, toiled
Singly; lost poise amidst such turmoils.
Naturally there were vistas surely enjoyed
As blithely cruised through fields of gold.

But with all those miles under my belt's share
With soul less often needing tuning, repair.
Learnt so; a lesson rare for my welfare.
Be it trial, trivial or critical, that does scare,
I try to see it as in a rearview mirror's glare.
Bearable seen with this perspective's stare,
Bugbears, nightmares and all such despair.
Looking back, seems so far the ride pretty fair.
Almost as if the Lord on vehicle does declare
With His stamp : " Fragile, Handle with Care."

JADE BRADBURY

ELEMENTAL

unable to know
my own expiration date
breath sustains until

LAND OF BROKEN PARTS

Sorting through handmade
textiles in a tribal crafts
exhibit booth, I caught the owner's
clear blue eye, and her other
softly closed one, fringed
with smooth lashes, resting
serenely above an aging cheek.
Fellow traveler, I guessed, living
forward differently.

She noted my uneven chest,
and swollen arm, didn't
bat an eye, but touched her resting
eye and said a brain tumor
had charmed it shut, that she
sees much better now.

We talk-storied, sifting
weavings in the bin; savored
threads and brightly patterned
sleeves; bonded over woven
wefts, until…our three eyes met,
agreed accommodation
works just fine. We hugged
as strangers do when kinship isn't
sought but found, knowing
in the land of broken parts,
a willing heart can see.

BLOWING IN THE WIND

The "Butterfly Lady" in Lonelyville
grows milkweeds migrating monarchs crave,
says, "they know you can't wall off the wind."
And they feast on her Fire Island fare
before flying to fir groves in Michoacán,
there, to reside as dense, orange, pulsating
clouds, cradling their royal progeny.

Meanwhile, we two-leggeds, feckless
predators of land, sky, and sea, prowl
among what remains of our careless
ways, seeking gourmet diversity.
We call on science and sometimes prayer
to challenge our very cells somehow--
maybe to wall off gale-force winds
we've brought upon ourselves.

LETTER TO GOD
After Hafiz

How like you to speak to me of trees,
piercing the feathered air as if
poetry could teach the heart of loss,
convey the constancy of change.

So much flux breeds excess caution—
I'm still not at home with it—how could
I be, who only wanted to love you,
as if it came to me naturally.

The mind that ever fears the worst
speaks volumes about its motives,
always asking what if and why not,
mainly intending, "Then show me!"

And that you do, more often than not
stranding me here on rock in sight
Of sky: What now, Love, is this all?
Will you love me eternally?

DAS BOOT: SIXTH EXTINCTION LOG

Note a lone fishing vessel
rocking in the ocean swells
like a seesaw, off the coast
of Maine. Ma Atlantic
delivers as best she can
scant scallop harvests
to this doughty trawler,
but it's pretty much bait
and switch, now that she's
almost all fished out.
Which is why the fishermen
had switched from cod
to scallop trapped in nets,
soon to vanish like all the rest.

They'll let bygones be bygones
anon, depart Ma's watery
grave to scour the sun-parched land;
become seekers of terrestrial
wash-ups until the face
of the earth is covered over
with living water again.

CAST UPON THE WATERS

Then one moon-fraught
night, it rained
silvery fish, thousands
arcing and pulsing
like stars or fireworks
streaming slowly
downward
in a foamy, twinkling mire
of mist as if nothing
unusual had taken place.

Some people keened
at the sight, their first pained
howls a grim sign
something had changed,
they didn't know what
and feared the worst,
the face of the earth a boggy
plain, the fish not sure
where to be when their world's
a shifting, dying sea.

JENNIFER SWANTON BROWN
SECOND POET LAUREATE OF THE CITY OF CUPERTINO

A GATE IN CUPERTINO
For the Cupertino Library 10th Anniversary, 18 October 2014

In Cupertino, there is a rickety gate in a redwood fence.
It hides recycle bins and drying laundry.
Cats sit on the gate in the morning
waiting to be fed.

For dreamers in Ancient Greece,
there was a gate of 'sawn ivory,'
and a gate of 'polished horn.'
Penelope asked the old stranger
if her dreams of her wandering husband
were false or true.

High in the mountains of Hunan province,
there is a gate on the Yellow River
where a strong carp, who perseveres,
who swims with courage and leaps up,
becomes a dragon.

We live in a modern city
without stone walls, without iron fortifications.
The gates to our city are freeways and wide boulevards.
Here, there is a gateway to learning—
shining with glass and flanked by
trees of fire, the library gates are made of fountains.

Enter these gates today.
You don't need a magic key.
Enter these gates today to dream,
enter to be transformed.

PUBLICITY
For AK

I sent emails to the people
who mean the most to me.
I invited my friends,
but some live in Maine, and NYC,
and one has to travel
to meet an old lover,
10 years isn't too long
in some lives.

It's hard to be someone.

Look at the geese!
I counted twenty-three
flying with their all-the-live-long-day necks
over Hyannisport Dr.
They move every fall
from the Percolation Pond
behind the 7-11 to the lawns
at Cupertino Hills Swim & Racquet.
They move above us
in their chevrons and lines, shape-
shifting in the wind
the way a piece of three-ply yarn –
black, white, gray – would move
held out in a child's hand,
or a cobweb spun from a crone's
spell. Almost Halloween.

The geese have very busy
lives of beauty
to perform
and do not worry
if their messages
go unread.

Being someone is for the birds.

CUPERTINO, WHAT IS YOUR MOON?
A Lunar New Year Sestina

Once a year, the year begins again.
The sun has made his one cycle, the moon
her twelve. The time has come to count your luck,
to launch anew – sure-footed as a goat –
your way, your goals and all your many dreams.
A city – like a woman or a man –

shakes off the dust. Each woman, child, man,
each teenager, each grandmother, again,
each grandfather compares today with dreams
long dreamed, imagined once under the moon
of youth. But truth is stubborn, like a goat,
and dreams as unreliable as luck.

And cities, built of stone, if they have luck,
are only as lucky as their citizens – men
and women – strong-hearted as symbolic goats
(or sheep) will be in the year to come. Again,
we will make plans and love under the moon;
nothing can keep the dreamers from their dreams.

So, Cupertino, what will be your dream?
How hard will you work to make your luck
as certain to come true as the full moon
surely shines in the night for anyone
who waits for clouds to float away again?
And what are we to think of the green goat,

with humble heart, who patiently waits, a goat
after all dreams only goat dreams,
and we are human. Will we try again
our hands at the same games of luck
and chance? Or aim higher, like the man
sent into space, sent to the moon?

Cupertino, what will be your moon?
Will you climb your mountains, like the goat,
will you, every woman, every man,
rededicate your life to those old dreams,
or strike out somewhere new and test your luck?
Now's the time; the year begins again.

May both the sun and moon shine on your dreams.
May you feel strong and peaceful as the goat, and may your luck
be human, and like the New Year, start again.

DOG PARK RULES
Mary Avenue Dog Park Dedication, 3 April 2014

Watch out for balls and feel the winter sun.
Remember who you came with, when you came.
Run and run and don't forget to run.

The most important rule is to have fun.
Smell all the smells, then smell them all again.
Watch out for balls and feel the spring-time sun.

Spin your body, spin and when you've spun
yourself into a puddle, change the game.
Run and run and don't forget to run.

Sniff the spots that human noses shun
Pee and pee and all good places claim.
Watch out for balls and feel the autumn sun.

Stay with that stick until the chewing's done.
Leap and wiggle your small body like a flame.
Run and run and don't forget to run.

And now the Dog Park rules are almost done,
and you will learn them as you learned your name.
Watch out for balls and feel the summer sun.
Run and run and don't forget to run.

IN A DRY TIME

September in California is a dry time.
Have you seen the madrone bark curl?
Have you seen the mountain lion on the trail?
Do not fear.

September in California is a new year.
Have you seen school children with backpacks thumping,
their bicycle helmets beaded with morning fog?

September in California is still a flowering time.
You have seen the pink and white oleander blossoms winking
between dark green, dusty branches, heavy
along the highway, waving as you drive by golden hills.

Soon the dark and wet will find us.
Already the first Liquid Amber leaves are turning red.
Have you seen them still high in the trees?

We are September in California together,
in festivals, in flea markets and garage sales.
We will walk the booths looking for a silver pin,
a ruffled scarf, a book.
We will finger the red, green and purple bounty,
the tomatoes, the long beans, the okra on the farmers' tables.
September in California is feast time.

Have you seen the moon as orange as a mango?

September in California is a waiting time.
Have you felt it, standing on-line for coffee, crossing the street
with your company badge banging gently against your hip?
Have you felt the changing angle of the sun,
the hot wind in the afternoon,
the air thick with that singed grass smell and car exhaust?

Soon enough the rain will come, but for now,
September waits with you.
September in California is a dry time,
but bright with glare glancing off the final days of summer.
Raise your hand, shield your eyes, we have a few more days.

PRAYER FOR THE YEAR OF THE HORSE
Cupertino Chamber of Commerce Lunar New Year Luncheon, 14 February 2014

for President Noynoy Aquino of the Philippines and me

Stay away from stress.
Don't dress unconventionally.
Praise a horse when you see one,
praise his haughty neck or humble head.

Watch out for sharp objects.
Your mettle will be tested,
but knife wielding can cut both ways.

Wear green or brown,
the lucky colors of California hills.
But keep your hand on your dance partner,
your grip may slip
on the handle of romance.

Above all keep your ratty nose down,
whiskers twitching with keen sense.
Horses have beauty and speed, it's true,
but you can escape under the fence.

SIXTY YEAR STORY & MORE

You can't be born or buried in Cupertino –
no hospitals, no graveyards. People come
to our city to work, to go to school, to live
with the likes of us, right here. Weirdly square
on the map, we stand on land both old and new.
Change is great and terrible and never ends.
The creek where first Ohlone stood – now dry.
The apricot cannery corner – gone – except
in memory. A father brought his family
to streets where paving over prune trees made
the modern way. Now buildings named for new fruit
crowd the proud roads, green with bike lanes glittering.
60 years of safe and happy homes –
You might just be the coolest city we know.

LYNN CAROLE BROWN

APATHY

I feel the creeping of the vines;
Inching their way toward my soul.
Their crawling fingers feel divine;
Strangling life, their rooted goal.

I cannot blame their weaving crush;
On nature's stealthy loom,
For nature did not bid them rush;
'Twas apathy, caused my doom.

I'll wait, to watch the flowers die;
Then wait for bloom again,
Not caring for the reason why;
My life was loss or gain.

Artwork: Edward Robert Hughes, 1895
(public domain)

WHITE LILY

White lily woman,
singing ancient ballads,
timeless geisha charms.

IF TWO CAN BECOME ONE

If two can become one,
let us merge so perfectly,
that fault can find none.

SPLATTER ME

Splatter me, with your love,
paint for me a heart,
that neither drips of promises,
nor brightens for the part.
Do not stretch love's canvas,
this will never do,
love is very flexible, but needs it's freedom too.
Add a shade to round my face,
but leave me not in shadow,
darkened eyes will search for light,
upon the colored morrow.
You have the brush of humor,
you have enlightened eyes,
so splatter me in colors,
which laugh and love and sigh.

MIDNIGHT GARDEN

Picking stars in my midnight garden,
white dwarfs, red giants;
all burning with a sense of delight,
shining a light of defiance!

I construct a starry string of white,
a cosmic daisy chain.
Wishing for all that is light,
for without it, what can we gain?

Meteor snails go speeding by,
leaving their galaxy goo.
Lunar moths flutter their wings,
between stars, there's silence and blue.

Beautiful Aurora -
her blushing cheeks fill the sky!
One by one, I pick the stars,
they burning, flicker, die.

KEDATON CAMPBELL

OCEAN IN NEED

The ocean is slowly dying
But it gets better if we keep trying
We'll reduce our pollution
And together we'll make this a revolution

Spread the memos
We'll be alright!
Yeah, then the ocean will be just fine

'Cause we love the world
We love the ocean
And we can fix it with our motions
We love the world
We love the ocean
And can heal it from our potions

OH C'MON!
Now, here's a little lesson
CO_2 can cause acidification
The ocean is acid
Because of our gases
And all the liquid from factories too

But we are the world
We are the ocean
And we must help
'Cause we were chosen
We love the world
We love the ocean
'cause our earth deserves promotions

Now, that you know what happen
We are hoping that you take your actions
Take away the CO_2 and plastics
And our ocean will be anti-acid

Save our ocean
Save it right now
Stop the pollution
So much but how
There are more plastics then people
What's it worth

Now everybody help clean up the earth
Squeaky clean

We are the world
We are the ocean
And we can fix this with our motions
We love the world
We love the ocean
And we heal this from our potions

LIFE

I work so hard everyday and night
But I just can't seem to get it right
And I wish I knew
I knew what to do

I could be famous
I could be smart
I could be nobody at all
But no one knows
What the future holds

How come life is so complicated
Love me till I am suffocated
Make it through whatever
I'll make it – yeah

Cause I love it
And I live it
Try to learn it
Memorize it
Oh that's life – yeah yeah
Why don't I listen

And feelings can be hard to say
But with my friends being around woah no way
Cause they make me feel
Feel like I'm at home
Life is hard – yeah I can relate
But you've got to work hard
Then you'll have a good day
And there's no other way
Yeah – no other way

How come life is so complicated
Love me or I'll be suffocated
I need the oxygen just to make it
'Cause I loved it
And I lived it
Tried to learn it
Memorized it
Yeah – that's life

Oh why don't I listen
'Cause I fight for my rights
To be by your side
Cause I'm not the only one who doesn't listen

I know life is so complicated
Love me till I am suffocated
Make it through whatever I made it

BEAUTIFUL EVERYBODY

Around all these people
They are starring at me
Oh what will I do if
I forget the words
My mind's slowly drifting
My heart's slowly lifting
Everybody's cool but
What am I worth?
Do I need to justify myself
Why do we feel that there's a need
To change this personality
'Cause there's a beautiful you
And there's a beautiful me
There's beautiful in everybody

WOULDN'T I STILL BE ME

If I cut my hair to a bob
Or dye my hair blonde
Wouldn't I still be me?

If I dressed as I please
Or put my diet at ease

Wouldn't I still be me?

If I was late on the trends
Or I didn't bend
Wouldn't I still be me?

And so you can see
We all can be free
And you would be you
And I would be me

FIGHTER PILOT SONATA

I love blue, because blue looks like the skies
I need you, so that we can fly sky high
We shine like stars in the sky tonight
May our hearts be pure white

I love you, 'cause you're one of a kind
I need you, because you're hard to find
We, the people of war; we've made history from the front line
May our hearts stay pure white

Oh I love blue, because I love the skies
I need you, so that I can see earth from up high
We're alike stars shining bright tonight
May our hearts stay pure white

Tonight
In the faded lights

PUPPY PLEASE

Please hand me a puppy please
I want one of those furry things
Please get me that puppy please
I'd like a Pug pre-fur-ably
Please hand me any puppy please
I'd like one of those too
Please hand me a puppy please
I'll give him bacon everyday
We'll go for a walk and play catch
Or we'll bike to Curry village

If you just handed me that puppy
We'll have some fun and doggy treats ASAP!

I'M SORRY

I'm sorry
I feel really bad
I'm sorry
I won't talk like that again
I'm sorry,
I promise I won't do that again
I love you
I'm sorry
I know I've made you mad
I'm sorry
I never want you to be sad
I love you
I promise I won't do it again
'Cause I love you

SHINE

Don't you know
The way to go
'Cause I can't find it on my own
So please take me home
I believe I can fly
Just gotta find the right wings
And as time goes by, still I try
'Cause I know it will be my time to shine
You and I will shine bright tonight

WE ARE STARS

When people ask me who I am
I get up into a great big jam
I wanna stay up all night long
Oh I wanna stay up that long
I wanna stay up and watch the stars
Flying right over our great big hearts
Oh I wanna stay long

We are stars
It's written in our hearts
Can't you see it
Can't you feel it
It's inside of who we are

SPRING FLOWERS

In spring there's a thing
That brings us flowers
March, April, May
And maybe June showers
Thought all of the flowers
May fill us with glee
All of this will end
September twenty three

YOU AND I

I know, I've heard
The rumors about us
But there's one thing that we can trust
It's a heartbeat sound
When we are down, we are down
Looking at the stars above us
Laying down on the ground
We will shine
Yes, we will
You and I

GAMER'S DILEMMA

I died in Fortnite
Oh darn it!
Why can't I buy immunity?
For all these things I login to
Alright, I found Cupid's bow and arrow
It had unlimited ammo
And some dude snipped me from the back-o
I re-spawned and waited till the end
And accidentally it dropped while I was trying to pick up some ammo

Here's what happened next
Someone stole it!

WE WILL GO FAR

We will go far
Touch the stars
And loose our scars
And without our scars
Our hearts will be free and fly
We will go farther
Then the others
'cause we are
The dream makers
Flying to the sky
Alright
Yeah, that's alright
'Cause we are not perfect
and that's alright

PERFECT PROBLEMS

These days we're lost and found
Going around trying to find our way out of this place
The clocks ticking
I turn around the bells are ringing
Driving me insane
There we are the perfect problems
Flying far away from this place
And I think we'll make it
Yes, we will
I know we'll make it

MELODY CHEN

SWEET, SWEET POMEGRANATE

Sometimes, I ought to be the one to tell the truth
The ripe, sweet pomegranate of truth—
Seeds coated in the cavity of lies and half-truths
Digging through the flesh until all the seeds have been turned inside out
I have always wanted to become a journalist
A dream tangled in the hairs of the bleak world
Money and respect rest in the crevices of its skin
Poking fun at its skin until the dents finally dig into the truth
What is truth anymore?—my dream or the reality of the job market
And then, I choose the path with dented footprints
The dents have already carved a path to the seeds of lies
Making way to the grab-worthy jobs in the tale of the two (Silicon) valleys
Sweet, sweet pomegranate ought to have turned sour, sour

DARA

A MONARCH BUTTERFLY

A Monarch
Butterfly

I'm so tired
All I do is flying
covering miles and miles
going on
forever

Life is a journey?!
Who was so
cruel
to make a metaphor
a reality?

I want to quit

But something inside me
keeps me going
keeps me flapping my wings
over the mountains
under the frying sun
toward unknown
destination

Somehow I know
that this journey
has
a meaning
that is bigger than me

If only I could understand

what is it?

Dear Keiko! Enjoy! Dara

RED BANDANA

I swim in my red bandana
To be seen from far away
To protect myself from the boats
So my Mom wouldn't worry

To be seen from far away
When I go too far from the shore
I hope someone would call me back

To protect myself from the boats
The only mermaid they can encounter
Doesn't want to be hit by the paddle
                    on accident

So my Mom wouldn't worry
But lately I keep wondering
If she still can see my red bandana
                    all the way from Heaven.....

UNEXPECTED

IGNORANCE IS BLISS

Ignorance is a bliss

Sleeping peacefully
in the middle of nowhere
Trusting the Universe
with your life

In the constant turmoil
of daily hazards
bombarded by bad news

I wish
I could just sleep peacefully
under full Moon
in the middle of nowhere

Full Moon
Shining like a flood light
Creating surreal landscapes
Casting shadows

The Beast
Dangerous?
Not really
It's a ghost
It's a dream
It's only imagination
It doesn't cast a shadow

Not real

How often
our troubles are just a fruit
of our own imagination?
I wonder…

*Inspired by
"The Sleeping Gypsy" by Henry Rousseau*

CLAIMING MY PLACE

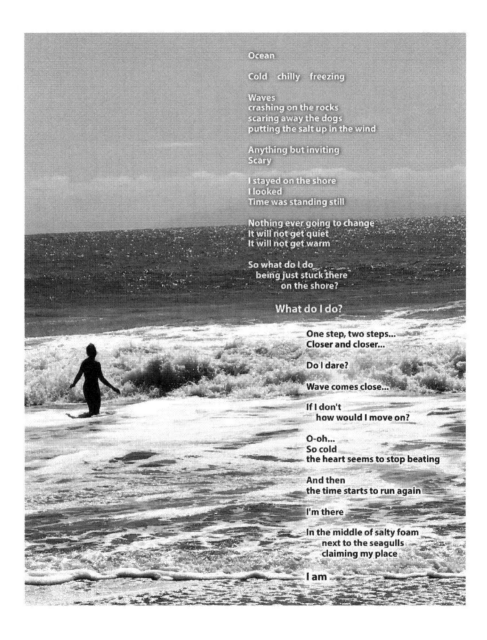

Ocean

Cold chilly freezing

Waves
crashing on the rocks
scaring away the dogs
putting the salt up in the wind

Anything but inviting
Scary

I stayed on the shore
I looked
Time was standing still

Nothing ever going to change
It will not get quiet
It will not get warm

So what do I do
being just stuck there
on the shore?

What do I do?

One step, two steps...
Closer and closer...

Do I dare?

Wave comes close...

If I don't
how would I move on?

O-oh...
So cold
the heart seems to stop beating

And then
the time starts to run again

I'm there

In the middle of salty foam
next to the seagulls
claiming my place

I am

GUEST

I'm visiting the Earth

I'm staying for a while
and nobody knows
for how long or why

I'm visiting the Earth

And I intend to stay
for couple of hundred years
or maybe for a day

I'm visiting the Earth

Don't cry when I will leave
I might be coming back
as fallen autumn leaf
I might be coming back
Forget about grief
I might be coming back
My visit might be brief
I might be coming back
You never know when

I'm visiting the Earth

You know who I am...

FIRE

I'm afraid
    of the fire
        dancing inside me

It shines through
        my skin
Reflects on my bracelets
Ignites the stars
            in my wine glass

Drizzling sparkles
    all over the
        green grass
            of your soul

I'm afraid
        to burn you....

I WAS BORN WITH A BROKEN HEART

I was born with a broken heart
(well, technically, malfunctioning…)
Used to live with the constant pain
Learned to ignore it
Considered talks about heartbreaks
nonsense
until one day
my heart
suddenly felt made out of glass
smashed on concrete floor

Thousands of sharp shreds
beating in my chest now

I'm afraid they will harm you
If you try to hug.....

THERE IS A TREE

There is a tree
on a sea coast
in Santa Cruz

Somehow it's just happen
        to be perfect

Old cypress
Gnarly branches
Odd shape

You'd ask what's so perfect
            about it?

I don't know
I just fell in love with it
from the first sight

I kept my distance

It was so majestic
that trying to get close to it
seemed to be disrespectful

Year after year
I was visiting
and admiring it
from far away

But then
finally
I gathered my courage
I inhaled deeply
I made a step

And I hugged it

Guess what?

The tree
    hugged me right back

MASTERPIECE

DAVID DENNY
FIRST POET LAUREATE OF THE CITY OF CUPERTINO

5PM CUPERTINO

I'm sitting in Peet's with my usual Cappuccino, reading.
I stop for a sip, trace the rim of the cup with my finger,
look out the window at Stevens Creek Boulevard.

Across the street cars are pulling in and out
of the Staples parking lot. The construction workers
who were tearing up the road when I arrived

have collected their orange cones and gone home,
leaving their gashes in the asphalt covered with large
metal rectangles. The sun is making its final effort

to illuminate the world for another day. The foothills
above town are ready for Cézanne to come along
and capture the geometry of dusk. Suddenly, light

catches the trees along the sidewalk for a moment.
Though the top branches are bare, a few amber leaves,
still clinging to lower branches, shimmer.

I take another sip, grateful for the way the milk
and the espresso both calm and excite the nervous system.
With my glasses off, the cars resemble logs

being carried by a river current and the leaves
look like fuzzy yellow stars and the foothills—
I'll leave the foothills to my friend Cézanne.

MARC CHAGALL COMES TO CUPERTINO

Until Chagall set up his easel in my backyard,
I hadn't noticed the depth of blue swirling in our sky.
Until that strange little man called Chagall came,
I never realized how many angels we had hiding

in the tomato bushes. (No wonder they're so delicious!)
What an impoverished life I led before Chagall
cried, "How can a man live without chickens?"
And now a flaming red rooster hides in the plum tree.

Until Chagall showed up with his palate in hand,
I never saw how much my meager barbeque
resembled the Ark of the Covenant, never knew
that my cat was really a sphinx, never heard the orchestra

tuning its instruments within our redwood fence.
See how my wife now flies above the rooftop!
Look—the smoke curling from the chimney resembles
a chorus line of Cossacks dancing the Troika.

Until Chagall set up his easel in my backyard,
I mistook this hot bed voodoo lounge at the center
of the hyperventilating universe for a bland little house
in a bland little suburb in the big bland state of California.

CAROLYN DONNELL

MY MOTHER'S NAME

Born with just my mother's name.
Father unknown they said, what shame.
Who needed a man's name to have pride?
Why was a woman's name so vilified?

Why? To cause us all that pain?
Father or not, I'm still the same.
My name is mine. I'm satisfied.
I'm who I am, my peace I'll bide.

I suppose a boy, a guy,
needs a man to identify
his own masculinity.
A pattern to follow, what to be.

But I'm a girl, a woman and more,
just like my mother and hers before.
I'll wear my mother's name with pride.
Hold my head up, and deign to hide.

She paid the price, she carried me.
No father where he needed to be.
To give a man more rights than she
is the opposite of liberty.

If my father ever looks for me
he will have to ask to be
allowed into our family.
Her rights, his privileges be.

A CLOSET ARTIST

He told me I was bad. My adopted father said
no one would ever love me.
But I remember. I was very young
when he and I squished toes together
in the black goo of the minnow pond
Co-conspirators against mother's disapproval.
No matter she was right. Polio still swam
in muddy waters then.
We wiggled our toes anyway.

He didn't like my music. Kicked the TV playing
Don Giovanni as if Mozart were a mortal offense.
But sneaked in to my recitals. Sat in the back.
And why read so many books? My favorite joy.
A waste of time, he said. But in later years I found
 a journal, poetry he wrote for mother, and writings about me
 and drawings. Horses running. Lightning in the mountains.
Electricity and equine snorting nostrils. Emotions
from a closet artist in a country boy's skin.

Now when I recall disapproving voices
in my ear, bad memories, I try to sense
the creative soul who may have lived
underneath that veneer. Disdain for artistic life
just an armor plate. Why hide away and not live
it out? He was Irish after all. Could have followed
Yeats and Joyce and what's more dear to the heart
of an Irishman than his horse?
He should have been singing out loud.
Not stifling the songs of his heart and mine.

ARMS OF THE ANGEL

Note from author: written 2009 after watching the homeless on North First in San Jose

(Listen to Sarah McLachlan's Angel)

In the arms of the angel
a line from a song
The hum of the music
rises to my tongue
whenever I see
gray-haired
bent ladies, wobbly
walkers crossing
at lights
insufficient time to catch the train
closed doors don't wait, schedules to keep.
Guy in the wheelchair. Unwashed,feeble, maneuvering down
Main Street. To where?
Veteran of wars
sent to kill
returned home
to die untended.
Mothers with children
no home to keep.
Bankers' golden balloon.
Others, no place to sleep.
Where are the families,
sons, daughters or friends?
Church and charity they say
but too often they pray,
"Thank you God, I'm not like them."
Where is the angel for all of these?
Are angels that selective and few?
In the arms of the Angel.
Do you have one?
Lucky you.

WHERE IS THE GREEN?

My heart is lonely for a tree,
a lawn that flows down green and gray
to a stony brook,
a meadow of grass and flowers
with deepening woods behind.

A place to walk
in solitary contemplation
the sights and sounds
obliterated here by urban noise
and polluted crowding.

Free from the roaring whoosh
of cars racing by,
motorcycles,
rock music cacophony,
loud voices,
outside after midnight.

Where is the cooing of the doves,
the chatter of the squirrels,
the lark's song floating
on a clean river breeze,
the rustle of fresh green leaves?

Oh to live outside of sardine cans,
these cardboard shoeboxes
we have to call home.
Even the howl of a mountain lion
in a backyard tree
would be better than this.

JUST ENOUGH OF A REMINDER

The road ends just behind
the long rows of upper yuppie houses. Cattle
graze on hills so verdant green you'd swear you were
in Erin's land instead of south San Jose where still some fields
grow ruby red fruit shocking pink-flowered cherries can be picked from trees
mist like dragon's breath from long lost Avalon coats the mountainside
sliding to valleys below
apricots then follow
popcorn blossoms
a few acres left
here and there
just enough of
a reminder
what the valley
must have been
when it was full
of orchards not the
sprawling shoeboxes
seen today.

TIMELESS TEAR

I sat upon a grassy hill, beneath a spreading oak
and watched as autumn sunlight turned green leaves to burnished gold.

A bubbling stream ran at my feet, its soothing sounds did flow.
The cool clean air did fill my lungs, refreshing flesh and soul.

A crackling in the brush did cause the reverie to end.
My eyes sought out the noise's source and spied the russet skin.

The Lord of forest dark and deep did pause to view his realm.
He turned and contemplated me with head, imperial.

I gazed into his sable eyes and saw there rise a dream.
He showed me hunters with their guns, defaming rock and stream.

I shed one tear, and as I stared into that regal orb,
I swear to you, I saw there too, a drop in his eye form.

Then in one timeless moment pure, we two became as one.
Our minds, our hearts, our souls did blend. At last, I understood.

I heard a shot ring from the west. "Go, run the other way."
I shouted, pointing to the east to try to aid escape.

But sportsmen had their way today. Mere contest was the goal.
Those antlers, just a prize to place for viewing on a wall.

I went to see that royal head, to pay my last respects.
For one brief instant, I did wish the hunter's there instead.

FATHERS LOST

The children and their mothers cry.
Left alone after a bomb
flies into their homes.
Or a lone plane goes down in flames.

Whether in Baghdad,
Or Kosovo,
Or earlier Nam
Even World War II.

The fatherless are millions.
The ones who are left,
who live without
their proper legacy.

My sister's father flew a plane.
A pilot, daring,
soared so bravely
o'er Korean fields.

Shot down one day. She was three.
They never found that MIA.
She has a photo on her shelf.
All that's left of him.

I never knew my father.
He may have died in the war before
the one where my sister's father flew.
Good old WWII.

But we are all alike, alone.
Whether the name is lost or known.
We are all fatherless, victims of
what war brings to us, everyone.

IF ONLY

If only
we could find
the promised
Balm of Gilead
the source of healing
flowing from the heart
 of giving love

some say it's church
the pope or cross
and fluttering white dove
others say go
look within
just breathe away
thoughts of yesterday
or tomorrow

but looking
at the world today
it seems that
Gilead has fled
to some far flung
stellar shore
and left us with
if only

SILENCED

It seems
this arm
has lost
its strength
to lift the
heavy
wood,
where
hand
can reach the
proper place, where
strings meet with ebony to
form melodic lines of grace.
Bow no longer strokes
the strings to flow
vibrations
to my ears
and back into my
heart. My viola's silenced
now, no more to merge, to
coalesce with others' notes and
beats and breaths. They create
the music now and I cannot
participate in making
sweet symphonic
sound
♪

HOLY GROUND

This is Holy Ground,
You have desecrated
our Holy shrines.

Words said throughout the ages
to excuse Mankind's warring
and destructive ways.

But what is Holy Ground?
Where battles were fought,
or won or lost?

What is a holy shrine?
Where a person was born,
or lived, or died?

Is Holy Ground a man made thing?
Or is it forests, mountains
and teeming seas?

Look at the universe far and wide.
Where else can mankind live?
Nowhere we have found.

Our precious blue planet,
humanity's only Holy Ground,
is all we have.

How much more death, war,
and destruction has to come
before we learn?

Will we reach out to one another,
to rescue, to preserve this,
our solitary refuge?

Or will we persist in slaughtering
people, animals, plants,
and lose the true Holy Ground?

We can preserve this rare and shining orb.
Or piece by piece destroy,
our blue and living Earth.

Time grows shorter every hour.
Leaving us with less and less.
What will you do? Today.

JEANNE FARRINGTON

CATCHING THE LIGHT

It's that part of town where I saw him.
He sat by the sidewalk with his cart
Everything coated with
Layers of dust from living outside.

It's that part of town where I saw him
He was reading;
Just that, just so
All attention in his gaze.

It's that part of town where I saw him
Where his dignity met the book, the day, the sun.
Right then, just there, was no time for words
So, silently I wished him well.

We were near there when I saw him again
Our paths crossed in afternoon light.
This time I said a few words and
Gave him something to eat.

We were still there as I saw him
"Thanks," he said, "I love these."
He shared the light in his eyes
For anyone to see.

AGAPANTHUS HAIKU

Sitting in a service.
Seeing her still
Eyes bright and alive
Like she's here, though she's not.

Sitting in circles
Folding chairs
Hardwood floors.
People I'd like if I knew them.

    Haiku with gardens
    Agapanthus remembered
    Read twice, so we hear.

    Delight and surprise—
    Seasons' changes caught in words
    Once again, said with love.

Sitting with my feelings I notice again
That the passing of mothers
Wakes up my own sorrow
In this part of now.

And so, I'm trusting you won't mind
That I borrowed my whole sense of you
To sit here next to me
Quiet, warm comfort from many miles away.

KAREN FRANZENBURG

RED POOL OF WHY

No chance to make up for missing words
I love you is now an empty heart
Cold metal stole your life
I hold your hand
Your future lies in a red pool of why

A SOUL CRIES

That September day
When she had to give you up
She cried forgive me

SOUND

Sound
Invisible fluid motion
Caressing spacial worlds of creativity
Wrapped in a composition
Touch intertwines instruments reverberate
A beautiful gift
Sound

MY TIME

Lounging in my quite place
Listening to raindrops
They come now
The words
Like music

HOPE

It rubbed her sun chapped lips
It exposed her raw bare bleeding toes
It tore her little jeans

It grew in her swollen hungry tummy
It was like a drink of cold water in a 100-degree sandstorm
It gave a dream in the still nights

It held promises

It put her to sleep on a long journey
It let her ride the big metal train
It saved her shoes from breaking

It brought her to the land of freedom
It brought them all to the promised land
It took her papa from her

It wrapped her in a blanket of fear
It is the tears running down her cheek
It is mama gently holding her and singing quietly

It is the long wait

CONSTANCE GUIDOTTI

CLOCK

Clock

Ticking time
Hands go around
Never stopping

Clock

Telling time
Going forward to nowhere
From no where

Clock

Hands moving
In a circle
No beginning, no end

Clock

His and Hers
His Digital forward to space
Hers round and round

Clock

In our bedroom
Ticking the rhythm
Of our lives

Clock

Never stops
Reminding me
Of Losses

IN MEXICO CITY

Paint peels uniquely while
Mariachi traffic
and hot blooded Toreros,
Matadors in the arena of daily life,
drive Chevies and
test their skills on the streets.

I watch some kids
slug it out on the street
from a rooftop in Mexico City
where roses and laundry on lines
mix freely with sounds of cumpleanos
and Mariachi traffic

Eduardo works in Mexico City
at fabrica Pepsi Cola, laboring
 twelve hours a day,
seven days a week,
while Magarita makes tortillas
and babies

and I drink Pepsi Cola
on a rooftop
where roses mingle with laundry,
and paint peels uniquely
while I wait to fly
United.

ON THE VERGE OF 60
Text version

On the verge of 60
So fast, but I don't mind
It's strange, I'm supposed to
Mind, but I don't

I had preconceived ideas
About turning 25
according to Glamour and Family Circle
A woman is downward bound
I bought makeup and a girdle
I never wore either

At 35, 40 was approaching fast
That was the cut off time I was told
It's all downhill from there.
Surprise! 40 was another springtime

Ah, but 50 I was told, that's when you enter
The desert of hot flashes
And you begin to disappear to everyone
Or you try to recapture your youth

Vogue gave a few examples of who I should be like
Elizabeth Taylor, Joan Collins, Cher
But mostly I was ignored

I stopped reading, stopped believing
Vogue
My mother in law, and Modern Maturity

Instead I went adventuring
To refugee camps in Pakistan, the Old
Tokaido Trail
Revisited pyramids and had tea
With a Royal Princess, near the Golden
Triangle
She was 60

I believed that Royal Princess
Her beauty shining through
As she served me tea
In her polished teak pavilion
In the middle of green jungle
Looking over a chocolate river

The driver was in awe.
"Why," he asked the princess
did you invite her to tea?"
Later he told me she saw something about me

With her third eye

ON THE VERGE OF 60

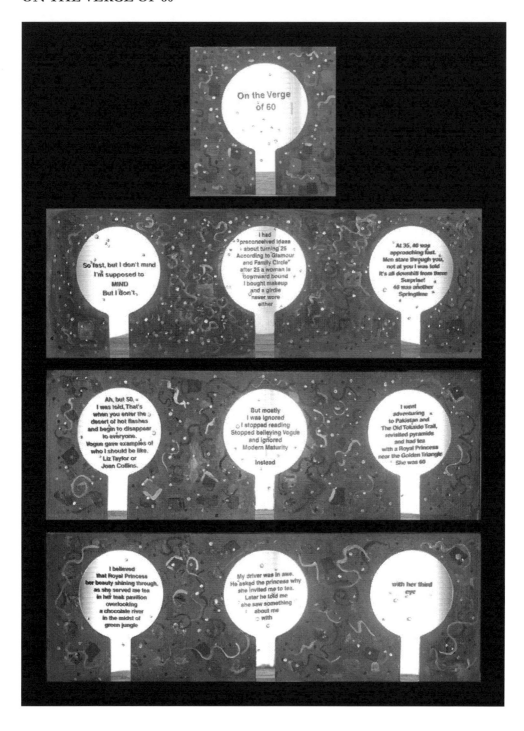

MORNING

In winter I write and he lights
the fire or opens the door in summer
to hear birds calling and in fall
wisteria pods popping.

       This is our morning.

He stirs in the kitchen then walks
out the door and returns with the paper
then I hear carefully carpeted footsteps
as he carries coffee to me.

       This is our morning.

I'm comfy in bed while I'm writing,
he returns to the kitchen to read
big bold headlines and full page adds while
I solve problems on paper and talk to God.

       This is our morning.

I look outside and bless blooming wisteria
or rain and the day then I pray for
family and friends and I stretch
and I stretch so my muscles wont ache.

       This is our morning.

Then I make the bed, no decisions,
I start and finish in a minute then
I start down the hall, my favorite part
and join Jim and the paper.

       This is our morning.

WHAT DID SHE DO TO DESERVE THIS?

He drove her to school, carried her books
Took her to movies on Fridays
Bought her burgers and fries
And taught her to drive.

                                        She loved him

He got a job on Monday
Turned twenty on Wednesday
And married her on Saturday
All in one week.

                                        She loved him

He worked hard every day
Came home every night
Gave her paychecks each week
And three babies.

                                        She loved him

He hauled wood and chopped it
For summer barbeques and
Long winter nights
To keep her warm

                                        She loved him

He gave her perfume and parties
Presents and flowers
Put gas in the car, air in the tires
And mowed the lawn

                                        She loved him

He still chops wood for barbeques
And warm winter fires
Still buys her burgers and fries
Brings tea to her bed every morning

                                        She loves him

What does she do to deserve this?

                                        She loves him

TO GO FOR THE GOLD

The easiest part is saying "I Do"
The next 50 years is an education with periodic tests of:
Endurance
Patience
Sense of Humor
Picking the Right Answer to multiple choices
Choosing between true and false
And essay questions with creative problem solving answers to difficult questions

Over the 50 years you will learn:
Compromise
Negotiation skills
Teamwork
Profit and Loss by your choices
Working for the Greater Good

Over this long journey of 50 years you will have many unexpected adventures
Bumps in the road
Smooth sailing
Bad weather
Fender Benders and a few serious accidents
You will laugh
Cry
Rejoice
Negotiate
Forgive
Forget
Remember
Say, "I'm sorry"
Say, "Maybe you're right"
Say, "I don't agree, but that's OK"

COLORS: ORANGE BEACH

Awake
Enveloped in warm air, moist
The hum of insects pervades
Night sounds fade
Bird calls, white cockatoos flying out of

Jungle
Dense, orchids wild, through the trees
Rustling, suddenly thunder
Wings beating, spanning three feet
Outlined dark against

Sky
Fruit bats against blue
Meeting aqua in the distance
Turning to turquoise
Fifty shades of green

Water
Deep, moving, containing life
Unseen in the depths of green,
Dark blue and turquoise turning
Transparent over white

Coral
Sharp, bright, blinding
Heat under noonday sun piercing
Exposing moving barracuda shining
Sparkling brass bullet

Shells
Joining coral, all dead
Jutting upward, one shell
Phallic, rooted in coral
That holds memories of

Orange
Water turbulent, red sand
Heat, sun and fire
Green against the red blood
On the white sand and sounds of

Thunder
From dark green caves hidden
In the jungle of the hills

Hiding orange rusting tanks
Facing in silence

White
Sand, deserted beaches
Of shells and dead coral
And memories of men
Who faced the terror of green

Jungle

VICKI HARVEY

FAREWELL LITTLE BUDDY

I almost stepped on you last night
as you slept in the landing outside
my room.
I see your shadow on the other
side of the shower door
as I have seen it so many times
before.
Whenever I want to take a
bath I have to shut the
bathroom door . . .
It terrifies you to see me in
the water.
I hear you purring as I lay
in bed late at night, giving me
the sense that all is ok in
the world.
You fall asleep on my arm
and if I move away you
nip my arm in displeasure.
I hear you coming down the
stairs to join me for our morning
ritual of coffee and writing,
but when I looked to the side
of me where you always sit
it is empty.
I remember the time you
tried to attack my yarn and
your leg became caught and
the needles chased you up
the stairs.
I see you sitting in front of me
lifting your paw ever so gently
not wanting to be ignored.
I saved your two Bullwinkle toys,
chewed and ratty, reminding me
of how much you loved them.
I still look for you as I open the
door arriving home from work
only to remember you are not
there.
As I carry my groceries into the
house I worry that you will slip

out the door – but you won't.

The water bowls do not need
fresh water.

The meds are no longer needed.

The spiders have returned.

The pain comes from out of
nowhere.

I have learned to breathe through
it

Keiko
Keep the
letters coming ♡

MOMMA AND SNOWBALL

Hi Momma
You came home today
After putting down the food and
water, I stepped away as I always
do. In an instant you were running
down from the hole in the fence.
You didn't even seem to mind that
I was fairly close. You know that
I would never hurt you. I studied
your notched ear and wondered if
It hurt some. I know you do not
realize it, but you will be a much
happier Momma now. One of the
light colored Tabbies squeeze
through the wire fence to get to
the food. Snowball appears next
and the Tabby bats her with his
paw. When you were away they
shared the food together with no
problem. I think you create competition
with your presence. That is
how they will survive. You didn't
eat as your tummy was most likely
full from your little trip in captivity
You looked so very beautiful.
Captivity suited you.
Snowball was licking your face and
I felt the love she had for you.
The other three kitties were feeling
much freedom with Momma sitting
right there. Snowball is the meek
kitty, the one I want to protect. She
has stolen my heart for sure. She is
as white as freshly fallen snow with
ice blue eyes. Maybe she will grow
Up to be just as beautiful as you are
Momma.

When I join the wild ones I am home!

TRIMERIC POEM OF NATURE

Hummingbird sits on ficus tree branch
Sweet nectar in eyes view
Hidden by soft shadows of lace leaf maple
Clik clik with anticipation

Sweet nectar in eyes view
So close yet so far away
One feeder to few

Hidden by soft shadows of lace leaf maple
Let it not be an illusion
Sense the sweetness

Clik clik with anticipation
The gift is almost here
Be silent and trust the transition

JACK HASLING

NUMBER, PLEASE

I must admit technology has brought us pretty far
In helping us communicate no matter where we are.
The trouble with invention is that everything is new,
And familiar ways of doing things are getting very few.

To get a person's number on the telephone these days
you have to know the system and its complicated ways.
Forget about the phone book—that's no longer what you do.
I'm sure you must have noticed that there isn't one, but two.

Finding names and numbers now is not a lot of fun;
The party whom you're looking for is in the other one.
It used to be so easy—we'd approach the task undaunted.
We'd just dial information for the number that we wanted.

It gave us some security that worked for us quite well;
we knew that all our telephones connected to Ma Bell.
So tell me now, as best you can within this world of strife,
How any kind of cell phone would improved my way of life.

I know it's so convenient sending photos with your phone;
Still, I wish those engineers would just leave well enough alone.
I much prefer the days when I could make a call with ease
And hear a pleasant sounding operator saying, "Number please."

FOOTPRINTS ON MY TONGUE

I have suffered apprehension many times that I could mention
When I've muddled up the messages I've sent.
It isn't very pretty
When I'm trying to be witty
To be saying things I never really meant.

I expect that no one wonders why my accidental blunders
Come more often than they did when I was young.
It's seldom I have ever
Been so absolutely clever
As to keep from getting footprints on my tongue.

I know I'm not the brainiest when I wax extemporaneous
And say things pretty stupid off the cuff.
As soon as I have said it
I invariably regret it
And my apology is never quite enough.

Now, I can't become a sage by simply reading from a page
Or reciting lines of poetry I've clipped
But I'd appear to be much brighter
If I had a decent writer
And my impromptu lines were written in my script.

WHAT'S THE POINT OF POWERPOINT?

Whenever the houselights begin to go dim,
I know that my chances are probably slim
To make an escape with polite hesitation
Avoiding a PowerPoint presentation.

The first slide comes up with a brief introduction
And tells of the people who did the production.
I don't need to know the technicians who do it,
It's me, after all, who is forced to sit through it.

 If only the speaker had something to say
Without letting bullet points get in the way
Graphics and pie charts are fine when you need 'em
But never stay long enough for me to read 'em.

It's nice when a background of music is playing
Unless I can't hear what the speaker is saying.
And where is it written, while this earth revolves,
That all slides must end with mosaic dissolves?

Will there never be laws in the states or the nations
Prohibiting PowerPoint presentations?
Let's pray for a voice that might come from aloft
Proclaiming our freedom from Microsoft.

MARIAN HIRSCH

TURTLE SANCTUARY

Over the gentle rise, we see
just an expanse of beach,
Cleaned for our atonement—
where vultures hold vigil over the driftwood.

Back in the estuary, the baby crocs
remain hidden, but two roseate spoonbills,
spooked by our motorboat,
fluster out of the mangrove.

At night, the sea turtles,
intent upon their task, let us
collect their eggs as they lay them,
globular clusters of little planets.

We place them in galaxies of sand,
enclosed in a styrofoam universe
to rest warmly for forty days,
until a scritch signals their hatching.

We cradle the batches of hatched turtles
to bless their exodus, and release them
skittering onto the damp sand, where
a lap of foamy wave sends them out to sea.

Will they join the ninety-nine that end
as food for fish or frigate bird?
Or, will there be one, twenty years on,
who returns where it was born,

When we have grown old,
grown lame, or have gone?

POETS IN THE ATTIC

Sometimes, late at night in the spring, I imagine strolling down High Street
and stopping at our old house, the one overlooked for demolition. The one
we coaxed back to life. With the traffic gone, and just a distant train whistle
for company, I can listen to the old poets' voices from the attic dormer window.
Thomas Wyatt holds court while George Herbert speaks of flowers.
Donne has a word with Will while Milton explains the ways of God to man.
Pope makes a witty quip while Chaucer silently observes, breathing softly.

Past the plum tree we planted, to the porch with the plaque reading "Built 1897,"
I creak open the door, admiring the parlor with the ornate trim we painted.
I climb the steep stairs, no longer to code, pull down the attic ladder, to search
again for my box of English poetry books, lost in the jumble when I left you.
The poets are here somewhere, beneath the tangle of loose wires and musty
curtains. They continue their cardboard conclave, but coyly hide. Above I see the
roof beams, the virgin redwood timbers that saved this house from the earthquake.

What must the poets have felt when Loma Prieta hit, and the house swayed like
mad, but then righted itself without a crack, except for the twisted chimney,
broken in the same place as 1906. With its strong bones intact, the house no longer
needed us. With voices for the ages, the poets no longer needed us. And we no
longer needed us.

One of these years, when we can no longer climb the attic stairs, someone else
might find the box. I hope they let the poets stay cozy in the attic, where,
on quiet spring nights, their voices might be heard by those with open ears and
hearts.

THE NORDIC CIRCLE: A MEDITATION

I.
On the glassy waters, sailing into the fjord, behind us
the sun refuses to set. But shadows lengthen on the shore,
turning the trees into the forest green of dreams.
At any moment, expect to hear Elvish whispers
calming us on the ripples of the tranquil inlet.

II.
About to awaken the gray snake that is the sea, the
wind whips the ocean against the cloudy coastline.
Ahead lies nothing but mist, until rocks jut into arctic air.
The water hardens, cracking the rocks, sharp as obsidian knives,
into splinters.

III.
Sailing in black waters, away from the spidery isles with their
crab-like points. The sun at midnight lingers with a sooty glow.
Arriving near the rim of the world, where directions have lost
their meaning. Atop the rocks of North Cape, a globe
crowning the bluff salutes us.

IV.
The water bright and smooth, leaving glaciers and mountain
cascades behind, winding through the archipelago out of
the last narrow fjord. Sailing slowly toward the fish farms,
toward the oil rigs, toward the bridges, toward the cities.
Elvish whispers murmur "goodbye."

MIRNA HIRSCHL

I AM OLD BUT DO NOT FEEL SO

Ha, declares the mirror, look well
and see that lives are limited.

I ignore it. Inside a dream-garden
full of pale-green fragile prim-roses,
it is spring again. The refreshing
morning breeze caresses the grass.
The grass caresses my bare feet.

Down the path among the weeds
I walk deeper in time—the wild roses
exude scented offerings to the temple
of summer. The sun leaning down
on fields urges nature to mature,
furrows the earth's crust and speaks
to the ears of corn.

Deeper, deeper—the aroma of ripening
fruits mixes with late summer flowers.
In my garden, the plants do not
age-discriminate. Some barely shooting,
some fully open, some with limbs
become transparent, veiny, needy of
consideration, as they verge on their winter.

And still I don't see it coming. I say
that I do, but I don't—this inevitable,
cold end of the cycle is for someone else.
I wonder off further in my garden
looking for violets.

They are not so conscious of the seasons—
they may bloom twice, three times,
or continuously, my little models, my darlings.
I tell them all about my dreams and failures
and how I would love to borrow their breath.

I pluck a bunch, roots, soil, and all,
plant them in a vase of amber, make them
face the mirror, survive winter. They tell me
that they want to be remembered,
and so do I.

By the family I raised. By the aroma of cakes
I baked. By the words I said, or wrote, or
by the mute ones because I acted on those
most often—the incongruent, unreasonable ones,
always the more memorable.

Remembered by anyone—a passer-by who noticed
that my scarf grazed the ground and told me so,
without knowing my name. Nor do I know his,
but I still remember him. By a child whose roll-away
ball I fetched and handed it back.

By the roads traveled or not, mapped, or planned,
or accidental. I believe that roads have memory.
It all makes beautiful sense now.
My life is a thousand lives and
many more opportunities.

Ha, I say.
Mirror, you declared the lives limited.
Mirror, you lied.

STAY UNRESOLVED AND I WILL LOVE YOU

de Chirico, Ernst, Dali, and Magritte,
for not spelling things out, allowing me
to fantasize, to brood—what does it all mean?-
and let my diverse feelings whirl unimpeded
about your whimsical, unchartered wheels!

Today I react to you thus and so, another time
not at all! But always, the freedom from having
to understand, and from boredom.

My dear Magritte, I choose you today.
I put on your black bowler hat and eat of
your green apple which invades everything—
a fugue from obligation,
a flight into imagination,
a thrill of the unresolved.

Tomorrow I may let the De Chirico birds fly
and wake up the antique marble bodies
strewn around like so many dead stones,
which they are not really, but are alive with
possibilities in these licentious landscapes
that confuse the physical and imaginary,
without censure, which is the delight of them.

And if I ascend with you, my Dali,
take me to the new time zones of watches
which melt and drip. I will send the rays of sun
to reflect on them and change their silhouettes.
I will stop a brook from flowing, just like you,
I will make the impossible real as long
as you let me inhabit your canvases.

But with you Ernst and your horses of the flaming
colors which speak the unspeakable of raw feelings,
I am shy. I need their boldness. I welcome them.
Please do come in. Meet your pupil. I want to be
a field without a fence. Teach me but beware!
Do not tell me everything. Let me keep my
inquisitive wings and I will love you.

JOHN HOGLE

CAROLEE WILL RUN AWAY
From El Sobrante Street Poems

Carolee will run away
from El Sobrante
when she's 18
(maybe sooner).
She's no longer Cambodian.
She's American all the
way, and all that
Buddhist shit and Catholic
shit and family shit
doesn't get her through the day.
Old Love Spirals Downwards and
Shing02 and Eminem and Lady Gaga,
older Nirvana, and ancient Robert Smith
are her gods,
are the family that gets her
through each day.
(She dances alone in the
bedroom she shares
with two sisters and
that bitch of a cousin.)
Carolee will run away
next year, maybe sooner.
So what if she doesn't
graduate. She's the
blankest generation yet
the expendables,
the ones no one cares about.
(Besides, 13 people in
one house is too fucking many.)
Carolee could leave
tomorrow. Kim has a crash
in the city. Carolee could
stay there until she found a job.
Kim wouldn't mind.)
Carolee dances alone
in the bedroom she shares
with two sisters and that bitch
in the house she shares
with her parents, two grandparents
one brother, two uncles,
one aunt, one bro-in-law, one niece

and that bitch.
Carolee dances alone
because all the rest are
at something cultural,
something traditional,
something Cambodian
downtown in San Jose.
Carolee is somewhere else.

THE DUELING MACHINE

The closet in the family room
is where he kept
the robot dueling machine.

6' wide by 7'8" high by 2'6" deep.

The manual and catalog of parts
he kept in a 1/3-cut vanilla folder
in the filing cabinet.

"Dear, the sink is clogged."

He used the machine mostly
on winter Sunday mornings,
at eight AM,
after a glass of lowfat milk.

In the summer
on Sunday mornings,
he would jog
at the beach instead.

He usually gave the machine
a heavy two-handed broad sword,
while he swung a light-weight
and faster rapier.

"Are you ever going
to repair the beam
that your machine
almost cut in half?"

He would set the height
and limits of reach and speed
of the dueling machine.
He knew his own abilities.

Shreds of air.
Shards of time.

Yet he rarely won.
And he did consider it a contest,
not merely exercise.

The flesh was reparable.
The machine expensive.

He would close up the machine.
He would bandage his wounds
and take a shower.

"Let's watch TV,
dear."

THIS SIDE OF PARADISE

Her index finger traced the door's periphery.
(The frail Turkish glass had shattered in his departure.)

She sank through the floor into the basement.
(The World War II Harley refused to start.)

Her lace-trimmed velvet dress remained in the hall.
(She looked through the broken door; he was walking down the road.)

In her slip she searched among the boxes.
(She would call, but she was right.)

In one with her name on it, she found her first porcelain doll.
(An unexpected breeze healed her afternoon.)

But the fragile clothes had mildewed; all that were left were the head and hands.
(It issued through the door and carried her upstairs.)

She cradled them to her wet cheek.
(To luxurious enervation on her silk sheets.)

CADENCE

Cadence,
Sally operates to no cadence,
no rhythm, no design.
Sally doesn't operate at all.
Sally is entropy,
anechoic chamber cushion
  to those around her.
She dissipates their energies
  into insipid nothingness.
She suffocates their striving, their desires
  until only regret is left.
She enshrouds their hearts
  until they are cloistered voids.
She scratches at their thoughts
  until they are unraveled shreds.
And only then does she depart,
  leaving chaos behind her
for the State to take care of.

ARKADY

Arkady keeps to himself,
a lot of the time,
but at least 140,000 people
follow his every action,
his every written word,
his every spoken thought,
his every relationship,
his life.

Arkady is a lifecaster,
one of those totally open people
who wears a digital video camera
and microphone and
broadcasts every moment
of his life to the Web
in real time.

Arkady has 140,000 followers
who want to watch him buy
that new cereal at Trader Joe's,
who want to watch him
unlock his girlfriend's phone
so she can use it in Europe,
who want to watch him muddle
the words to an old
Chapterhouse song,
who want to see him to flip off his boss
because she said he could not wear
his lifecasting equipment
while he was talking to
customers in the optician's office
where he worked.

He does all these things
and so much more,
but he doesn't feel that he has a life.
He feels like an image
projected on a screen,
two dimensional,
with an audience
sitting in their comfy seats,
just waiting for the projector,

digital or analog,
to shut off.
Then the audience
will go home.

NOT SO SUPERFICIAL

You always see Dinesh
and Kalyani walking.
Kalyani in her choli, lehenga,
and sari of the day; he in his
chinos and plaid sportshirt
and windbreaker.
You always see Dinesh
and Kalyani walking because
they always walked
almost everywhere
in their home village
in India.
In India, Dinesh was a teacher;
Kalyani was a homemaker.

Here, on this suburban,
Silicon Valley street
they are appendages
to the lives of their son
and daughter-in-law and,
even, their three grandchildren.

Dinesh sometimes helps
the grandchildren with their homework,
but they often have difficulty
understanding his accented English.

Kalyani cooks frequently,
since their son and daughter-in-law
both work,
but the latter prefer
Thai and Chinese and KFC.
The grandchildren prefer Togos
and McDonalds and sushi.
But a chicken pakora is still a hit.

India lingers.

LOSING MILES

I saw the last few moments of Miles,
three months before he died,
He was on the stage with his horn,
but he seemed like the old dog,
verging on senile,
circling the yard endlessly
with no real voice,
just a whimper.
He seemed like the grey parrot
bored in his cage,
pulling out feathers,
until he is almost naked.
Miles was naked.
The music flaked off him
like shedding skin,
an almost invisible process
except to the mites
in the audience
who were waiting for
nourishment, waiting for
what was once
valuable.

THE MUSIC OF ONE BLIND AND DEAF

You think because I am deaf and blind
that I can have no music,
no band, no lullaby, no symphony.
You are wrong.
I have each morning a symphony of touch,
an art of touch in each morning's shower.
As I stand in the shower,
I conduct the streams of water
from the showerhead,
each a cascade of notes
touching my body
here and there
in brief rhythmic staccatos
then long chords, washes of
notes, of drops, of waterfalls.
My fingers weave through
the streams, conducting the
notes to fall here, to fall there,
to give me my rich and varied music,
to give me the wonder of sound
as vibrations on my chest, my face,
my hair, my arms, my legs.
And as the complex melodies play
across my body,
I draw the fingers of my left hand
across the tiles and the grout
between the tiles in cool counterpoint.
It is only with greatest difficulty
I draw myself away from this
symphony, but as the last chorus
dies with the turning of the
handles hot and cold,
I step from the shower
and dry off the notes, the chords,
the pavanes and partitas,
the sonatas, the symphonies,
and depart fortified for a world
that knows little of the music
of touch.

THE SHAPE OF LIFE WITH SEASONS

South-of-Market Sharpie
stands with black aluminum
baseball bat at
the corner of 11th and Harrison.
At 9:38 Thursday night he waits.
He waits for the right car.
He does not know
  what a "right" car is.
It does not matter;
  it will happen soon.

The windshield implodes,
particulated glass hail storm enshrouding
  Maxine Hasem and Ted Nelson
  as they turn the corner onto 11th
  toward the night clubs.
(They had driven from suburban Colma
the town with all the graveyards,
to hang out South-of-Market. It was
the in-thing to do if you wanted
to be cool in Colma.)
"Fuck, what the ...?"
Ted's words cut short
by the perverse vision of
Sharpie with his bat
raised high like a liberty torch
to illuminate his glory.
Maxine brakes and wipes the shards
from her cheeks as Ted opens the door
and leaps for Sharpie.

South-of-Market Sharpie
does not move,
a Statue of Liberty
in Docs and black leather.
Ted charges him,
shoulder into breastbone.
Sharpie makes no defense,
  no attack, no supplication.
He falls, his head cracking
  on cracked concrete walk.
Blood.
That is not enough for Ted,
who rips the bat
from Sharpie's giving hands,

slamming Sharpie's head
again and again
with the bat, the glorious bat.
Maxine screaming.
Ted continues,
till all that remains of Sharpie
are memories on the corner
  11th and Harrison,
till all that remains
are shadows sullied,
  never to be so opaque again.

Sharpie's dead
but not forgotten by his parents
who do not know where he is
in any case.

Sharpie's dead.
His few friends remember
  for now,
but in 20 years
two have jobs and kids,
and no memories of Sharpie,
and the third is dead
(two years after Sharpie).

Sharpie's dead.
Ted's in jail.
He'll be out in three years.
He'll die in 42 years,
  metastasized cancer of the colon,
  his family at his side.

Maxine still screams.

WHAT JILL?

Jill's nom-de-radio
is The J. Ward.
        (Every morning she shrouds in her
        mortgage-broker wool-macho suits.)
She's a volunteer DJ
at Foothill College's KFJC.
        (By 7:35 she's in her Lexus
        By five-to-eight she's at her desk.)
Jill hosts the graveyard shift
on Sunday mornings.
        (With paper and computer
        she links lender and borrower.)
She calls her show
"Patients in the J Ward."
        (Jill turns down dates
        with the other brokers.)
She plays gothic and noise,
industrial, and hard trance.
        (So the men call her dyke and
        lesbo bitch behind her back.)
Her listeners love her,
some of them archive her programs.
        (The macho crap pisses her off,
        so she out-commissions them 2-to-1.)
Her boyfriend Lemmy was a listener.
Now he's the station's Publicity God.
        (That pisses them off even more.
        Someone punctures her tires.)
Lemmy works at a used record store.
He wants to be an A & R man.
        (Jill's boss says he'll fire all the men
        unless the guilty one confesses.)
She wonders why she fell for a
semi-slacker like Lemmy.
        (Three brokers rat on Bob Quince.
        He's shown out the door.)
But she's so fucking happy, she
thinks Lemmy should move in.
        (Tracy, her house mate,
        thinks one-half of Jill is crazy.)

LARRY HOLLIST

EATING ICE CREAM WITH JESUS
For my niece, Emily

The other day Jesus knocked at my door.
He asked if I wanted to go out for ice cream,
He was buying. I said sure.

When we got to Baskin-Robins
He ordered Chocolate and Cherries Jubilee in a cup.
I ordered Wild 'n Reckless Sherbet and Rocky Road in a waffle cone.

He said most people won't even answer the door
Once they see who is there.

I said I never check and I never turn down free ice cream.
I should be the one buying since I feel like I owe you.

Nonsense, spending time with you is all I want.
Then there was a long comfortable silence
 As we both enjoyed our ice cream.

I then asked, is there anyone you ever didn't want to forgive?
Well… a long pause
No,
You were worried I was going to say you.

You know Jesus has a great sense of humor.
He told me a joke,
"Did you hear about the time when
Moses, an old man and I went golfing?"
It was a joke I had told hundreds of times before
But it seemed better coming out of his mouth.

He was in a lighter mood.
So do you think I should've told Peter
About the stepping stones on the Sea of Galilee?
Dramatic Pause,
Gottcha, there were no stepping stones.

As he dropped me off he said
We should do this again.

Sure, anytime.

How about now?
Then he winked and drove off.

SONNENZIO ON A LINE FROM SHAKESPEARE

When in the chronicle of wasted time
If you take your time you will see my name listed,
Maybe even four or five times.
In very little time I have perfected the art of laziness.

One time I taught my hard-working farmer friends to goof off.
This was not easy because in the previous 20 plus years they had never goofed off.
I often stop playing video games the same time I started the day before.
Then being tired I take time off from doing nothing to nap.

I take bathroom breaks in the time it takes to cook my frozen meals.
I keep the backdoor open year round to save time letting the dogs in and out.
I wash all my clothes at the same time
And from time to time I wear the same thing for days.

These are just some of my time savers
So I have time for my idle behaviors.

I REMEMBER WHEN
After "When you awaken in the morning's hush," Mary Elizabeth Frye

I remember when
You had your first shots. Normally you
Would kick your legs up three times, then fall asleep, but now the pain would awaken
You. I felt helpless standing next to your crib in
Your room hoping the pain would leave before the
First rays of morning.
Hush my son, Hush.

LARRY'S LOVE SONNET #1

When the reaper walks near your door
Is when you realize how deep you are.
Depths you have willingly dove, going
A little deeper joyfully, ecstatically, everyday

Slowly you have become attached
Thinking that the two being one has always been
Feeling all of each other's emotions.
So attached that phantom pains develop when not physically near.

It is when you think they are not doing their part
They seem to be a little further away
So you think, "What can I do for them?"
You become closer just with a change of your attitude.

It is the thought of losing you is my biggest fear.
Yet, to have something so strong is all I have ever craved.

SORROW
After Taha, Muhamad Ali

"His God-given rights are a grain of salt tossed into the sea."
                                                    – Taha, Muhamad Ali

This sorrow was his.
His alone by God!
This was a given.

By rights,
Revenge was his to dole out, but as things are
How do you take revenge on a a a
A thing that started smaller than a single grain
Of wheat, a mustard seed, a piece of…

Thinking about this is like cleaning his wound with salt.

His wife's cancer gave him less control than a surfer tossed
To the ocean floor then dragged into
The surf over and over again by the
Sea.

I AM THE GREAT I AM
After "Do not stand at my grave and weep," Mary Elizabeth Frye

Who am I?
I am The Great I AM.
I did not
Die. Or rather my death was not permanent. My body is not there.
I did not do this for the glory of me, myself, or I.
I do what I do
For you and the glory of the Father, not
The glory of men. My love does not sleep.
Let's you and I
Walk together so you can become as I am.
I tell you be not
Afraid. Blessings are there
That I
Have reserved for you. Did
I not say to Mary Magdalen and now to you, "Be not
Afraid. I did not die."

PLEADING
After LDS Hymnal #185, Joseph L. Townsend

Pleading humbly on
My knees. I plead for the
Peace of believing on the cross.
I plead to know of
The truth of Calvary.
I wish that I
Can say I have
Been a believer. I have suffered
To say this. I plead to know there is life after death.
I plead, I plead, I plead for
A peaceful voice comes. It is true I have done this for thee.

ANITA HOLZBERG

I AM RIVER

I am River
I am tree
I am a bird
Flying aimlessly
I am a flamingo
Tall lean with skinny legs
Not putting my head down in the sand
I have come to be humbled by God
Humbled by not walking
I awake alone
Join friends
Present my poems
I am comfortable in my skin
I am loved too!!!

BLANK PAPER

Blank paper
I sit before thee
Fill you up
My lines pristine
Truths
I write to save myself
Others also

Blank paper
La tabula rasa

Focus on inside thoughts
Self is rained on everyday

I wait for the sun
To wash away old wounds
I have mended
I have seen life turn positive
Amen!!!

WHEN I GROW OLD

When I grow old
I shall wear purple
My trousers rolled
I will eat my Wasa cracker
With a big fat crunch
And sometimes even forget lunch
I will watch 'I Love Lucy " at 5
How she does really jibe

Amazing how when you are old
The world can pass you by
But I shout out loud and clear
"Look out world
I am still here"!!!

KELVIN HU

THIS TOO SHALL PASS

Remember: warm summer nights
Whiling away wistfully
The – long – grass welcoming light,
lying still as the Sun clocks in early

Your mother reminds you:
this too shall pass

Remember: cold winter days
The Sun shining on snow
Your sudden heartbreak,
after spring love is wont to follow.

Your mother comforts you:
this too shall pass

Remember: a climate-controlled room
clean curtains cannot answer
The coughing comes so soon
Corrupted–Malevolent–

Your mother holds you tight,
and whispers in your ear:
the passing gets easier, and
you too shall pass, my dear

And O! Wasn't it lovely, while it was there—
Remember: in the end, there is Nothing to fear

CONVERSATION BETWEEN A MAN

Remember those nights when
you cried so hard that
your heart almost burst from
the pain?

I held my arms around
you and hugged you so
tight but the tears just
came and came.

And I felt so helpless
and you felt so hopeless
that the two of
us should split;

That one becomes two,
and I part from you,
and those arms were imagined,
not mine
nor yours.

And the future you had
wanted with me right
inside it had faded from
sight on shore.

But on distant
waters a boat blew its
whistle and you (as I)
manned the helm.

Hold yourself fast,
you who is past,
your future is
coming home.

MEDIAKITTY

There is a cat on my chest,
a fine beautiful specimen
with mottled grey hair
and a decisive curvature.
I could be anywhere else
but here I am tonight
watching the channels go by
like flickflickflick
a glimmer of worlds that could be.
It's not sad, really,
and I don't blame the cat,
but I can't move
with him on top of me.
All beautiful and stunning,
All that I am not.

JANNAH HUSSAINI

HIDDEN SHINE

Everything around us has much to see
Each thing on it's own
Each thing unique
Each thing with it's own spark to be

As things magnify a new world is seen
With tiny ants together working
Overlooked, a melodious sheen
That is only noticed if you look deep

Each one has their own world, the way they see unique
Their family, their friends, there is no end
Of the beauty their eyes continuously seek
And legacy to who they can be

But to some what's known for shine may seem dark
For to their eyes they have their own
Their perspective, way to make a mark.
No matter how small or large

For on this world that's what everyone has to do
As one's talents can only be done by themselves
And one's stories untrue or true
Can only be told by the holders who know.

And above are stories told by stars
For each has their own system around
And under them planets, Mercury, Venus, and Mars
Not forgetting our beautiful Earth

Each has their own world to host more wonders
Where boxes are opened
And there are glories and blunders
Wherever eyes wander they see opportunity

Look up and down, everywhere
More boxes are waiting to be unpacked
For everything is full of beauty and care
If you only bother to look within.

NHI HUYNH

INTRO

nighttime used to be the time i dreaded most
it used to mean i didn't make the 11:59 deadlines
and the best time to sleep at
and the time where i shouldn't be awake or i'll think too much
and the time all my inner demons came to plague
inside my mind

it's now the time i look forward to
it means time to a new day time to a place where
i can restart and live though my vicariously wildest
Fantasies

it's the time i can see you.

ONE

just for tonight
i'll let you whisk yourself alive
i'll let you fox trot me slowly across
the bedroom floor
into the universe of our maybes
i'll let you kiss me on the forehead
the grassy meadow
where i'll always find you
waiting just for me
i'll let you tell me you love me
the breezy bright night
where your eyes shine like a thousand diamonds
my midnight fever dream
i tried my best to let you go
but just for tonight
i'll hold on tight
- this idea of you

TWO

two am.
too many sleepless nights
too idyllic is the thought of being with
you as you are
too good
too perfect
too beautiful
to be real
i must let go of this idea of you before it's
too late
-    it's too late

THREE

tonight i no longer dream of you because
it's three pm in the afternoon actually
and this fruitless
reality has caught up to me
i wish i could say i don't think of you
but thoughts of you still consume me passively
            of
"how are you doing"   and
                  "i miss you"
                     and   "do you think of me at all"

?

(this is embarrassing.
because i know you don't
third time's the charm They say
but it's been wearing off.)

128

RESOLUTION

your beautiful smile
a hallucination
your cold dead eyes
a reality

You were a glitch in my stimulation.

no recognition
we're back to being

strangers

the illusion chipped
and i am malfunctioning
error of 01001100 01001111 01010110 01000101
-    I don't know how to function without you.

DEEYA JAIN

MOTIVATION

sometimes it feels like everything is falling apart
and things aren't going the way you wanted them to
it often happens that
the only thing stopping us from moving on
is ourselves

STARRY SKY

like a painting
spread across the night sky
the stars shine brightly in the heavens

like a feeling of comfort
never changing, always staying by my side
the stars shine brightly in the heavens

when the day fades away
and the night comes to be
prevailing like a mighty goddess of the dark
the wind howls and terrors roam the streets
but the stars still shine brightly in the heavens

orion on one side
and the little dipper on the other
the stars, they envelop me on the darkest nights
even when the clouds mask their luminescence
the starlight breaks through and shines brightly in the heavens

SELF-LOVE

this new feeling
that makes my heart flutter and the butterflies in my stomach come to life
what is it?

what is this feeling that makes my cheeks turn pink
and makes me smile at nothing for no reason
is it love?
yes.

but who is the love for?
my dear,
all my love is for me
because I love myself
and my body
and my smile

whatever other people say
your clothes are boring
your hair is tangled
your skin isn't clear
it doesn't matter to me anymore
what matters to me is
what I think of myself
and nothing else

i love myself
more than I could ever love anyone else
it doesn't happen easily
it takes time
to love yourself
and accept your flaws
but my dear,
you can do it
i believe in you

YESTERDAY, AND TOMORROW

sometimes it feels
like life is flying by
faster than I can capture all the memories.

no sooner than it was yesterday
it is tomorrow
i don't even remember when the day turned.

to capture all of life's little moments
is truly a skill
one we must learn so we live to the fullest.

let go of the regrets
and the worries about tomorrow
and live today, this moment, as if it were your last.

VEENA KARTHIK

AN ALPHABET BOOK FOR THE REST OF US

A is for Amen
B is for Blessing
C is for Courage
D is for Dare
E is for Empathy
F is for Faith
G is for God
H is for Happiness
I is for Inspire
J is for Joy
K is for Kindness
L is for Love
M is for Mercy
N is for Noble
O is for Optimism
P is for Priceless
Q is for Quality
R is for Righteous
S is for Sweet
T is for Trust
U is for Uplift
V is for Victory
W is for Worth
X is for Xcellent
Y is for Yes
Z is for Zealous

R.E.S.P.E.C.T.

Note from the author: I was stuck in traffic and pulled over to the side to merge back later. The goal was to unblock the cars making a left. A young adult on a bike seemingly angry showed me his finger as he zoomed past. This poem is dedicated to him.

My greys are brighter than your pearly whites
My years more golden than your hair
Why then my friend did you show me your finger
When all I did was care?
I could have been your mom
I could have been your teacher
I could have been your little sister's music teacher.
We are human, we make mistakes
Be more tolerant and up your stakes
Show more respect is all I ask
For a better future, For a better life.

EVA KASHKOOLI

WHY WRITE POETRY?

To ease the pain,
To appease the strain,
To expose the stain,

To assuage the ache
And the thirst slake
And for sanity's sake,

I pen my lines
And partial rhymes
And worry less
About happiness.

COLORS

Wrapped in white blossoms, trees
Sense Spring six weeks early.
Just yesterday
Enameled leaves
Adorned their branches –
Crimson, copper, gold –
All fallen now,
Enriching soil.

Grey doves at my window
Bow and wobble
Beg for seed.
I rush outside with feed.
They thank me with their coos.
Their droppings green the lawn,
Revive me from my blues.

PAUSING AT STARBUCKS

Pausing at Starbucks
To savor some joe,
One the way to my gym
Where I frequently go.
I pen a few lines
To share with my class
That gathers tomorrow.
I'm at an impasse.

My story's not finished,
Refusing to end.
Therefore, I will shun
It and chat with my friend.

I'll work on another.
I have quite a few
That cry to be finished
Ere I start anew.

Perhaps there's a market
For unfinished tales
Like the "Unfinished Symphony"
My spirit wails.

RUMINATION

I lie in bed
And gauge my spread,
Assuage my dread.

I must arise
And face my thighs
And adipose
That grows and grows
And join a gym
Where I can trim
My size.

But, I resist
The call to twist
And sweat and strain
And incur pain.

Why is it great
To look so straight?

Perhaps, I'm bound
To live life round.

Upon this thought
I'll meditate
And stay in bed
And vegetate.

DANIA KHAN

WILTED

Bright pink flowers bloom along an old fence
By the rough sidewalk where two children sprint
And look up to see tops of their apartment complex
Their bare feet seem to fly down the pavement,
there's summer and light in the air they breathe
And their laughter echoes off cracked walls and eaves

A girl picks flowers among thick dark bushes
A neighborhood boy, looking mad, approaches
"To pluck them, pain them, is to make god sad"
He says, and he unfurls her hand

She looks at her palms, feeling shame and guilt
Cradling soft petals and leaves that have already wilt
And agreed. Some things are better admired from afar
Five years old, she knows nothing of beauty or power.

Years pass. She remembers the flowers, undisturbed
now knows how it feels for petals taken away,
By men who did not appreciate or obey
Searches for what once belonged to her dreams
And wonders, sometimes, if god still weeps.

SANDRA KHOURY

HER DEATH BEAUTY
For Denise S.

Portrait of joy
in midday bright light
that streams the room
during winter dark days

effervesced eyes, moon-shaped face,
nestle deep in the folds of her final vessel
skilled hands spread soft,
stilled fingers relax,
once captured bounties of beauty.

Vision of beauty in muted mask,
rounded lips, upward turn of mouth
the awe of wonderment

body rests white
purified of life,
now not far her destination

body awaits the moment,
stir of wind, a whisper,
released

Legacy of art, absent of pain
pardoned life now departs
immersed in ethers,
alert gods and goddesses.

TO DAUGHTER

you were not conceived in the wound,
it did not take nine months to hold
you, you did not arrive by modern
reproduction.

captured from a photograph,
youthful gaze of contemplation,
I ponder your life, daughter of
desert, ochre and umber.

to keep you in my life,
I create you,
two-dimensional, paper-thin,
one pencil stroke at a time,
with love as fingers define
pensive grey gaze, crescent brows,
pursed lips, tilt of heart-shaped face,
tight-knit braids tumble to tap shoulders
on fragile frame

you emerge on blanketed white paper,
each stroke announces your presence,
entices you, assures your arrival.

daughter of desert ochre and umber,
of steeped dunes, starked skies
desert dense nights,
swirls of heavy heat twirl and tumble
no more.

now…you with me
in city of ordered existence
entwined in hurried meals shared
imposed by stare of eyes,
your quiet gaze replies to all
and I imagine, you, my daughter.

THEN AND NOW

Mary, mother
  stilled
    in her recliner,
  midday nap, sun
  streams patio,
Head angled down
  right,
she lightly breathes,
  mouth muted,
    turned to deep frown,
  as gravity sculpts her
  face.

In quiet sleep
  secrets revealed,
  tucked-deep dreams
  dormant desires vanish
her frown mesmerizes,
  unhappy mask
  lifted to my gaze.

Mother Mary,
  exhaustion of
    rules obeyed,
  unquestioned life
    pursued.

rest now, mother.

JOYCE KIEFER

REFLECTED

The mountains and sky double in size
The lake repeats their beauty in reflection.
Endless sky in depth without measure
Only the mountain understands.

The lake repeats their beauty in reflection.
It says "Look at my world,
This is perfection."

Endless sky in depth without measure.
The sky contains infinity
The lake is infinitely deep.

Only the mountain understands
It rises over the lake and under the sky.
And knows it will crumble and the lake will be filled.

NATURE GUIDE

I expected
      a starburst of lupine
      and poppies opening
      to the warm kiss of sun on a hillside facing the ocean.
I'd tell the class these are the grasslands
(You eat grass if you like popcorn, Cheerios, or a bowl of rice.)

But minor surgery intervened.
I couldn't climb the hill that day,
      consigned to the woods around the pond.
  (The hillside badger would have toughed it out)

The morning of the hike
      mist sucked up the hills,
      wrapped the woods in spongy silence.
Poppies wound their petals tight as wands,
      what they do when the sun won't come out.
The teacher cancelled -
      It might rain, she said.
      (The newts would rejoice at this prediction.)

           ****

I walk back to my car through
      woods that smell of wetness.
In the deep green
      wild strawberries pour creamy blossoms,
      white milkmaids light the path.
      A Douglas fir shines with chartreuse tips
      (The needles make great teas)
Not even birds sing through the silence.
I breathe deeply to receive this gift

DELTA TOWN

Clapboard buildings lean together
  Sharing old secrets
  Of brothels, bootleg, brawls.
 Their balconies have seen it all
  On the narrow street below.
All that passion over gold, women or loneliness
  Staunched by a stab or a shot.

The ground floor
  Of a white building bulges out.
  Names, hearts are carved on the door,
  On the walls, faint but everywhere.
The tacked-on second floor,
    Dark boards, stain worn off,
    Seems to restrain collapse.
    Love is too fragile.

At the edge of town a yard sign says "Chinese Food"
  But nasturtiums choke the place.
  Nothing but dry rot served here.

We sit in a windowless room at Al's.
  Put on glasses to read the menu.
  Talk loud so the other can listen,

Outside,
  we walk carefully along the cracked street.
  Slipping is easy to do here.
  The levee above the town
  Holds back the river.

HILARY KING

U-TURN TOWN

When my husband makes the U-turn
towards our house, I flinch and cling to my seat.
There are no street lights in our new town,
a local quirk we don't yet get. Our street runs

dark and narrow. In the middle, a median full
of tall pine trees produces missile-size pinecones.
The neighbor's orange tree masses over our driveway
like a childhood monster. Here, what you want

is often over there. The roads have two left lanes,
one for turning, one for reversing your course.
Left on El Camino, left on Page Mill, left on El Monte.
Left, left, left.

It was his job we left for, his dream. An adventure,
we agreed, our opinions sweetly merged, a turning
towards a bigger world. It's a damn tight turn, though,
to make at mid-life. We keep getting bruises.

We can always go back, we tell ourselves,
back to our old life, back to when we were happy
and an orange tree was a wonder, not something
we hit one night as we make our way home
        broken branches raw and sharp in our driveway.

THE SILICON VALLEY DREAM HOUSE

is a time machine, built before the housing crisis of '08,
before Facebook went public and made Menlo became impossible,
before Proposition 13 rendered my neighbors rich simply
by aging in place. The Silicon Valley dream house is

someone's mother's house in Atherton or San Jose.
Available, inherited, paid for. I never met so many
grown people living in their mother's house.
The Silicon Valley Dream house is in Carmel or Half Moon Bay when

the pumpkins are out but the traffic isn't. I'd take
an Eichler on one of those leafy streets in Palo Alto
or anything with an ocean view in Sausalito.
I'd even take this rental, this brown house, brown

cabinets in the kitchen, brown grout between the tiles,
brown the weeds the landlord refuses to cut,
brown our envy, too bitter to be green.
We'd buy it if we could, brown house. We love

the schools, the walk to coffee, the twenty-three
fruit trees in the backyard. Twenty-three! Lemons,
plums, loquats, apricots, apples, and a palm so tall it hurts
my neck trying to take in all of it. We sit in its shadow

and say to each other, this is why we moved here.
For work, yes, for the dream yes, for someone's dream,
 but to be here, breathing distance of coast and mountains,
where fruit falls into your hand.

LOST ORCHARDS

Once, after the first gold rush
        and before the next,
apricots grew here thick as grass on a prairie.
Settlers planted the seeds, hoping this rich soil
and dry summers would yield a fruit small, perfect,
                and sweet.
Every street here had an orchard. Every yard here
had a tree or two or 12. Men worked the orchards,
laid down at night between boxes of drying fruit to sleep,
their dreams clouded with the scent of invisible flowers.
Children picked apricots at in their yard,
laid down at night between the fruit and slept,
their dreams unclouded.
        Then.
If you could grow apricots, you could grow
        code and computers
             and companies.
Farmers sold
        and families sold until
            all the land was gone,
until the last apricot orchard became
        a museum
a relic, a lesson of what ripens, what grows
but time, season after season.

PHYLLIS KLEIN

THE STORY I DIDN'T TELL

When I married you, a thousand
of your wives' corpses covered my path
to the altar. My father tried to dissuade me,
I only wanted to save those remaining,
and put an end to your vengeance
if I could. In private I'll admit I cringe
from your tainted touch, your criminal mind.
My thousand sisters murdered to avenge
your one cheating wife. My dreams overflow
with them when I sleep at all.

That's how my thousand and one stories help
us both, distract us from your cruelty
and violence. In the book about me,
I am not afraid, but don't believe it.
How have I done this night after night?
Thought up the genies, the djins, the wandering
mysteries like water drops forming a lake,
forming an ocean, keeping me alive
another day and then another.

Don't be sad for me. I have used my mind
for peace. I have done what I could in a disaster.
I have travelled in secret, I have altered
the veil of bedtime forever.

LIFE IS GLASS

There are so many fragile things, after all.
People break so easily, and so do dreams and hearts.
                                    — Neil Gaiman, Fragile Things

Breaking: Buzz of a bone fractured, burst of a bowl hitting the floor,
boom of a heart splitting. *Please like me.* A dream as it shatters.
Please think I'm good. Whistle of a word as it severs from itself into the air.
Of a scream demolished.

Moments of breaking:
Hand over the mouth, gagging, pushed into a room, door locked from
the inside. Parties, drinking. *Why did I do that?* The seconds it takes to get
lost. Smash of consciousness as it disappears. Disillusion's waking
croak. *Where are my clothes?* Fragmentation into terror.

How it happens: remembering, forgetting. *Was I drugged?*
After school, at a party, pungency of impact, taste without
permission. No proof. In the sacristy, in a back seat, a hotel
or a bedroom, *did it happen?*

Breaking: dust of collision, whiff of dreams burning, nightmares strike,
cymbals snarl in the brain. *I'm repulsive.* Floating above it
all in a disappeared body.

Why she didn't tell: Pretend. It didn't happen.
No one will swallow it. He threatened, laughed, was stronger, bigger.
It's my fault. They won't believe me. Pretend. Have to see him sneer.
Hide it.

What happens next: Cracks. Panic, a plane taking off in the gut.
Armor, as involuntary as neurons saying run but all there is is a
wall. Looking ok, nobody knows. *Get over it.* What is PTSD? The thing
that won't leave, the image, the smell, the taste that's a plague.

The crush of shame. Lack of sleep. *When is it over?*
Feeling it, numbing it. Not understanding yet that greatness
comes from damage.

DISASTER RELIEF THANK-YOU PARTY
For the Trauma Recovery Network

The summer after the fires, empty spaces
where houses were, trees disappeared.
The dead might also be crowded into the party

room, with the scorched minds of the five hundred
survivors we helped to heal. We are women doing
what has to be done. We will do it time after time,

offer up what is needed after a crisis. How you know
it could have been you who lost everything, still might be.
And what's a great party without food, barbecue, salads,

three different pies. Dedication to the volunteers, also survivors.
Everyone a survivor of something, along with the dead, passed
into the magic trick of inferno. They look okay again,

in case you're afraid. And the creeks, the rivers still running
towards the ocean. It all seems to move on as it always has,
the restoration, the healing, the celebrations, the love, also red and hot.

SOMEONE ELSE HAS BEEN ACQUAINTED WITH THE NIGHT
After a line in Rereading Frost *by Linda Pastan*

I could write to Linda with gratitude. *Thank you,* I would say,
for easing my sleepless mind in the 3AM dark, in the middle
of a crawlspace dark, in a somber movie theater in the winter,
even in the dark of a sunlit summer afternoon. It helps so
not to be alone. I could travel toward the sun, let myself go

away, board a train, listen to its sounds and sway. I could sit
in a hot tub on a mountainside in the moonlight. Notice a hare
spring into the forest. *I've been to that forest,* I could tell it,
and I know where there is shelter, where there is safety.
Where it is scary and what to do about it

MISSING OUT

Last night it was between Maggie
Nelson, MacArthur Genius Award
winner, genre bending poet reading live,
it was between the sublime Maggie and the gym.

The gym, its mundane machines rising
to meet my faltering muscles. Drudgery
of the treadmill. Me just back from Hawaii
needing that sauna like an addict craving opiates.

So easy to miss up, mess up, my schedule
an overripe banana. So hard to choose,
decide, follow the peel as it falls or follow
the fruit. Which is which?

My apologies to Maggie who didn't miss
me, I'll never know now how she looked
when she read that poem I so hoped to hear
about green, how she was surrounded by it

after a year of planning to write a book
about blue. If I had time I would read that
one. I would think of her, so beautiful,
in front of the group at Stanford, everyone

so impossibly smart, the dress she wore,
its color, her face as it went from serious to grin,
I would see myself being there.

THIS POEM USED TO BE TITLED *OLD TREES, NEW BUDS*
For Cam

Originally, this poem was for a spring hike over
a rain softened trail. Originally, it was for you,
friend over these forty five years since grad school.

This poem, formerly known as flora reblooming, told
about what a noteworthy Dad you were, your children popping up
like wildflowers, how your wife went the way of the flowers

so many years ago. The Christmas at your mother's house
in Vermont, you and your wife, two nesting bowls. Your laugh,
the familiar way you have of walking, not exactly a strut, your good

looking smile. Basically a springtime friendship poem that becomes
something else—maybe it's winter still, and we're back in the snow
banks, the avalanche of losing your wife. My move across country

to California, how lucky I was to visit with her one last time. Maybe
it's summer, your grandkids with you on the beach. But I'm not there.
Or how time and distance change everything, until you're having dinner

and it's all the same again. We're young, not 70, the future still climbs
ahead on the trail, along with the new treasures, along with
the grief. And the love. And the seasons.

SUNDEEP KOHLI

PAINTINGS नक़्श

ज़मीं से आसमानों तक हज़ारों नक़्श बिखरे हैं
मुनासिब है मुसाविर का किसी इक पर फ़िदा होना

There are so many things of beauty from earth till skies
Painter's falling madly for one of them is always justified

ज़मीं का रात भर जगना सितारों को तका करना
समंदर की रवानी पर भी वहशत का गुमान होना

For earth to stay up whole night and watch the stars
The tides of the ocean give an impression of being in frenzy

इक उम्र ए जावेदां लगती है उल्फत की रसाई में
मुहब्बत का सिला मिलना सुख़नवर का सुखन होना

It takes one whole life for love to reach culmination
To get result of love is like a poet to become a poem's body

पहुँच कर मंज़िलों पे रास्तों की भूख ना मिटना
हमारी किस्मतों में ही लिखा है ला मकाँ होना

The hunger for journey not getting satisfied even at the destination
May be there is no place of dwelling in our destiny full of wilderness

LITA KURTH

SILICON VALLEY 2019

Through my bedroom window
at five in the morning
already the large and steady roar
of cars and trucks on their way to work
Mother and fathers
got up at four or even three
kissed their sleeping kids goodbye
left notes:
Microwave the Hot Pockets.
Don't use the stove!
Do your homework.
I love you.
And prayed somehow their children
will remember the dream
of a parent's touch.

GENE F. LEE

DANCING WITH YOU

sweet young girl
you dance with me, swirl
to my lead, hand in hand
follow the drum beat of the band
like Ginger and Fred
my shyness shed
you let my arm embrace
your womanly grace
the band swings hip
my lady I dip
ah, to be so young
you take me back among
my long past friends
where childhood ends
and I danced once before
with a girl who wore
a dress like yours and her hair
tossed through the air
as we whirled to the tune
on a wedding night in June
now dancing with you
I feel so true
and time itself bends
as old remembered friends
come to me quick and gay
not as ghosts on a lonely day
but to me with you swinging
to the beat and bringing
out the youth inside
I long denied
sweet young girl
you dance with me, twirl
with the tune follow my lead
step forward, smile, recede
we spin and turn in rings
the music swings
the music swung
ah, to be so young

KEEPSAKE

For you this poem, words to show my mind,
Much like a photo would depict my look,
This little trinket to throw out or find
One day preserved inside a favored book.
We're guided by the choices that we make—
You with the world to grasp, explore and change,
I with my pledges and a path to take—
That comes a time we go is not so strange.
May this remind you of a friend who came
Your way one summer when we shared a dance
Too brief, and went our separate ways, whose name
You should recall with fondness and romance.
Our deeds will fade, as life will push us old,
Let's not forget these days, before we're cold.

NATHAN LEE

EXIT WOUNDS

the gun goes off
in a walmart
at a food festival
in a high school

thoughts and prayers
and the gun goes off

in a theater
at a university
in a club

and the gun goes off

like fireworks,
like the fourth of july.

home of the free
land of the

bravery shouldn't have to be existence.
every time i walk into a building
i look for the exit

wounds that we cannot heal.
exit wounds like bullets lodged

in our teeth
in our lungs
in our throat
exit wounds like

candlelight vigils.
like the fire alarm screams

and the gun goes off.

how many more?

RECOGNITION

MAYBE I'VE ALWAYS BEEN THIS:
YOUR SWEET LITTLE GIRL.
YOUR BOY TOO BRIGHT TO TOUCH.
TAKE A MATCH TO MY GASOLINE.
WATCH ME DISAPPEAR / REAPPEAR.
THE BEST SLEIGHT-OF-HAND TRICK
YOU'VE EVER SEEN.
I'M THE SAME AS I WAS. OKAY?
BURN THE BABY PICTURES IF YOU WANT.
I'LL BE THE SAME. I'VE BEEN THE SAME.
FLIP A SWITCH. SPIT MY NAME LIKE A CURSE.
I'LL BE RIGHT HERE WAITING.

SEPTEMBER

i burn my tongue
on august. she leaves
me scraped raw,
skinned knees, bare-
handed; no salvation
in the crush of her palms.
but the summer fades
(as it does) &
september brings
cool wind to my aching body.
among orange & gold
i relearn how to breathe &
on foggy mornings i could
fall & fall & never hit the
ground.

DEFINITIONS

nathan
/NAY-thən/
noun

I.   boy with lungs too small for poetry. boy with hollow living in his bones. boy with scars, skinned knees, bruised knuckles. boy plunges his hand into his ribcage and comes up empty.

II.   this is the self-portrait of the artist, i guess / slice my heart open with a scalpel / wipe dry my rose-petal veins / stitch my sternum up with the fraying threads of sunrise

III.   my father calls me a stranger. and yes, i don't recognize the face in the mirror. i locked up my heart put the key in a box pushed the box out to sea flung the sea into the sun waited till the sun came crashing down. yeah, maybe i was not meant to be known. but i'm done holding on.

AUGUST

stretches around us
like a sunday afternoon
honey-slow, firefly-golden

there is basil growing
on your kitchen windowsill
peach juice staining your lips
your hair corn-silk soft

oh, i want your blue hour
your six o'clock sunrise
your star-strewn sky
just you,
       you,
          you.

DEBORAH LeFALLE

AUTUMN HAIKU

whirling wind drift
yellow leaves dance gracefully
into tree hollow

ROCK MUSING

Pick up a rock// examine it closely
and imagine what it might tell you
about its journey.
What is its texture, color, form, shading?
Does it have spots, patterns or lines?
Is it translucent, solid, dark, or light?
Smooth, bumpy, or jagged?

People are sort of like rocks.
We come from a host of lineages
and we all have distinct characteristics
that contribute to defining who we are
and the spaces we occupy.
Our stories are intertwined, yet varied –
lived and told in many ways.

Rocks make up mountains and riverbeds,
the ground beneath our feet
and people make up communities.
Be grateful for the *goodness* that thrives
amidst our earthly existence
and seek beauty in the myriad rocks
that sustain mutuality in our landscapes of life.

TWO WEEKS AFTER
in San Jose CA, on aftermath of 2017 North Bay wildfires

the sky is blue today
absent murky gray-brown haze
valley's surrounding mountains
in full panoramic view

makes me think of places
north beyond the Golden Gate
people piecing back together
what destruction tore apart

the blackened landscapes
lives lost, the injured and missing
charred remains where homes once stood
possessions reduced to ash

here – I breathe freely
glad smoke packed its bags and left
there – distant neighbors still wear masks
and cling to thoughts of fresh air again

CAROLINE LINDLEY

55 BULLETS

The number of bullets they fired to kill a man.

A man, unexplainable asleep in a car
in the Taco Bell drive thru lane.
Not explained why.
Now, not ever to be.

Just 55 bullets.
In 3 and a ½ seconds.
From 6 policemen.
1 man dead.

They said a gun was in his lap.
He was coming to, waking up.
His left hand made a motion towards the gun.
They said.

55 bullets.
3 and a ½ seconds.
6 policemen.
7 lives ruined.
55 bullets.

The number of bullets to kill 1 man.

ALGEBRA

You don't understand.
How could you? It was never explained.
You were sent for help, only for help.
An important old man,
they said he knew the subject.
His house next door,
a small dark room,
heavy curtains drawn,
one lamp.
Your school papers,
a pencil laid out on the desk.
You still don't understand.
Your glossy hair falls over your face.
You feel your nose begin to drip.
How can letters be numbers?
You can't think about the letters on the papers.
He rises heavily,
walks behind you.
One hand goes slowly down your yellow school blouse.
His large hand goes over your small breast.
Hold still you think, don't make a fuss.
Not a sound.
Everything stops.
Don't breathe.
Now impossible to think at all.
You sit so still. You can't move.
You say I still don't get it.
Suddenly he pulls his hand away.
Straightens up. Says
you better go home now.
You go home.
You don't understand.

HOT SUMMER GUILT

Eating ice cream with a fork.
Standing in front of the kitchen sink.
Silky, cool, coffee ice cream
swirls into your tongue.
Deeper your fork goes
bringing up a bit of brittle
dark chocolate so cold
that you can't even taste it,
only feel it.
But then, its dark, smooth texture
begs you to dig your fork deeper
into its carton.
Again and again the mark of the fork
appears in the ice cream.
Only one bite, you said.
But the fork doesn't seem to hear.
A noise!
Someone coming?
This is your solitary pleasure,
shameful almost, no one must see.
You toss the fork into the sink.
Quickly you smash the sticky lid
back on the carton.
Into the cold freezer the ice cream goes.
Waiting for your next visit.

TRYPTOPHAN

Thoughts pushed into my mind worrying its edges.
The noise and clutter of the house made me jagged.
To soothe myself I walked into the clear sunlight.

The sidewalk was warm and empty.
Suddenly quietly there they were.
Five turkeys drinking from the sprinklers in the green lawn.
One tom and his four ladies.
Their heads bobbed down to the bubble of water
then jerked up and blindly stared.
Each movement very distinct, very random.
Across the asphalt he walked,
slowly peeling his feet away from the ground,
as if they were glued to its sticky surface.
Pretending not to see me, or really not seeing me,
he walked into the tall, gold grass.
His ladies followed with their own reluctant movements.

So deliberately calm and focused.
My mind now empty as the birds'
I walked back to the house.

BC DOG SONNET

Writing a sonnet about our old dog
I thought about Billy Collins sitting
writing in brilliant sunshine or dark fog
his ideas clear his brilliance biting
or was that the ugly dog he mentioned
maybe some novice poet's poem read
that has brought about this awful tension
headache that will send me often to bed
until this dog sonnet will write itself
and Billy asks me advice for unruly
dogs or poems it will go on the shelf
never to be voiced or treated cruelly.
If Mister Collins now reads my poem
for dogs and verses I truly owe him.

FROM THE FENCE WHERE MICHAEL SHEPARD WAS STRUNG

He hung for hours on me.
When they strung him up on my posts
I held him tight, what else could I do?
He was a delicate, a sprite, a true faerie boy.
When his frail frame hung
and the blood from his broken body dripped,
what could I do?
Sap from my long dead cells
mixed with his blood and tears
and fell to the dry hardpan dirt.
I would later be roughly pulled from the earth,
thrown into the back of an old pickup
and burned to grey ash in a furnace.
As if that would clear the evil.
          ....

When his frail frame hung
and the blood from his broken body dripped,
what could I do?
When his broken, jagged teeth and his blood streaked salvia
dripped from his open mouth,
I could do nothing, only hold him.
What could you have done, if you were me?
          ....

People used to admire me, my handsome work.
They would feel proud, I would make them think
 of Lincoln and rolling green country sides
and honest men.
We are named Buck fences
and have graced beautiful landscapes
in this harsh West.
Now, I feel a shame that was not of my making.
Too late, I burned in disgrace.
I preferred to call it in honor.

CITY OF COLOR

In the Target parking lot in Cupertino
the Jacaranda trees are in full lilac splendor.
Their spent blossoms carpet the blacktop
with a purple rug. My little white car
looks absolutely festive sitting under
the glowing lavender boughs.
A purple stencil is left when I drive away.

Down the sidewalk come two ladies.
The white hot sun rains down
and up come delicate turquoise and pink umbrellas.
They walk talking to each other,
 holding aloft the colored umbrellas so careful
 as not to let the bright sun touch their ivory faces.

Down Bubb Road men walk,
their hands clasped behind their backs,
dressed in white pants with long white shirts over all.
Behind them women walk slowly
in saris of brilliant scarlet, lime and gold.
Some are made of a long skirt and top
that reveals a middle of warm, cocoa brown skin.
Rainbows of pink and green
glitter from the sequins strewn on the fabric.

Elegant Teslas speed by in apple red, brilliant blue and sharp silver.
Green lines painted on the streets
guide brave bicyclists to late classes while crossing guards
in yellow vests with orange flags warn cars
to watch carefully for students.
These green lines also guide bicyclists as they weave their way through traffic.
Their tight tops of neon yellow, red and orange clash purposely
with their black and white striped helmets and black tights.
Young brown, tanned legs pump quickly
as they cross the street between white lines
along with grey beards on riders going faster.
Their sliver bikes streak past on the warm street.

The hills above us turn grass green in spring.
Summer brings its warm tones of gold.
We are a city of color.

PAUL LIU

HELLO BUT GOODBYE

the wind blows through my hair...
   She comes—she goes
   to another place–
      chased by poets.

The wind tousles my hair
   like a mother to her boy.
   She creeps along my arms to
      my fingertips...

She skims over skin–
   pebbles skipping over ripples
    my lover
     just a minute...
She whispers in my ear
sweet little secrets about
      the trees, how the leaves gossip,
      why the willow droops, the
      wisdom of the old yew tree
          that lives many lives.

The wind embraced me–
     a warm gust,
she was really rushing
     through my arms in farewell...

the wind blew through my hair,
she was just passing through,
   so I said "pardon me," and ducked,
     as to not crash into her,
        my ever-leaving muse.

FINE

"How are you?"

"I'm fine."

fine, fine like mother's china,
breaking with a touch.
fine, fine like a fair maiden,
for whom only tragedy awaits.
fine, like the thread of life,
flimsy and anxious.

"I'm fine,
thanks."

I SPOKE TO THE GUQIN ONCE

I love spouting nonsense / like the man down the street / somewhere in the world where / fairies dance in the meadow / jiuweihu, where are you? / I sat down once / and wrote and wrote / until I was writing no more / the willow quivered / suddenly / the little lady by the river waved her little wave / and I sipped tea from tea cups wiser than me / and I wonder whether / the wind swept me here / or if the words became alive / and took me into their arms / suddenly / existentialism unravels / nothing but now / as I twirl / with my nine-tailed companion / sing with the sirens by the sea / farewell to the gray / settling in little stone houses / and / suddenly / the quiet song of the scholar rises / like odorless smoke / curling around the trees / singing to the universe / in sophistication / it begs simplicity / here is loneliness / here is a beautiful lotus / drowning after her lover / in the Qingshui river / here is the Summer monsoon / precious rain of life / here is the harsh winter / suddenly / death / I spoke to the guqin / I asked him if he knew / what it was I needed to do / to escape his claw / he said / *shift your perspective* / I laughed / what a silly guqin you are! / yet his whisper resounded in my mind / *you are as sad as you think you are* / and the willow quivered / and I realized in my waking / I *am* as sad as I *think* I am.

THE WOMAN WHO WAS A DRAGON

And I strolled on the paved road with
  cracks like creeping vines on bark
    through rows of skylights called trees
fracturing beams and spilling them
  on the floor in the form of little
      bright souls who wander in the day
       and I flew away with the spirits–
         forgetting where I set out to go
     grinning like a swaying leaf in
       forgetfulness—Then I came upon
    a queen who was really a dragon
she sat on an obsidian bench and
  all the drifting spirits glistened
on her skin as if finding the place–
    the infinite where lost dreams go—
  and the she-dragon raised her claw
    inhaling—the firefly spirits part–
and I see upon her face the festering
       pains of the universe—
    catharsis or a similar miracle in
exhale and my brilliant friends
  scatter with the dragon-smoke
    that smells like charcoal embers in Winter
    or dreams slipping out of grasp
      gray dissipates…
      She puts out her
       cigarette.

ORPHANAGE

white marble cookie crumbs
gingerbread houses and frosting-white snow
            or absence of these
stepping out of bed or stumbling
onto uncertain shores and deafening waves—
each morning the sun rises in red
            loud mornings hurt ears
we scavenge to fill the restlessness
but the serpent-like chill whispers—
in darkness fear keeps us still
            we must live
                  or do we?
whether the orange-bellied robin sings
or the lonely crickets mourn together
it is always night in this place
            there is no night
                  like death
sift through the ruins—
tattered infant's blanket—
a wreath for the old
broken grandfather clock
            don't listen to them
                  it is too late
and it all becomes undone
somewhere a desolate dust scatters
peer aimlessly into the mirror
            empty baby photo albums
                  who's the thief?
half-drawn murals of our demons
vying for tortured lost souls

TINGES OF RED

a couple
aromatic
roses

those
flushed
cheeks

pools of
rusted
blood

that
bittersweet
death

tinges
of
red

AND I SAW YOU AGAIN

I lied to the moon / said that the sun is just around the corner / like an old friend / waiting / for fiery topaz chrysanthemums / or tears like rivers / or even just a glimpse / at the lost grains of sand / coming together in / a strange wind / forming a familiar stranger's face // I lied to the moon / the silver mirror in the sky / reflecting lovers' radiance / or unbounded sadness / I was fearful / of the reflection of the night / its personality frightened me / as I stared into my own depthless eyes // I lied to the moon / I promised him / the day had come / many days ago / until time left us faded / time is no friend of ours / and like my reflection / with silver hair / a tired smile / and foggy eyes / my spirit sighed // and I saw you again / my fire topaz / solid lifestone / my vital muse / I see you / in the weakness of my spirit / in the fading moonlight / in the golden sunrise / I see you again // *Smiling back and waving farewell / I saw you again.*

LEAVING MYSELF BEHIND

Most things we don't realize
                 or don't know / won't
Like how the people
                 sigh with their eyes
with a smile along their lips

No, no, *you don't know*
         not until you are
                 what you are

I am the crackled lips of the
                 Methuselah tree
         the slender,
vermilion fox with bushy tail
you come around
                 by and by

And we all fall away
                 with our eyes shut
         half-gasping
             half-asleep

No, no, *I don't know*
         not until
                 i leave myself behind

PUSHPA MacFARLANE

NATURE-MADE

I walk in the shadow of the glistening edge
the setting sun—a golden orb
a low hanging fruit on the horizon

I trace my fingers along that line, as the evening
August breeze flutters through like a Monarch
butterfly sweeping across my face

sweetness—ripe and full, fills the air—wild berries
and seaweed, makes me hungry. A sprawling black furry
spider like an anemone, crawls out from under the bench

I breathe each pearl of air—the blue waters, the smell of raw,
rough surfaces, and grainy wood benches. Soft sounds of air
bubble, pop, and burst, leaving a pungent peppermint smell

the sky soon takes on a plethora of colors, as if an artist
waves an invisible brush across, painting unexplained swatches
in gold, orange, ultramarine, and smoky blue

white puffy clouds and lighter shades, dissipate in the soon
darkening sky. A sense of autumn filters in the edges of a canvas,
and gray seagulls take off mysteriously, into the clouds

THE DOG AND I: A DOGGONE CONVERSATION

Hmm. A quiet pause.
Oh, such cute paws!

I'm looking at her frown.
I'm watching her smiley face.

I'm hoping she will smile.
Is she going to jump? I'm getting eager.

I have my smiley face
But I have to wait—"Stay"! I say.

My tongue is lolling, I'm almost dripping wet—I'm still waiting...
Can't believe I exploded when I first saw her

Should I reach out and sniff?
Well...I was only thinking about the huge responsibility.

Will she think I'll pounce?
I can't stop looking at her.

I'm getting excited! I'm panting now.
Now I'm anxious. Will she snap?

Can she not see my wagging tail?
I'm a bit scared. But I know she likes me.

I can hear her think, "she's frolicky"!
I'm going to try a hug—but what if she growls?

No! I'd better be polite...I'm restless.
I scream: "Come here!" and hold her paws.

I am startled. Should I get closer? Will she be afraid?
She is stunned. She's bowing down—her face between her legs.

I can't wait! Oh gosh! I love her, I love her, I love her!
Drat! I missed my chance. Drat! Drat! But I truly love her!

THE SILENT STREAM

The first time I saw the stream it crept over
rocks and twigs without much hue or cry—

the bubbly sound evident like the chirrup
of birds in the area—tones you understand

when you see the evidence—there's no surprise
or wonder—just acknowledgement of its presence.

In fact, seeing the chuckling stream frolic and froth,
and bubble with no sound, would be an abomination.

Listening to the regurgitating sounds of happy normalcy
put me at ease, conscious of its beauty—the reflections

it carried with it, as it tripped over the dry bits of wood
and tender saplings—friendly, gentle, calming.

Who knew what tensions grew within, when the
rains came. Gathering force—like years of abuse,

it kicked around, throwing tantrums forcing out
its gravity, swelling and spewing like volcanic

lava over and onto the humble banks—turning
into something treacherous, profane, and frothing

at the mouth—it swallowed whole, in a matter
of minutes, buildings of brick and concrete,

evidence of tar and bridges, dissolving mud and
sandy soil into bogs, pulling down automobiles,

fences and large acres of productive land. A horror
exploded on humanity—the curse, inflicting

the innocent—damning intellect, then watching
humans scurry like rats for safety, nature

waiving arms like wretches—the abomination
of something gentle, natural, now demeaning—

irresponsible, demonstrating hidden rage,
exposing rapacious instincts, and silent screams.

HAIKU AT MCCLELLAN RANCH PRESERVE

Kigo

budding leaves
unfurl
unclenched fists

charcoal twigs
etch a story
a canvas sky

****

stray words knit
tales at
McClellen Park Ranch

creek wrestles
over rocks
a swallow dips in flight

green clovers look up
as yellow stalks
sun themselves

a heron stalls
undisturbed
standing on one leg

brick red barn
blushes
in sunlight

an old fence folds
in courtesy
to the fallen oak

denuded trees
break out in pimples
in spring

a waft of fresh
cow dung sparks
yearning for bundt cake

red-shouldered hawks
haunt
the Douglas fir

owls screech
past the red
and white barn

CENTO—THIS EVERYTHING DANCE

Cento: A poetic form composed wholly of quotations from the works of other authors.

> *I like to live in the sound of water*
> *In the feel of mountain air . . .*
> *This motionless turmoil, this everything dance*
> > *—William Stafford (Time for Serenity, Anyone?)*

look at the silent river and wait
there are comings and goings from miles away
that hold the stillness
I like to live in the sound of water
this wilderness—this motionless turmoil
this everything dance
is it magic?
wrapping a new piece of time
around you, a readiness
for a meadowlark
great waves can pass unnoticed
whole mountain ranges, history,
the holocaust, sainthood
listen! a bell sounds—then leaves
a whole countryside waiting

SOMETHING ABOUT TREES

All my stirring becomes quiet . . .
    —*Wendell Berry, "I Go Among Trees and Sit Still"*

There's nothing better than walking among the trees, being right in the midst of them, smelling the freshness, especially after the rain has washed down the leaves. Sun-dried ground—a strong foothold, my mind not distracted by puddles or soft footing. I look around, listen to the sounds of birds retreating for the night, the rustling in the trees, the sky—as it turns from blue to blush—I switch on a mental video in my head to record every moment.

There's something about the trees. Just looking at them gives me joy—I've never really questioned why, but I think because the trees remind me of the human life cycle. They grow from a little seed, have a reasonably long life, then get old but continue to live their life till a calamity strikes—either a lightening, or a storm, or the ill-fated woodsman's axe to its trunk that lends to its tragic disintegration, then back into the earth. I think I've always been fascinated by a tree.

Even as a child, I've secretly harbored some kind of veneration toward the lordly and beautiful trees my father planted in the house where I was born. Enamored by the rugged trunks and lofty branches, that reached out to the sky—protecting everything in its shade. My Dad, mostly silent, except when he found something hilarious, then shake himself with laughter and tears dropping down his cheeks like dew—a momentous occasion, since he was mostly quiet otherwise.

When I look at the marks on the tree where a limb might have been, they stare back like dark eyes—my dad's eyes. They say a lot. One never knows what goes on behind them, but they're deep pools, where I can wallow, see myself, and feel a sense of warmth. To me, the tree is a symbol of my father's inner strength. He was always there for us—his family—no matter what. Over the years, I've seen myself increasingly, doing the same thing with my children—just being there for them. Some day they will do the same for their own.

It takes courage, love, and mostly it means taking care—like the tree standing up and always giving it's all throughout it's entire life-span: Its shade, its leaves, its fruits, the moisture in the soil, and the wood and warmth, when it surrenders its life. All this in silence—we accept what comes from silence.

Something to be treasured in trees.

PAPER NESTS

I love to read, so I collect
books, printouts from workshops,
and my own notebooks—end
to end with free writing—
poems that hover like wasps
hanging on to memories—
some sad, some happy.

I walked across the McClellan
Park Ranch, and the first thing
I was surprised to see was
an enormous nest flattened
in layers—a vacated wasp's nest,

where once the queen and her
sisters resided. Busy little
creatures tidying up, the queen
laying her gems and packing
some away for posterity,

like me—hoping
one day my children
would enjoy going through
my notebooks, to see what
I couldn't talk about with them.

Words laying bare
my thoughts, looking
into my mind—as I
looked into the windows
of the paper nest
the wasps left behind.

THE REDWOOD SAPLING

What pressure must it feel—
the young, slender redwood
sapling. What ambition conquer,
to be like the elders?
Born with the genes of a giant, such
greatness—what imminent pressure
it must feel.

Standing by a two-hundred-year-old
Titan forged with a hefty trunk, brick red
with bark revealing its maturity—
its toughness, height, its roots
spread far and wide into the soil—
what history must it repeat?

And yet, when morning comes,
the young redwood dons
its brightest green. Its stems
fresh and eager to meet the sun.
Its tender leaves ready to shed
its dew—and listen to the
wind passing through—
the fiercest test it will
have to endure.

THE NURSERY

Out in the patio under a thin gauze-white
canopy, is a lined up parade of pots,

at intervals of twelve inches or so—
glazed gargantuan, Moroccan earthenware

in varied shapes and dimensions,
wide-brimmed in ultramarine and jade,

gold, glazed veneers marble-like, resting
atop another, hour-glass style.

The plants invincible, unseen behind
the stretched canvas, unless you crane

over inquisitively, and stand on your toes,
when you walk under the canopy.

Wooden pallets propped up—a make-shift
counter on cardboard boxes, black pots

overturned in piles, white plastic
and green wide-mouthed, yet silent—

empty, waiting for a pit full of earth.
A promise of sunshine, seed, a germinating

cotyledon, root, stem, and leaf. Bees
whipping up a buzz. Pollination.

Progeny. A new life, and hope—
the start of a new generation.

IN THE GARDEN

Swirls of white feathery clouds,
wisps of dog-hair strewn
on a light blue carpet
the moon winks—ticklish.

The more I stare at the clouds
the spaces in-between appear
like faces looking down—
frowning at my bedraggled,

drying jasmine, as it clutches
the green sprightly twines
creeping in the shingles—
unreachable, without a tall

ladder. Rusty stragglers strangle
the Juniper branches that reach
out like tentacles—a green octopus
against the gray sky.

Pendulous sprays of bougainvillea
tumble from thorny dry stems—
the last vestige of magenta,
reminiscent of plump purple grapes

redundant on age-old vine.
Clik-klak, clik-klak, the fluted
wood, lantern-shaped wind
chime rattles in the breeze.
.

If I peek out from half-closed
eyes, it looks like an old
oriental peasant, knee deep
in a muddy paddy field.

A dove coos somewhere,
as if the flute suddenly spills
a halting harmony—coo-coo-coo,
then a prolonged silence.

SINEAD McCAFFERY

GO LIVE

Go live
Go do what makes your heart pound
And your hands shake
Until your goals
Those daunting monsters
Lurking in the dark
Are defeated

MAGGIE McCORMICK

THE HORSE & EARTHWORM ARE ME

I am loud, I am strong
I know what my task is
And I know how to complete it

I writhe, uprooted from my home
Nowhere to go except out into the open
Waiting to return to my hole
Only to be flushed out again

Running, I feel no fear
Everyone adores me, admires me
I am groomed, loved, and accepted

I am ugly, unloved, avoided
Stepped on and thrown into the dirt
Picked on and scared

I laugh and smile, I feel the wind in my hair
I am free, I depend on only myself and the blue of the sky

I am suffocating, buried deep below
I only come out in times of rain and I struggle to return

Maybe I am only loved for my strength and good spirit
Maybe I am only detested for my repulsive form

I run to hide the pain that I feel so that it may never consume me

I fear to feel power for it is more than I can endure

Still, we push forward together

*for Keiko -
with love
and poetry!
Lesa*

LESA MEDLEY

DRIFTWOOD

Years ago
while walking the beach
on the Oregon Coast,
Mom spotted a
large, gnarled
piece of driftwood
she just had to have.
Dad drug that driftwood
for 3 miles down the beach
back to our car
so that it could become
the centerpiece of our
front lawn landscaping.

Fast forward
some forty plus years:
to a pleasant,
sunny Monday afternoon,
late August;
my sisters, my Dad
and I,
parked across from the old house
on Wright Street
in The Dalles.
That same piece of driftwood,
weathered with age…
but still in place.

We began to plan a covert
night time mission
to take it back,
but couldn't agree
on who should keep it.
In the end, we left it there...
and went to Big Jim's
for ice cream. ~

3,000 MILE ROOTS

I was born in Beckley, West Virginia,
raised in Oregon, and I have lived here
in Silicon Valley for the majority of my life.
I am quite a mix.

I come from West Virginia coal miners
on my father's side and Oregon wheat
field farmers on my mother's.
My roots run deep and they are 3,000
miles strong. I come from proud, sturdy
hard working people. Salt of the earth
comes to mind, again and again.

When I think of Oregon, I think of
wheat fields rolling softly in the wind
like green and golden ocean waves.
I think of mountains, lakes, rivers,
farm lands and fruit orchards.

I think of early mornings and early evenings
in summer and fall in the alfalfa fields with
irrigation sprinkler lines running, against
the backdrop of snow capped mountains.
I think of the fishing platforms along the
Columbia River Gorge where members of
the Wy-Am nation used to catch salmon
the old way, with huge nets.
I think of the mighty Celilo Falls,
buried by The Dalles Dam
in 1957.

Thoughts of West Virginia invoke a misty,
foggy, smoky, shadowy part of myself that
has been dormant and out of focus for a very
long time. Memories and images are trying to
step up, come back into focus and be clearly
recognized, claimed and embraced.

I'm noticing more and more that an occasional y'all
will slip out from time to time or when I happen to be
talking to someone from the region, even for just a few
minutes, and I can hear my accent slowly creep back in.
This makes me smile. The movie Next of Kin,
especially the scenes in Kentucky, the movie Coal
Miner's Daughter, bluegrass music and John Denver's

song Take Me Home Country Roads all bring out
powerful emotions and hold great meaning for me.
My body remembers where I come from.

When I think of West Virginia, my mind pictures
miners coming out of the mines, tired, covered
in coal dust, carrying their silver lunch pails,
with big head lamps on their helmets. I think of my Poppy,
in the mines for 30 years until black lung
forced him out. My Poppy is a whole 'nother poem!
I think of my Uncle Boots, my Dad's brother, he was also a coal miner.

 I am very proud of where I come from, both
sides of me, my history, my roots. I am working
on discovering more about these pieces of myself and
merging them into a cohesive whole, where all of my
history comes together and all of my 3,000 mile roots
can grow strong and shine!

SOME HAIKU

quiet, ominous
dark sky and blustering winds
a storm is brewing

from my patio
summer evening sparkle leaves
my best time of day

leaves falling gently
darkness comes early now
autumn's golden light

fragile miracles
white and pink cactus blossoms
only last a day

HANKIES IN HER POCKETS

Last Fall, in Oregon
after my mother passed away,
my sister, aunt,
cousins, and I
were going through her closets

In her jackets, sweaters,
and pants
we found tissues,
"hankies" in nearly
every pocket

Her nose was notoriously runny
due to allergies
and she always carried clean
"hankies" in her pockets...
just in case

We all got such a good,
much needed
laugh finding those
"hankies"
and remembering

Shortly after returning
home to California,
it was time to pull out
my own jackets,
cardigans and sweatshirts

In most of the
pockets
I found,
you guessed it,
"hankies"

I just laughed
then smiled
and thought to myself...
"like mother,
 like daughter"

PREPARING 4TH OF JULY DINNER
Preparing and cooking a meal surrounded by memories

I decided to oven barbecue
chicken thighs
using homemade barbecue sauce
my Mom's recipe
haven't made it in years
brown sugar
ketchup
finely chopped onions
vinegar
Lea & Perrins (Worcestershire sauce)

Memories started to engulf me
maybe because it was
my Mom's recipe,
or maybe it was the tangy smells
wafting from the saucepan
either way, I felt her presence
and the memories flooded

As I stirred the sauce
and added the Worcestershire,
I remembered my Mom's little brother
my Uncle Paul
Uncle Paul loved Worcestershire sauce
and he ate it on just about everything

He always just called it
Lea & Perrins
I don't think he ever called it
anything else
it was always there
on their table
in its tan paper wrapper

Chopping the onions for the sauce
and the potato salad
brought memories of my Dad
and my cousin, "Little Paul"
they neither one liked onions
and would not eat anything
with onions
there always had to be a separate
bowl of "no onions" potato salad

Paul would always ask
"is there unnies in it?"
about everything
His brother John
and my sister Paula
would torture him
by telling him
there were "unnies" in
everything:
cookies,
milk,
ice cream…
well, you get the idea

Just. Plain. Mean.

WHITE 4RUNNER
For Steve

Driving to work this morning on Blossom Hill Road
In front of me was a White Toyota 4Runner
Just like yours, complete with the black rack on top
I hadn't seen one in a while so it took me by surprise
Sometimes when I see them, I just notice,
But other times, like this morning, it hit me
Right between the eyes and in my heart
Over 23 years later, it all came back

The last time I saw you, my brother, was in January 1996
You were getting ready to get into that 4Runner
And head back to Oregon for a brief trip
You said you needed to take care of some unfinished business
You said you would be back,
I think I knew then you wouldn't be
I waved goodbye and watched you get into that 4Runner
And drive away
You said you would be back,
I think I knew then you wouldn't be

We had just celebrated our birthdays together that December
You were here for Christmas
Although I didn't know it at the time, it would be the last time for both
I was just so happy to have my brother back in my life again
You left shortly after New Years

But about 6 months later I got the phone call that forever changed my life
You were gone, at the age of 33
You chose to die, alone, in that 4Runner at Colliding Rivers in Glide, Oregon
And I am left to forever miss you and wonder… why?

POSTING FROM A NIGHT TRAIN

Friday, May 3, 2013
On a night train,
no, not to Georgia,
but the #14 Amtrak Coast Starlight
8:25 pm to Eugene, Oregon
My final destination: Roseburg, Oregon.

There is a Rod Stewart wanna be
in the seat in front of me,
with yellow-orange spiked hair,
he is standing in the aisle
smoking an electronic cigarette.

After sitting for a while,
need to walk and stretch my legs.
I wander down to the sightseeing car
nothing to see out the big windows
except dark and my own reflection.

I get a turkey sandwich, peanuts and water
from the snack car and head back to my seat.
The train rolls northward.
We stop and pick up more night travelers
and the seats fill up.

3:43 am. Well surprise… I can't sleep!
Finding it hard to get comfortable,
and it is not so easy to sleep
next to someone I don't know.

We were stopped for 2 hours earlier
outside of Martinez
due to a medical incident
requiring paramedics.
Hoping for a good outcome.

Advised family meeting train
I may be late.

Now we are just lumbering along in the dark,
I am not sure where.
Quiet,
except for an occasional cough…
from somewhere,
and the creaking of the train.

BORED LONELY SHOES

One pair
Black Mary Janes,
One pair
Brown, sensible
Walking shoes,
Lined up
Side by side
Ready, waiting
No place to go
Waiting for me
To slip in
My feet and
Take them
Somewhere, Anywhere…
Work,
The bookstore,
Shopping.
Instead, they just sit…
And wait.
They are jealous
Of the flip flops
And white tennies
Who got to go
To Hawaii.
Yeah, they are
Pretty unhappy
About that.
Now I have been sick
So I've just
Been shuffling
Around in slippers
And socks.
Poor bored, lonely shoes.
The black ones
Will forgive me
Tomorrow though.
Tomorrow, we are
Going to work.
The brown ones
Will go to work
On Tuesday.
Now the flip flops
And white tennies
Will sit, and wait.
Poor bored, lonely shoes.

RODRIGO MURALLES

RAIN

Rain…
A solemn cry of the heavens above
A
downpour attributed to sadness
A
saddened heart sympathetic day
The
rain form puddles
A
never ending rain, or a crying heaven
The
clouds blocking the ever gleaming sun
The
rain forming an endless solitude
Causing
an eternal like loneliness
For
some… a blessing
For
others… a curse
A
blessing is for some for they, their hearts sympathize
Others
a curse, for they hate the darkened day
A
curse for some, for the light and happiness is blocked
A
blessing for some for the rain causes an enjoyable day for them
A
day where they are most used to, accustomed, love
Rain
of the crying heavens fills the sky we share

REGRETS

Regrets
of the past
Close
or long ago
Chiping
at the mind insistently
Of
what could've been done differently
No
control over the situation yet
Only
a deep regret is founded
Even
if it is disappointing
To
want a different ending
To
make a difference
To
wish to go back and fix what went wrong
Even
if there is no happy ending
The
way to make it right
Hidden
from sight
Lost
and gone with an endless pain
Even
if the sun goes down
Rises
the moon and once more
The
sun rising
Nothing
will have changed
With
only regrets….
As
everything comes falling down
Everyday
a bitter reminder how what happened before

VIBRANT

With
an energy never ending
With
the happiness to rival the sun
A
painter of fun
The
light emitted to light a dark void
A
darkened day lighten up by her
To
a day of a gleaming hope and joy
A
figment of joy and silliness
The
innocence of young light
Silly
as she is
Yet
hopeful nonetheless
With
a never ending beautiful light
She
is a light within the darkness of the night
A
warm burning flame in a winter storm
A
light with a purity and light as strong as a sun

GRATITUDE

Friends
who care
She
said "You'll be okay because I said so" many times
"Are
you okay?" They all asked
She
had cared
They
all had cared
Even
if they themselves are scarred
Hurt
and burned
They
still cared
A
warm happiness feeling in my heart
Gratitude
and a quiet happiness
Warming
up replacing the bitter cold
It
was cold being alone but warm with the cold bitter wind
But
with them it's always warm
No
regrets living a blessed life with them
Even
if they are the opposite of me
It's
always fun
My
heart is clear and warm
My
mind relaxed and free
A
surge of life in their grace
If
they grief then as am I

To
repay them for this gratitude
I
promise to always be by their side
I'll
never forget this great gift you all have given me

GOLDEN SUN

A
day arises once more
Hope
and light dawn thy world
Beckon
the crow's call
Justify
a day to wake
The
sun and it's glory they love
Bringing
upon it's golden rays
Bright
and warm
Yet
chaotic engrained to its core
A
contrast to its partner's cold and cool light
Thy
golden sun tall and steady
Staring
down bright and happily gleaming
Looking
upon its stars
Such
beautiful flowers
Rely
upon the kind sun's warmth and light
As
they gently bask thy home

What
hardships it has suffered
If
any at all
We
will never know
For
the golden sun never rests

ANN MUTO
FOURTH POET LAUREATE OF THE CITY OF CUPERTINO

BE LIKE *OVIE*

Note from the poet: My aunt's name "Ovie" was a take-off on Ovaltine beverage.

Accepting what surgery couldn't fix,
solving a crossword,

ordering Five-Spiced Chicken at Beacon,
dropping dollars in slots at Vegas.

Giving us pleasure,
chatting with us on the phone,
teasing us about poppies.
Accepting
an arm to step up,
rides to Trader Joe's,
dinners at Woo Lai Oak,
gift cards from Drapers,
yet another coffeemaker.

Your example shines brightly.
We are grateful
we can still enjoy
the gentle lightness that you are.

Happy 95th Birthday!

SQUARE ONE

Drinking fresh-squeezed oj,
chewing Nueske's bacon,
I almost forgot
why we could walk
to Square One for lunch.

Two blocks over
in the Kaiser complex,
Dr. O'Connell's scalpel
sliced out the pernicious
tumor in *Ovie's* abdomen.

In the tumult
of anxiety and fear,
Alan brought us
to this welcome oasis –
an escape,
a passing of time
and more …

a warm memory.

REFLECTIONS

I know how ominous fear can feel,
how it tempts me to hide or run away.

Poetry lured me out of hiding, offered me access
to questions I didn't know to ask, linked me
with neglected memories, revealed pathways
that delivered me to unexpected vistas.

Poetry forced me to bypass the cliché,
expose what had been elusive, search
for my essence, honor what's true for me.

Poetry begged to be shared with others, read aloud.
At first, applause as hard to accept as critique;
over time both became welcome, even sought.

Being Poet Laureate intensified my zest for poetry.
Other poets enthusiastically joined with me to explore
      poetry's power to reimagine our past in memoir,
      its power to connect us with the majesty of the sycamore,
      its power to invite youth to stand up and be heard in Slams,
      its power to celebrate creativity with all ages.

Tonight, no hiding or running away.

Tonight, poetry rules!

CINQUAIN COLLECTION

ANZA BORREGO CINQUAIN

Color Bent

Desert
sunflowers bend –
a jerky, random dance –
form flowing layers of golden
ribbon.

On the Edge

Asters –
lavender orbs –
gossamer polka dots
float over sumptuous carpet
of green.

POINT LOBOS CINQUAIN

June's Radiance

Glowing
golden yarrow;
add lizard tail yellow,
monkeyflower gold, buckwheat buds –
rich, lush.

YOSEMITE CINQUAIN

Warming Morning

Sun crests
over Half Dome.
Gooseberry blooms – pink. red –
woken by warming light. Leaves moist
with dew.

Bees and Buckwheat

Buckwheat
blossoms vibrate;
bees' floating barrage, a
busy, buzzing universe of
pink, black.

Unbroken

Half Dome,
stained by lichen,
bares her face, breasts, shoulders,
daring forces to shatter her –
still there.

TAHOE MEADOWS CINQUAIN

Nature's Design

Gurgling
wee waterfall.
Ophir Creek enriches –
keeps Tahoe Meadows flourishing,
nourished.

Joyous

Dogwood's
pale yellow bracts
rim lime green pin cushions,
leaves praying, open to the sky,
aglow.

ODE TO CASTLE VALLEY

Ode to Castle Valley

Your quiet introduction:
purple wandering daisies
peeking from the undergrowth,
lining the dusty rut-filled trail.

Your first mixed garden of
of creamy corn lilies, yellow
butterweed, orange paintbrush,
purple lupine delighted us.

More corn lilies, wandering daisies,
butterweed splashed ever wider
over meadows, up hillsides.
You sprinkled coral and yellow

crowns of crimson columbine and
magenta Lewis' monkey flowers
along the trail, making us smile at your
scattering of small surprises.

Castle Valley, we left you with regret.
We bade farewell to the rich mélange
of color behind us. Puffs of dust
followed our boots up the barren
ridge leading to Round Valley.

Ode to Round Valley

What could you, Round Valley, offer?
We had come this far; we decided to
proceed. Conifers crowded switchbacks
blocking any views of what was to come.

Yet, we spotted Leichtlin's mariposa lilies,
glistening white, nestled amidst dark pine
needles. Your purple carpets of wandering
daisies flowing down steep slopes began
peeking through the conifers,

until a vast sea of daisies spilled down
an entire hillside – nearly a hundred feet –
to the floor of the valley below. As the
trail flattened out, between tree trunks,

we glimpsed flashes of pink and red. As
the trees parted, a foot-high deluge of
pink and red elephant ears flooded the
wide expanse of your valley floor,
matched beyond by a spread of corn lilies

larger than any we had seen in Castle
Valley. Suddenly a room-sized pink
oriental carpet greeted us. Inch-tall tufts
of pussy paws boldly dared other species
to encroach into their territory.
Reluctantly we left you, too, Round
Valley.

We chuckled how once
we were so smitten with Castle Valley,
how once we could not imagine
how anything else
could possibly amaze us.

BACHAN'S EGG SUSHI

Bachan made it for New Year's.
Eggs whipped with salt and *shoyu*,
poured into oiled square hand-hammered pan.
Egg sushi, one of Bachan's delicacies.

Eggs whipped with salt and shoyu,
fire kept low to avoid burning.
Egg sushi, one of Bachan's delicacies,
egg square so carefully flipped over.

Fire kept low to avoid burning.
Her entire being engaged as she
delicately turned egg square.
Bachan's special treat as the year began.

Her entire being engaged as she
rolled egg sushi in handmade bamboo mat.
Bachan's special treat as the year began.
Bachan made it for New Year's.

Bachan – grandmother
Shoyu – soy sauce in Japanese
Sushi – Japanese food: rice and other fillers usually wrapped in dried seaweed

208

AUNTIE DON (MITSUE)

My aunt left this world
as she entered it:
carefree, playful, unfettered,
yet determined.

After school, my brother and I raced to the "Old House," burst through the door, searched for our playmate – our aunt who could not see. She immersed us in play – hide n' seek, Candy Land; constructed papier maché cowboys, Indians, horses for us to paint and gallop across bedspreads; tickled us until we howled; picnicked with us at beaches.

One day, the house was empty,
only *Bachan* was there.
No dramatic notes chasing notes,
the piano silent in the parlor.
Day after day after day,
our playmate gone …
without a word.

*   *   *

A trip to Oakland. Up the porch, into dark white rooms. *Bachan* silently surveyed the rooms, looked in drawers, examined the bathroom. She said, "It's because she cannot see," as she washed a bit of blood from a sheet.

Our aunt arrived,
cane in hand,
defiant in step
up the stairs
on her own.

*   *   *

A late evening phone call.
Bachan wanted us at the Old House.
Sitting in the parlor, not at the kitchen table, our new uncle sat next to our aunt.

Bachan - grandmother

Shocked, he was not Japanese!
Still, *Bachan* served them tea
as if nothing were wrong.

*   *   *

Bachan stayed with them, helped, when my cousin was born. *Bachan* told my mother, "Bob really takes good care of Mitsue."

Surprised! not that *Bachan* said that,
but that she said it out loud;
my aunt heard.

*   *   *

They helped us when we were students at Cal and hired my husband one summer to paint their house while they were gone.   He left the key on the kitchen table, locked up the house.

They called, asked about the key.
They only had one key.

*   *   *

Joys bubbled through their lives:
his work, her piano improvs,
the daughter they adored,
political debate, operas
by Puccini, Verdi and Wagner.

Her cuisine, varied, well-seasoned.
Fingertips measured liquid,
skipped over braille spice labels.

Suggestions from radio shows produced a family favorite –

"Pot Roast with Snail Beer".

*   *   *

Alzheimer's took from her
what blindness never could –
the reality of her loved ones.

At the end, secure in her own world,
unworried by daily events, even cancer.
Nothing that bothered us, bothered her.

She chose
to live her life
undeterred.

My aunt left this world
as she entered it:
carefree, playful, unfettered,
yet determined.

Note from the poet: "Pot Roast with Snail Beer" – my aunt heard over the radio that beer improves a pot roast. The only beer they had was the beer they used to rid their garden of snails; therefore, snail beer.

LEGACY

Imprisoned in Poston,
the mother, her family
looked happy in camp photos.

Behind those smiles,
the mother kept asking:
   What did I do wrong?
   I should have known.
   What's wrong with me?

She brought no answers back
with her children to Salinas;
only the same questions
along with an unspoken mantra:
   Be a better American
also left unsaid:
   so they won't send us away again.

She scraped pennies into dollars;
typed furiously at the Credit Bureau;
sewed skirts and suits late into the night;
controlled her children's perfection
as well as her own; raged
when anyone faltered or failed.
She ended up hating herself
because she failed her children.

No one told her it was not her fault.

The daughter took in her mother's words –
swallowed them whole.
She was just not good enough.
Her unspoken mantra:
   Be perfect
She avoided her mother's rants
by following the rules.
She hid within herself,
so her mother's rage couldn't touch her;
she did exactly what she thought
her mother wanted. She craved
"perfection" seen in others.
She was ashamed that she was Japanese,
that she wore homemade clothes.

No one told her she was good enough.

The daughter had a child
who was perfect just as she was.

The daughter was now the mother
who swore she would be the perfect mom
and give her child all the "happinesses"
she craved growing up. When her child
was not happy enough,
she hated herself.

No one told her she was good enough.

One day her bottled-up rage exploded
when her child's birthday balloons
lay limp in the closet
– helium gone –
surprise deflated.
She had failed again!
Her ugly voice growled,
berating herself.

The child shrunk inside,
thinking she had done
something wrong,

No one told her she was good enough.

Today the same mother can see
the humor in limp balloons.
She lets herself off the hook
more often, appreciates the goodness
in her life, and recognizes miracles
with greater humility.

Today the child is seeking who she is –
finding pleasures of her own.

The mother's job is to just let her.
She prays her child knows
    how much
     she trusts her;
    how much
     she loves her.

SEPARATE AND STRONG

helplessness
powerlessness
finally engulfs me

severs old beliefs
old habits

frees me
from stepping
into her sadness

still my daughter
still the one
I love beyond measure

separate and strong

C. M. PANNELL

A COLOR-LEAFED PATH

Down from the hills
we finished our hike.
Down to where the gravel
became sand from the river.
And covering this path
were drifts of gold, red, and brown maple leaves.
Ankle deep, or knee deep on me.
We swished, swirled, laughed and danced
with this sumptuous surprise ending to our hike in the woods.
Now when I see maples change color
I remember the fragrance of those fallen leaves,
the crunch of leaves underfoot,
and how the dirt under those leaves was feathery soft.
Soft from so many autumn leaves having fallen
over many, many years.

BAKING WITH LOVE

Our kitchen time is full and bright in my mind
The sunshine, the smiles, and the colors are
embedded in me.
But loss and fear approach,
grey fog brings nothing-ness

Mom and I were once where time is.
In color, in conversation, baking with love.

Is it that Alzheimer's has extinguished
our kitchen colored memories? Or
are they just temporarily
forgotten.

FAREWELL IN BONNY DOON

Under a tree in Bonny Doon
We buried our father's ashes
Beneath his favorite tree he rests.
I like to think he can live in, and see the world again.

We buried dad's ashes
Brother dug the hole, we cried tears, and murmured a prayer.
His sacred ashes are safe and hidden.

Beneath his favorite tree he rests.
Beneath the vine maple at the end of their garden
The maple now takes up his essence.

I like to think he can live in, and see the world again.
The parent branches giving life to leaves,
the leaves living, seeing, and being in the world.

Then returning, in turn, to the earth.
Rest in peace.

JANE PARK

THE BAY

My future was handed to me like a
creased menu in a restaurant
a waiter with a wavering smile, impatiently tapping her foot
wondering how long I will take to
actually
order
something
My parents screaming at me, telling I just
choose
something
Crying into my lap because
it's been 16 years and
I still don't know
what
I
want.

WHEN EXACTLY

When exactly did I forget
The discreet cavity in which I hid the blades that
Carved into my skin like a knife into a soft pumpkin
And stained the bathtub red with carnage

When exactly did I forget
The familiar habit of tucking myself in my bed
And crying into a worn out pillow, thinking I'd be better off dead
Planning out my funeral like one plans a party

When exactly did I forget
His gentle lips and curious hands, the feeling of his eyes looking lazily into mine, the
Air around us a hazy mist
Our toxic love and the wince of bitter endings which connect with his name

When exactly did I learn
To smile at people with my teeth and my eyes and
Sincerely care when I ask, "How are you?" and have concern over their well-being
Rather than being clouded in rage and depression over mine

When exactly did I learn
To think for myself, not worry about what everyone thought
Forgetting to plot each move and debate every choice
And instead, the queen does as she pleases

When exactly did I learn
That churning disquiet was not equivalent to love, that having
Butterflies in your stomach does not always mean that your
Heart belongs to them

When exactly did I realize
That I was perfectly imperfect the way I was
The ridges on my thighs, the thick flesh that dangles over my stomach when I wear
tight shorts, they are meant to be there
And I am meant to be here.

JESSICA'S HOUSE

Her house
Is beautiful
large
expensive

Her house
Is cold
Bone dry
Bare

There is art on the walls but it does not mean anything
There is food in the fridge but no one eats it
There is a hole in the wall met with no acknowledgement
There are shards of glass on the floor

There are fights
And screaming
And silence

It is a house, but it is not a home.

ROBERT PESICH
PRESIDENT, POETRY CENTER SAN JOSÉ

XENOPUS LAEVIS: AFRICAN CLAWED FROG

Abandoned, likely by a scientist,
in Golden Gate Park, just east
of the National Academy of Sciences.
The lily pond, your new home
and with no natural predators
you flourish, ravenous
even against your own young.

Xenopus, show yourself
to the lovers and the children
before the Department of Fish & Game
arrive to eradicate you
with explosives.

Show how you hunt
whatever moves
including their fingers
and reflections
among the yellow lotus
as they throw coins
large as their eyes
for a wish
while trying to taste a petal.

If you claw my palm
I'll call it a sign
that you are naming us
according to a ruptured light.
The scar will remind me
during the coming droughts and firestorms
that the song can survive detonation,
living underground, consuming its own
shed skin with plans to return
with or without us.

CUP READING

I.

You will begin a long trip next year
to collect baby teeth.

>Before that
>many night trips
>to Natural Bridges.

II.

How is your health?
You can't avoid doctors.
But avoid your doctors.
You're already taking something
you don't need.

III.

>See this? Up close, it looks like nothing.
>Your handprint, it remains
>on a secret wall
>flying among birds and fish.

IV.

Come the summer solstice
you will meet a couple.
Unclear what they're doing, studying
nothing it seems.
Follow them.

V.

>All the caves you enter
>have a secret exit to the ocean.
>See the feather moving your mountain?

VI.

Now, touch the bottom.

PRODUCTION OF THE NEXT, SAFE HAPPIES

Years after they privatized the reservoirs, rivers and lakes
they finally took even the mountain peaks,
leaving us with nothing.

Our nothings mumble in abandoned schools.
Our nothings accompany us across empty fields
as we migrate now in search of our names.

Rumored to be durable and pliable,
a new-age psychoactive neo-material,
they returned to harvest our nothings.

Substrates for the synthesis of new therapeutics
marketed as the next, safe Happies,
users remember good-times they never had.

Although only a little better than placebos,
our new-and-improved nothings sell well at their Costcos,
effecting a new normal, the side-effects yet to be reported

as we migrate North in search of our disappeared,
their names on watchlists and school bulletin boards.

ELECTION SEASON

Time of the headless
horsemen delivering midnight mail
little brown boxes
full of dried eyelids
fluttering inside
to the sound of the voice.

Time now to answer the door.
Time when our home hides
inside its dirty dead-
     bolt.

Time to admit Baba Yaga
has not left our neck
of the woods.

Time for you to count
the number of baby teeth
hanging around the neck of your night
says the card on the box…

They eat through the lid
fly straight for your breath
the eyelids
eating away your face
eating away your name
as you sleep.

I SPY

a chicken egg dyed white
a beehive high in a pine
and crocodile crosswalks

I spy a fire-truck with a ladder made of letters
a little girl waving the Queen of Spades at her baby brothers

That's nothing. I spy the letter A shot twelve times
and an ambulance rushing a wrench to the ER

I spy a hummingbird perched on a bulldozer's blade

Dump-truck. I spy a dump-truck full of stones and clothes

Here's a trail of baby-teeth inside a bibliotheca

Combat boots full of fingers
a school-bus with black windows
women and children pounding the doors of the Dew Drop Inn

I spy you spying me spying you pushing your baby-stroller from the hospital
the postman working our street
his pockets full of flies

NUDE CHALLENGES THE ARTIST

Don't use your old brush.
Find me in all the edges
of your palette knives.

I'll gleam dark as clay, loam, blood,
a relief map for the blind.

DRY GRASS

Lightning loves me

Sometimes we bite each other
and I burn for weeks

My smoke drives you
                            out
of your house
and into your breath

Coyote on the road
wants to know if you will follow
if you can now taste yourself
in the air

NILS PETERSON
FIRST POET LAUREATE OF SANTA CLARA COUNTY

SNOW FALLS FROM THEN TO NOW

Pluvius couldn't make up his mind between
snow and rain – so he sent small snow, small rain
together. A small quiet joined them, so dog
and I walked with all three, a little wet, a little white,
a little inward. Last night, when I rose to comfort
him from some disturbing doggie dream, I could
see whirls of whiteness dancing in the streetlight
and heard myself think, "Silent Snow, Secret Snow."
Early waking let me watch the fall continue through
a blue-gray dawn sky. Morning walk – short, dangerous,
ice beneath the white coverlet. Greystoke didn't
like it either so was quick, though I had to push
my walker across the tundra to pick up his leavings.

So, this is an ordinary poem about ordinary,
but I'll add a small quiet blesses it all.

STEPHANIE PRESSMAN

KATY

K-K-K Katy did it; beautiful Katy
with keen eyes and careful smile.
She charmed the kilts off Canadian
Scots as they marched through Amiens.
A far cry from the tamed Kate, khaki clothed
she drove ambulances into killing fields,
carrying back the shell-shocked, the wounded.
Kinfolk at home wondered how she stood it:
in Ypres landmines shattered limbs;
machine gun fire punctured kidneys, lungs;
flamethrowers in trenches scorched skin;
frostbite plus bacteria caused gangrene.
Katy, idealistic at eighteen, came home
quiet at twenty-two, her nights broken.

VULTURE

Nothing to love about a turkey vulture's
head, featherless, its white hooked
bill, beady eyes. But how it soars
wings held in a V, tips fingered.
It vacillates, seeking victims
of disease, various remains of prey
viands that otherwise would foul the bottoms
of ravines, trash heaps, dumpsters, before the decay
of carcass renders it no longer fresh,
its sense of smell acute, although it lacks
vocal organs, just a kind of hiss
or growl when fighting for its share of snacks.
Though some avoid it, think it ugly, vulgar,
violent, Nature values the scavenger.

IN THE BEGINNING

the mother—
bacteria multiply
in hot volcanic vents,
photosynthesize,
oxygenate the air;
sponges draw nutrients
into their bodies;
jellies float, microbes mat
in watery layers;
trilobites roam
the seabed, scavenging
in weed; cells cluster.

the mother—
moss forests, algae,
leaves, spores;
seeds on wet loam
bore between magma
and sandstone.

the mother—
ray-finned, lobe-finned fish,
armored bottom dwellers
with jaw bones
troll the depths;
arthropods crawl
from sea to land
hatch eggs
spew young.

the mother—
gardens of Eden sprout
everywhere
new species develop
go extinct; new species
develop go extinct; new
species develop;
ice age,
growth.

the mother—
creates and creates
vertebrates, tetrapods,
mammals, primates,
apes, great apes,

humans.

the mother—
Eve.

ERECTA

Prometheus gets the credit,
but she drags rocks and piles
them into a hearth—
dry twigs and mosses,
fallen branches sapped by fungus—
flints a spark until it catches
flame. No gods. Just
the lore of mothers
grinding rye: cakes baked
on stone, rabbits flenched,
spitted, turned then torn
with the teeth. She renders
fat in clay tubs, rubs
it into the pelt, ties one
skin to another. Strips
of leather bind the whole
to poles: a booth for shade.
She uses quick branches
for smoke to ward off
gnats and wasps, smudges
a nearby cave. Lays a granite
rod in hot coal, cauterizes
a hunter's gash. Tends
the fire, teaches
her daughters to tend.

LOT'S WIFE, *A PANTOUM*

No one knows why she looks back.
Salt, salt, pillar of salt.
Her eldest daughters wed godless men
who laugh at Lot when he bids them flee.

Salt, salt, pillar of the earth.
She packs dried meat and hard dry bread.
Children walk to school as her family flees,
the road exposed and pitted with traps.

Will they have a home? will they have bread?
The future too stark, nightmarish, tasteless.
The road in the open mined with traps.
The life they leave: neighbors, friends.

The future like stew: without salt, tasteless.
Routines ingrained, sand rubbed in skin.
Mama leaves Aleppo, her sins, her friends,
won't ever return. Does she turn to wave?

Routines upset, sand etches skin.
Shirtless men by a burning couch
won't ever return, caught in a wave
of refugees crowding the camp.

Shirtless men kept warm by a couch,
asylum in limbo. Unsleeping, unbathing
refugees crowd ten to a tent in camp,
scrabble for food or fight or forget.

Asylum in limbo, unsleeping, unbathing.
The future makes its oppressing mark.
Scrabble for food or fight or forget.
Sin and sin. The cycle's complete.

The lack of a future presses its mark
on hard-working people swept up
in others' sins. Destruction's cycle completes
itself. These gods who are so quick to destroy.

Hard-working people, their child swept up
on a beach from a downed boat.
Itself a reason to stop not destroy.
And what would I leave? Could I even go?

On a beach flotsam from a downed boat:
my grandmother's candlesticks, archived photos.
Would I leave them behind? Could I go
without my children, my family of friends?

Her grandmother's candlesticks, the tokens.
I think I know why she looks back.
Her children, her family of friends;
she'd save even those wed to godless men.

Salt of the earth, on Mount Sodom she stands,
dumb witness to burning cities and the dying sea.

CHARLEENE PUDER

THE FUTURE
After "Dreams" by Langston Hughes

What pursuits might a stingy future hold?
When once feasting on time,
I now must frugally fast.
Hoping to avoid a landscape left barren,
But soar above instead with what remains.
And find a field of unexpected dreams.

AN A+ HEART
After Ted Kooser

I've abandoned those red
construction paper hearts.
Although I've made more
than 30 in my time.
And encouraged at least 30x30
to make their own.

Any of those tattered love tokens
might remain
collected in a drawer or a box
or in hearts and memories.

Assembled with rubber handled safety scissors
held by tiny sticky fingers.
Aided in the cutting by the tongue
gliding over the bottom lip
so they'll be careful with their heart.

BOOKKEEPER'S CHILD

Forty years ago, a woman's place was in the home.
But my mother didn't buy that.
She was a keeper of books, at an office all week, 9 to 5.
What did other mothers do to fill their time?

On weekends our house was bursting with domesticity,
Cleaning, cooking and shopping for groceries, once a week with a long list.
Selecting each item very carefully,
Better not forget things, do everything efficiently.

One weekend we went to buy a car, just mom and us kids.
Reveling in the surprise and excitement of that new car smell,
power steering, and the ride home joyous and lazy.
It's rich smooth brown color so much like her good gravy.

She had signed her own name, and hers alone,
on to that very official car loan.
A privilege women hadn't controlled.
She might have been one of the first.

And now a car payment would be part of the ledger.
For all the changes to come, was she a trailblazer?
Or just doing the math of a bottom line,
That didn't add up.

MY HAPPY PLACE
After "My Happy Place" by Irene Edwards

I smiled
looking at the photos brings me back
memorable experiences
inspired
distinctive
my love note to creative communities
a gift to take part in
grateful
an even bigger gift to share
what we love
with all of you.

POLINA RUNOVA

Polina

OLD FASHIONED

My poetry isn't slam material.
It never was.

Because I write in the fashion that makes you think of butter yellow meadows
And drizzling butterflies flashing colors into the perfectly blue sky.
The way I write makes you smell the sweet smell of honeysuckle flowers
It lets you feel the gentle fluff of the faraway peaceful clouds,
        floating without a worry in the world.

The way I write makes you know that these words
        were written on a curling scroll of parchment
                with a big feathered pen.

Not slam.

It's not that my poetry is bad. It's just not the type you would present.

It's not the type where
you get up with adrenaline rushing
and you press it out of your soul,
and once you start you can't stop,
and your voice is ringing even if it's cracking at the same time,
and everything goes away
it's just raw, raw emotion bursting through you
because it is you,
and you are it,
and as it expands so do you and,
and,
and that's not me.

In my poetry there are no flames of love and hate twisting,
uniting under the same sky,
        the same stars,
           the same shattered dreams,
and together
burning away the very soul that gives them life.

There are no gifts of words that blow your mind,
your thoughts,
not just away but also towards.
Towards a place where there is nothing but the fear,
the anger,

the joy,
the sorrow,
a place you can't wait to escape
but a place in which you could stay in forever.

My words tend to stay on paper.
My poetry reads out loud with a rhythm.
Like gentle ripples in the lines,
like clear water that sways your reflection,
but doesn't tear it away.

So no, no slam for me.
At least, not yet.

A CHILDHOOD IN SUMMERTIME

The pale rocks lay near the sea
Warmed by the endless golden sun
Nowhere is a place so free
As one that's now forever gone

A childhood in summertime
Running barefoot down the road
Everywhere a rock to climb
Everywhere the good signs bode

Grandma's chocolate mushrooms
Grandpa's stand for photographs
Nowhere were there city fumes
The town was powered by our laughs

Then one day Grandma passed away
A war for land turned dark the sky
Never got a chance to say
To the freedom there goodbye

A PENCIL

A pencil
A small yellow number 2
Pencil
So simple
Yet so complicated
In it
Is the effort that it took
To get the led
The time it took
For trees to grow
And be cut down
The exactness
With which the eraser and paint
Were created
A pencil
So simple at first glance
But with such a tale to tell
A pencil
Taken for granted
But with such a journey behind it
All this is hidden
And unnoticeable
In a plain yellow number 2
Pencil
Nothing more

PEBBLES

On the beach
Lay smooth pebbles
They are
Like people
Give them some movement
And they will interact

Different sizes and strengths
Will destroy each other
Rub rough edge to rough edge

But two that fit together
Will polish each other
Smoothing over
The flaws
And regrets
Finding new colors
For each other
With every layer
Until
They are washed ashore
And the movement stops

And there they lay
Different yet the same
They may stay together
They may part
You never know
What the next wave
Will bring
People
Are like that

PATCHES

There.
Look there.
There, beyond the strangled weeds
There, beyond the dust of time
The memories of worthless deeds
Lying covered with this grime

Look there.
See beyond these tangles lies
Filled with thorns and fading hope
Look beyond these woeful cries
Falling down this endless slope

Look there.
There, where there is joy to catch
There, where life can be rebuilt
Because here is just a patch
On an ever growing quilt.

WORK OF DREAMS

A tired day, a busy day defines
A normal day at work, many agree
But is work really that
Which it's made out to be?

Sure, factory smells can be harmful
And due dates can be an armful
But some work is also charmful
Or is that type of work not work?

If I sit by a window and wonder
As I hold a big feathered quill
If through crossed out phrases I blunder
Down a path that is only uphill

If I stand in front of a canvas
With my buckets of varying paint
And I see the potential it has
Even if really, it's faint

Then am I worker or dreamer
Or are they both one and the same
Both can share sorrow and humor
Why can't we share a name?

POETRY

The art of words
The flow of feelings from a pen
They pool in a dark inky mess
Waiting to be sorted
For someone to understand
The scratch on parchment
Is the sound of the soul breathing
Spilling out the secrets
That kept it buried
The stories that were never told
The thoughts that were ignored
The dreams that it always knew
Would remain dreams forever

IN MEMORY OF AN ARTIST

I waited for a final word
To wrap up all that we had learned
But only silence joined me
And told me there was something I must see

Still then I hope things were the same
Until along a stranger came
And next to me sat down
And pulled a cloud across the sun

There's nothing left to wait for here
He said, and from the graying sky
Then fell a single silent tear
It might've meant goodbye

Later, I did not find it strange
When from the empty frozen blue
The skies began to change
Movement, color, gentle hue

For I knew somewhere out there
Near the sky that we all share
A new spirit had gone by
And thrown some paint across the sky

MAYA SABATINO

37°18'19.7"N 122°01'02.8"W

In P.M.
I

The summertime is rough
crickets chirping
my sweaty body and

Even as the sun sets
Sunsets do not bring rest

The same hushed house
Empty swimming pools
The lone ducks in parched creeks

All just a reminder
when I sleep

                                        a.m. you.

                              Sleeping without
                            tucked sheets
                    wrestling with the empty spaces

                    the heat persists night in and day out
            and the mantel clock ticks the degrees and days past

                    the nights suffocated by a tropical heat
                            become orange streams of light
                    flooding from behind screened windows of memory

                                        when you wake
                            it will be at the same time

                            39°00'27.9"N 117°42'39.6"E

In P.M.
I   a.m. you.

The summertime is rough   sleeping without
crickets chirping   tucked sheets
my sweaty body and   wrestling with the empty spaces

Even as the sun sets   the heat persists night in and day out
Sunsets do not bring rest   and the mantel clock ticks the degrees and days past

The same hushed house   the nights suffocated by a tropical heat
Empty swimming pools   become orange streams of light
The lone ducks in parched creeks   flooding from behind screened windows of memory

All just a reminder   when you wake
when I sleep   it will be at the same time

37°18'19.7"N 122°01'02.8"W.   39°00'27.9"N 117°42'39.6"E

LISA SCOTT-PONCE

MALAYSIAN MOON

My final night in Kuala Lumpur
An ivory moon peeks from behind inky wisps of clouds
Tiny Caroline is nestled in my lap
The moon will be like this again, but she won't

An ivory moon peeks from behind inky wisps of clouds
Her silky black hair reflects sparkling moonbeams
The moon will be like this again, but she won't
Beloved Malaysian granddaughter, wrapped in my arms

Her silky black hair reflects sparkling moonbeams
Creamy, dreamy, mysterious moon!
Beloved Malaysian granddaughter, wrapped in my arms
Cold and uncaring, the moon overlooks us

Creamy, dreamy, mysterious moon!
My final night in Kuala Lumpur
Cold and uncaring, the moon overlooks us
Lucky moon, watching Caroline always

SPICE CABINET

Today my eyes are cinnamon brown,
Mildly warm, with a capacity for burning.
Tonight I'm smoked paprika,
Garnet, sensuous, exotic.
A little goes a long way.
I am the salt of the earth,
Reliable and righteous.
In the deserts and beaches I became sage,
Calm and knowing.
My true name is rosemary.
I taste of fresh, verdant needles and tiny blue flowers,
Beckoning bees to make honey.
My hair is as dark and fragrant
As vanilla beans.
In my next life,
I'll have plenty of thyme.
The world is bland without me.

DAD ON THE DAY OF THE DEAD

Assembling an altar of memories.
A bowl of soup is a must.
You'd cook the best, most delicious clam chowder,
Steamy, creamy, flecked with clams and bacon.
You could be so generous.

A plate of savory Caesar salad?
Such a showman, making it tableside,
Brandishing romaine leaves with a flourish.
All the ingredients are standing at attention on a tray,
Just like I stood ready to do your bidding.

I shall include a glass bottle of ketchup,
A memento of the tiny Mom and Pop market
Where you lost it on a simmering summer night,
Where with one furious sweep of your arms
The store display of Heinz became shattered glass and
Gobs of sticky crimson on the damp floor.

Any memories of you will always be tinged
With ketchup on the floor,
Slick and spilled and sickening.

A CLOSED UNIVERSE

Today I chatted with my Chinese friend,
Older, dapper, wordly, a kind Christian gentleman.
Unexpectedly, we moved beyond the usual chit chat,
Discussing bigotry in our small corner of the world,
Recalling lifetimes of slings and arrows we've both endured.
Our heads whirled, remembering cruel, cutting comments.
He recounted a mutual acquaintance complaining, "Too many Asians here."
Silently we shared our world-weary disgust.
Elderly, grumpy, and opinionated is our pal,
Traditional, old school, old world.
That guy doesn't remember when he and his family were called wops.
Then my companion peered at my New World face and pronounced,
"Mexicans are really good at manual labor in the work force."
Stunned, my other-worldly thought is that my friend's a dark horse.

SAMHITA SRIVATSAN

THE SONG OF THE BLUEBIRDS

With the rising of a swirl of flame,
It chirps to all it's kin.
From atop a tree, where all is seen,
The song of the bluebirds begin.

The light casts directly overhead,
As the children come out to play,
The bluebird sings a melody,
All through the summer day.

Shadows silently dance,
The sun tumbles into the night,
The tune of the bluebirds fade away,
Dimming with the light.

Darkness makes way,
For skies of pale pink hues,
Its cry, pure and sweet,
Another tune it coos.

LOST

Sands of time slip through my fingers
Memories fading like echoes
A desire, pulling me far away,
A glowing star in the distance.
Urging me to leave myself behind,
To start anew.
An ocean of doubt swelling around me,
And envelope of pain and uncertainty,
As I fall slowly, down
Sinking.
From where I will never return.

IF ONLY YOU KNEW

I don't quite remember how to
Move my hands the way I
Used to.
I don't quite remember how I felt
When you walked
In and took my pen and paper
And you read aloud the stories
I had written.
You sang the songs I sung in the
Silence of my room.
You played the melodies
I wanted to hide from the world.
You promised it was all in good fun.
Now my fingers pluck
Absentmindedly,
Wishing they remembered
How it used to be.
The strings are limp and out of tune,
Worn from childish dreams,
But in their distressed chime,
I hear what you stole from me.

SPROUT

An old cobblestone path,
Destroyed and black,
Filled with cracks,
From the aftermath.
Little green sprouts,
Intertwine,
Hoping to grow,
Into soft green vines.
A hidden dream,
Within the seams,
Of the old cobblestone.

CHRISTINA STUBLER

THIRTEEN

I wish I had known sooner.
This intertwinement, the pushing and pulling of fine thread.
What we were creating.
Slowly. Painfully.
The strings chaotic.
And the waiting. I thought it would kill me.
It asked me to be gentle instead.
All the while, I didn't know what we were making.
Lace.
More delicate than imagined.
More durable too.

AABHA VADAPALLI

FINDING STRENGTH WHEN WE LOOK WITHIN

Sometimes life throws curveballs and forces us to introspect,
Then we see ourselves under a white light and notice every blemish and scar,
We feel judged by the world and try to be what it expects,
We assess where we really are right now, and question whether we can go far.

In tough times it is natural to doubt ourselves and second guess,
We wonder if we should still work hard, and plough ahead,
It's times like these that test our mettle,
For failure we should not settle.

When we know who we want to be and have a worthwhile goal in sight,
It is usual that we will face failure in the process,
We might miss something or do something not right,
Such a situation will test the resolve in our heart's recesses.

It's important to know deep inside us that failing is a part of life,
Failure is only one step closer to success,
The problem is when we think about it in excess,
In our mind it causes turmoil and strife.

Roosevelt said, "The only man who never makes a mistake is the man who never
    does anything."
Nothing is easy or simple in life, be strong,
Look within to see how far you can go, even if you fall get up again,
Keep going no matter how rocky the road gets, stopping is the only wrong.

Don't be afraid to make mistakes, it is our imperfections that define,
Even if everything is not fine, keep going till you reach the finish line,
Look within and see the hero you can be.

AMRUTHA VAIDYAM

THE CUPID

I strike the emotions of gods and mortals
Hearts I flit, against my morals
The arc, the line
Gave me a sense of power through my spine
I hide among the tenderness of the locals

I clutch my quiver
Satisfied, my wings shiver
But I had my own mask I tethered
I assembled out of my plucked feathers
I was known as the sinner who was his own killer

They snatched my heart
Unbridled, violent I fought
Eros, let go of your inked rose and suppose
Your vultures will turn to crows
Everyone knew the demise would take part

Now I would like everyone to know
Greek and Roman fairy tales end in sorrow
Red was love, and yet the color of my own blood
I thought I was invincible, yet I was so cynical
That I am the cupid who dropped his bow,
And held onto the arrow.

DOUBLE-EDGED BLADE

Doves turn to crows
As the sharp edge of the sword meets its foes
The weapon made of bronze and tin
Could not help but hold all of the centuries' sins

Dignity and Respect
Two words the truth certainly did not expect
Power, A word held with the weight of a thousand tones
Listening in as the consequences are soon to be overthrown

A massacre of dreadful destruction
Changes the limpid light blue skies to polluted and darkened gray air

Virtuous screams are brutally silenced
As bravery and authority have astonishingly vanished

Innocent families who have been slaughtered see no tomorrow
As Terror trembles through the people who are filled with sorrow
The answer lied in the face of the tyrant with the blame on the blade
Children who run and play, hide till their nightmares fade

Vengeance and Aggression
Kingdoms shattered as society was once thrall by royalty
Worn out Tarot Cards whispered their name graciously
For the suit of swords to declare its absolute oppression

Hundreds of years later
Bronze and Copper has turned into Steel and Aluminum
With strength and weight, once more put into the hands of the unreliable
We should have known the repetition of history is inevitable

An innocent promise morphed into blood shot eyes of remorse
Out of control, the rush is still an authoritative overdose
Lives taken by a slash of the sword or rather by a heavy bullet
Naive enough and too late to see it

Power turned to Ignorance seemingly unjust
And when holy water hit the rapier it turned to rust
The dirty inescapable truth rose alive

And left everyone in pools of blood left alone to die

FIRE

The fire
that my heart conspires to be
Rage burning
and twisting with spark you won't see
Yet a beat
in my chest begging to be released
However,
one match is more than enough for me to be free

I have no
secrets down and deep
Call them
secrets or call them a need
Grab my
hand and I'll take your lead
Otherwise
you'll catch your own demise at your own speed

Loving me
is like playing with fire.
Any moment
any time, you could go around me
But if you
learn me right
I'll let
you tame me.

ARIKE VAN DE WATER

HOMESKY

Vlogen naar het westen, curious
The sun peeked over the horizon again
Made it blaze, evening after night
Regenboog tussen inktzwarte grond en
Sterrenhemel, kissing the moon
A little foggy still en geen koffie want
We wenden ons af naar goudzilveren grond
Hart van oranje met aderen wit en rood streaming
Tin bodies flowing into the night
Tussen fakkels van huizen

En lantaarns, flickering through tree shades
A bridge die schittert over het water, teasing
Will o' the wisp that'll take you home
Late, nadat je haar verleiding volgde
De nacht leeft, it bleeds, a livestreamed kaart

Schokt de stoel als we landen neussmeer
Wat overblijft op the oval plane window
Fixed to the planet, people, luggage leaving

DOUBLE LEVEN

Flinterdunne tissue barrier
Opaque membraan flaring
Als ik adem, fluttering
Hiding wat ik versaag to say
Fitting between days we do share
Ik draal met gebalde vuist
Slam that thin skin to lay
Flayed, opengereten
I flinch, de gedachte alleen all
Nee, I hate and ik wil
To pass as familiar friend
Access without challenge
Geaccepteerd voor wie ik ben
Blood held below paper skin
Blauw waar your blow fell

FANART ON TUMBLR

A girl, sixteen,
Saw a made-up man
And wanted

She picked up her pencil
Drew a body
With budding carnality

She wished to share it
Under an alias
With anonymous friends

Because breaking her
Illusion of innocence
Would cut her parents

Amateur art
Proceeding from desire
Exhibited online

Until another platform
To show her growing self
Decides to delete it

ICE QUEEN

"Ice Queen," because I didn't burn
On your pire of sweet sizzle whispers
Wrapped in the flames of your own fever
Blind to my heart brimming, languid
Full of you and your fingers, stirring
Water where you wish for explosions, so
You breeze arctic out of our cotton tent
Breaking our marshmallow huddle against
The long night. I curl up when you count
Only that hot/cold moment when I was never
Made up of the same elements and you said
My easy ripples and your fiercer friction
Could meet in the middle but you left
Me wishing for a friend, he, she, who cares
To stir the coals only to a glow, bright
Neither of us working up a sweat, leaving
Me to dispose of salty wet blankets

ALL OPTIONS

After school lets out, I pause
By the children on the green
Not a mother

My hands hold children's books
Collected in hope, used in class
As a substitute

Old enough that someday looms
Over a mould long broken, left open
What I want

A slow untangling, say
Children does not mean pregnancy
Pregnancy does not mean sex
Sex does not mean desire
Desire I do not have
Where do I start?

You a mother? one asks me where I stand
At the gate, meaning, why are you so close?
I am on my way

PETER VERBICA

WHY

Grace,
that promiscuous virtue,
which confounds
both professors and dunces

warmed her perfect ass
under woolen blankets.

She held a pillow
to her breast
as if it were a baby

and a naked bulb
hovered in a halo
above her.

I was coming out
of a blackout,
making cowboy coffee,

the kind where grounds
weep bitterly
at the bottom of the pot.

I lifted the kettle off
of a blue flame.

The window yawned
at the Bay

and I could smell kelp and
the sea's memento mori.

My hands shook
and I spilt on myself.

"My cup runneth over,"
I joked.

A gull laughed outside
at my folly.

"You damn right,"
Grace answered.

I stopped drinking from
that day forward,

but for the life of me,
I don't know why.

DOG, HAWK, LASER

I drove down to the Desert
to save money.

No one told me
I'd be almost hypnotized
off the shoulder by the windmills.

I'm in the hotel room,
hiding from the heat
and casinos.

Another convention
booked on the cheap
in the off season.

We're all bean-counters,
so I can't fault them
for saving money.

I'm playing hooky,
thinking about
how to write

a letter to the greatest poet
in the world.

I'll have been dead for years
by the time it's read.

(Just as well,
as it will be a computer program:

a money ball poet
which will weigh all the stats:

and blend them in
with haunting hyperbole.)

From the balcony,
I spy a curiosity by the pool.

She's wearing a lion tamer's
dark green uniform
and sunglasses.

Walking around the edges,
slowly as if counting her steps,
her profile halving clouds
under the misters.

I've been under the sun plenty.

Hiked to the Indian water falls
and swam in the cold pool
beneath with immigrant children.

Breathed in hot breezes
and white flower sage.

Tired of the canned music
emanating from
fake rocks.

I meet her face-to-face later.

It's at least 110 Fahrenheit
but she's young
and used to it.

I guess she's from Cambodia.

Is she entertaining children?

"No. Scaring off birds
which shit by the pool,"

she explains,
"with a dog, hawk and laser."

'TIL DEATH DO US PART

I promise not 2 surprise
you in the tub
while you pleasure yourself

or ask you about

your fantasies of making love
2 my best friend

so that you can understand
me better.

Our minds and bodies
are curious things

and some of this is none
of my business,

despite my clairvoyance.

So, listen.

I promise 2 endure traffic
for an hour each way,

2 pump the brakes,
check my rear view mirror,

and flash a peace sign
rather than the finger.

I promise 2
open doors for you
zip up your dresses,
and listen 2 your dreams —

even the one
where the world rips apart,
the ocean drowns out humanity,

and you are the last survivor.

Wake up,
orient yourself
with the compass of coffee.

It will keep your teeth
from chattering
and serenity will come upon you

like light
through stained glass.

You know that I'll entertain you
with stories.

It's the weekend,
so sit on a bench and
overlook the harbor,

with its drawbridge
and fishermen
who pull nets from

their brightly-colored boats.

(I'll leave you 2 lounge
with an old censured novel
while I commune with the locals.)

Know this:

I see your beauty
even in the dark;

I hear you playing your violin
even when I am at work.

I hold you when you pose
alone in front of a mirror,

while you wipe tears
from your eyes

on the days you think
about not having
your own children.

And if you read this years later,

when my ashes sit
in bronze at a columbarium —

I urge you 2 shut
the damn book immediately.

Run out into the warm
tropical rain;
hear the birds argue
over their breakfast.

Live the poem
most read:

come up and out of it --
like a dolphin break through
the surface of the sun.

Feel no remorse
for me or my memory —

for a statue of Moses himself
will be there
2 keep my bicameral mind company,

2 chat about the days of dangling
my feet in creek-water,

if just 2 watch brook trout
dart under a ledge.

Leave me 2 reminisce
when I was a boy
and my wrist
was without a watch,

when the sun
hopped unhurriedly through
the Sycamores,

when I could taste the air
salted with cinnamon
and summer straw.

And, if you remember
when we stood before an altar

in front of our friends and family,
congratulate yourself

for making it 2 the finish.

For your own sake,
move along.

There's nothing to see here
but the supernova of
your brilliant epiphany.

I'm so proud that
our love,
more often than not,
has been unconditional —

'til death do us part.

THE LITTLE ISLAND

Years ago,
I took a float plane
out to an actor's little island
to discuss a script.

Over the engine's noise,
I asked the pilot
to circle once

so that I could eye
the tan ribbon of beach.

After skimming
into the lagoon,
I clambered out
with my travel case

and expectations.

I followed a narrow path
choked with plumeria shrubs.

The main house
languished in front of
dormant volcano and
was covered in pastels.

A cook with gold teeth
and bright eyes
met me at the door.

After my eyes adjusted
to the light,
I was taken aback
by the size of the host
who sat in his living room.

He had sunk deep
in a padded chair.

He wore a large white shirt
interrupted by stylized
blue flowers.

He waved at me as I

was shown a room in the back.

After dinner,
while smoking filter-less cigarettes,
the man asked me
to look at his cellophane albums.

It was like Caesar insisting you
share fortified wine --
that kind of munificence.

Except the host giggled strangely;
I wondered if he was doped up.

I didn't need to look
past the first page
to figure out the contents…

Polaroids of
French Polynesians:
flesh trophies.

The faces were hidden
to the camera.

I abandoned the book
and set it down
on the porcelain tile floor.

I left early the next morning
with the dew evaporating
off of the palm trees.

It made them seem as if
they were burning.

I was out of words
and glad to leave
while most were still sleeping.

THE LITTLE AMBASSADOR

François leaf monkey
orange as a pumpkin

Beijing's little Ambassador
making his way
around the harem.

First emissary
like a Jesuit
with his delicate hands

studying the ridges
of a leaf.

Such focus!

Like Chinese mining engineers
eyeing the purple mountains
and Eucalyptus

of their most recent acquisition.

The shepherds come in white coats
to count the lambs in Mandarin.

They paid
too much now.

Us? Too much later.

A VISIT WITH QUENTIN

I stand on a bluff
which faces the ocean
and wear a wool coat in the wind.

Once again,
I have come to speak
with Quentin.

The hill is covered
with white crosses.

I am reminded of Abel's blood
calling to God from the ground.

I have been asked to carry
a message back to
the States.

The ink burns into the paper
I have folded in my pocket.

A simple sentence:

"Father, mother,
forgive me for my sin
of dying before you."

These men buried,
the echoes of their hearts
still beat beneath me.

The smell of morning
and wet dust on the leaves.

Tell me the story
of your sick brother
and how you brought
a pony into the elevator
to make your sibling smile.

Your flight jacket,
as brittle as crisp bacon,
hangs in a closet
at Sagamore Hill.

I promise to clean it
with saddle soap and oil it
when I get back to Oyster Bay.

You fly over Auvers,
follow La Cambe,
and wag your wings
at Saint-Laurent-su-Mer.

I see you lean forward
in the cockpit
of a Nieuport 28
with her closed bolt
Vickers and
the 95th's red, white and blue tail.

They have the advantage
from above,
blotted out by the sun.

You could retreat,
but instead,
you engage.

Is it a grin or a grimace?

Rest in peace,
with these good men.

Know that we are on the
side of right.

Know that despite the odds,
we are winning.

DREAMS OF A BURNING MAN

Flames shoot from the head
of a metal duck.

It entertains a crowd
held in captivity by the lights.

Sojourners,
they enjoy the freedom
of the open desert.

(The closest fence-line
is miles from sight.)

A fine alkaline dust
gathers around the moist spots
of their nostrils, mouths

and the wet rocks
of their eyes.

A silver balloon
of helium reflects
bicyclists milling around
in figure eights

upon the arid earth.

Thin and thirty,
an anti-hero gnaws on a stick
of dried meat
and drinks from a plastic jug.

He is everyman,
but special enough for
the sun to blow him a kiss
before setting
into the horizon.

Tibetan prayer flags
flutter their muted colors
from a row of lean-tos.

At night,
he smells the burning oil
of kerosene torches

caught in the wind.

He showers under
a bag of warm water,
hanging like an udder
from a pole.

The darkness provides
him and a woman he meets
some privacy.

He has no idea
what she does,
where she lives,

or the color of her eyes
underneath her goggles.

Despite her anonymity,
he would happily
marry her.

Her hair is in dreadlocks
and the coils of her pubic hair
rub against him
rhythmically.

Laying naked inside a pup tent,
he drifts into sleep.

In the cocoon
of his re-discovered youth,

he dreams
of a burning man.

BLANKETS ON THE LAWN

All morning searching
for my grandmother's letter,

the one with a list
of relatives
so I could write their names
on the back of the canvases.

I nervously rub
the tops of my ears
with my fists.

Outside,
hummingbirds
hover at the fountain.

If I could only describe
to you the light
on the drops
as they dart into the water.

Too late!

The jangle
of the front door's buzzer
and I open the portal.

I can smell the smoke
of dry grass burning
in the hills

and see the outline
of a large truck
in the driveway.

The oleander bushes
surrounding it
are in full bloom.

A man with wire-rimmed glasses
has arrived with his clipboard
to seize the furniture
and personal effects
for unpaid taxes.

His shadow falls upon me.

He brings three big men
dressed in overalls
with him.

I expect the piano,
rugs and clock to scream
as they are bound up
and removed.

They are silent
and leave without protest.

All will sell at auction.

The naked house
will go next
with its pale rectangles
on the walls where the paintings
used to be.

Even the ghosts
of sheer curtains have
disappeared.

Obscurity is a sea.
Wave after wave,
it washes the memories
off of things.

Or is anonymity,
I ask myself,
a fire which burns down the brush

to feed the soil for
the next generation.

The Bay trees will be the first
to return
with their pungent leaves.

We would pull them
from branches
while horseback
and crush them
in the pocket of our palms.

The taxman leaves
a bright white card
on a window sill.
His first name is Matthew.

I am in no mood
for entertaining
the irony —

sitting on the cement steps,
looking at the willow tree
and lava rock gate pillars.

Only the heat
of the wind feathering my face

as my dead family
arrange their blankets
on the lawn.

TENDER OF GOATS

The English tourist and travel writer
came to visit
the tenders of goats

just before the onset
of another war.

She paid too much
for the local cheese
and bread.

The herders would
pay a price as well.

The faintest smell
of bootblack was in the wind,
as they sat on hardscrabble.

But for the absence of trees
one could mistake it for pine.

For years,
the shepherds warmed their hands
over the fires
of simple folklore.

My ancestors gathered sticks with them.

But the Russians,
Turks, Austrians and Italians
keep arriving without invitations

to carve up
the same meager carcass
on a wooden platter.

The West's visit was
just after a baptism
by bearded priests.

The couple sat
and did their best
to peer through
the steam-covered windows
of their automobile.

They could just make out
dark shapes exiting the large doors,
looking a bit like large lambs.

Hats off for the wit and
turning of phrase,
for the mythology and long words.

But, with their engine
idling in front of the old church,
I hope the two didn't miss the cue.

For generations here
the women hide
their reoccurring epiphanies
with stoic faces:

There is no comfort for them
in knowing

that Orthodox incense,
Holy Water
and a baby's crying portend

an unbearable suffering yet to come.

THE BEARS

We've all been there.

Forced to drink our own urine
to survive.

Different bears get us there.

Drag us into a cave after breaking our spine.

Storing us for food.

In the desolation,
the animals have no fear
of persecution.

Their skulls grow larger.

Thank God for the barking dogs
which guide our rescuers
with an insistence.

The hunters brave the image
of our mummification
and the stink of our necrosis.

"Why were you
alone and unarmed
in a God-forsaken country such as this?"

the men wonder.

Perhaps the beast ambushed him
from the pines
when the campfire was dimming.

More probable he was drunk
and defenseless.

Whatever the reason,
we've all been there.

Epistemic.

Forced to drink our own urine
in order to survive.

VIVEK VERMA

EPIPHANY

I have been here
Oh, I have been here many times
each time I thought of doing things differently
each time I ended up doing the same thing

Am I running in a time loop?
Why I keep repeating at the interval.
Often wonder, if the result is different this time
even though, I am doing the same thing.

why life is like, running in a circle now
running endlessly but not getting anywhere
time is slipping like sand in the hourglass
Still standing in the same place as a rock

How to break this wheel of misery
when all I know is, how to run in it
is it wheel's design?
Or my unwillingness to change.

whatever might be the reason
I am just a hamster in the wheel

KATHLEEN VIRMANI

POPOVERS
Written for Ryan Salladay, age 4, on the occasion of baking with his Grandma

Today we did your favorite thing
To do when we're together
You got your Mollie Katzen out
I thought we'd take forever

to choose that special recipe
Among the many listed.
"Popovers," we both said at once.
To think we almost missed it.

Now you are busy whipping milk
And eggs together neatly.
"Don't worry if they spill outside,"
I whisper to you sweetly.

You take your job quite seriously
As you stand upon the stool,
Your clothing covered with a towel
When cooking, that's the rule

I remember back when I was four
And helped my mother out
with making cookies, cakes and treats,
Those things we never bought.

But later, as I grew a bit,
And cooking was MY chore,
It wasn't fun, 'twas never done,
There was always one meal more.

"Get ready to eat!" I say to you,
"Because they're almost done."
You squeal with joy, but I don't know
Who had the greatest fun!

Then out of the oven our popovers come.
They smell scrump-dil-e-icious!
Thank God for you, my grandson dear.
Now who will do the dishes?

ARYA VISHIN

SPACES

Every time I close my eyes I'm
institutionalized again. Phone
number in pencil on paper. It
will be my bible even though
that's not my book because we
pray to whatever is closest &
can hear us best. My hallmate

is worshipping is watching a
movie is using plastic cutlery
is forgetting her own name is
trying to leave is not allowed
to have a birthday cake with
candles on it is singing One
Direction until 3AM, I know
because she's been singing for
so long I got up to check the
hallway clock. The nurses

are telling her to be quiet are
moving her to the cell we call
the quiet room are pretending
not to hear the girl who tells
us her next attempt date as
she leaves are taking away our
plastic cutlery are taking away
our movie privileges after we
make too many jokes about
Blade Runner are taking away
the number in pen on paper,
my law, my guide. Every time

I close my eyes I'm there, I'm
in my bed at 3AM I'm cold
because the blanket I got in
the ER is thin & I'm hearing
my hallmate sing offkey.

IN THE FAMILY HOME ROTHKO PAINTS IN BLACK AND WHITE

And everything blends into each other, because without color,
blocks of color are just that: blocks. All of us have been thirteen,

trying not to interrupt your uncle's brother-in-law at Thanksgiving
as he dissects people like you. It's where we exist in the smallest space:

condensed into a chair at the dinner table, in between the tongs of
the meat fork, reaching out for the salt and hoping that your hand

will come back with all its fingers. I'm withdrawing the invitations
from my funeral because mama already mourned me for too long and

I've already written my own elegy.

FORSWEAR IT

Picture it. Summer seventeen and the only thing left to do
was to find something to do, as most things go when we're

left without purpose. It was far enough from the party that
we could hear the music but we weren't listening anymore.

June is hopeless. I wish we were people who said words
like forever less easily, because I'm already all in and that only

tends to end in tragedy. Eyes were eyes and fish were fish, and
the whole tank was this brilliant shade of turquoise and a

school of neon-yellow tang blurred as they swam. I could
stare straight on and still not see you coming - it's collision

theory. Humans won't ever fly but if they did it might feel
like this. It might feel like swimming. It might feel weightless.

KRIS WELLER

PLATONIC LOVE LETTERS

Advertisement for a Permanent Roommate

i want someone who reads to me
as i fall asleep
or maybe i want someone to read to
as they fall asleep
sometimes i cant help but think
theyre really the same thing

i want someone who invites me
who asks but does not expect me to answer
who is okay with sitting in the same room
and not talking
who forgives me when i say "if thats alright
with you"
too many times

someone who understands that
when i ask "do you want to take a
walk with me"

it means "i love you"

someone who doesnt mind that i like eating alone
who gets it when i say
a house is not real without
footsteps
and that i hate it when mine
smells like a stranger

someone who thinks the circular
water stains on my coffee table
hold memories within their borders
memories of little things
like tea and paperbacks
and that art is always more beautiful
when you know the person who created it
not out of biases
but because you can see
the tiny piece of themselves that
resides within it
hidden between words and canvas

i want someone who understands
that i cry
silently
because i know the only way for me to stop
is to sit alone
and process
to pull myself out of the usual state of non-emotion
most of us wander around in
and understand where i fit in everything
and for a moment i become so achingly

terrifyingly human

i want someone who doesnt mind that

Zone 3 to San Francisco

i rode the train with a ghost child
in my lap
he fell asleep against me
his breathing in time with my own
i did not wonder why a ghost boy breathes

i looked at him
small
all round cheeks
and smooth skin
and thin limbs

when awake
he haunts me
but asleep like that
i could only wonder who he is
rather than who he was
and be grateful
for this ghost child i can hold
without fear that he will leave
leave
leave me
leave me alone
alone again
because now i know
this
this lack of obligation
how easy it is

and i find myself becoming greedy

White Noise

A static ocean
Making me lean closer
Just to immerse myself
In your electric waves

A dull drone
A comforting presence
That you only notice
When it's gone
An undeniable there-ness
So forgettable
So vital

The rustle of breath
The rush of blood
The hum of unused energy
The thud of barefoot footsteps
These involuntary reflexes
Only remembered when they cease
Sensory deprivation

The world would be
A little greyer without you
A subtle thing
A slow insanity

The Wanderer's Requiem

he comes to you
he comes to you with a book in one hand
and a flower in the other
he comes to you with eyes illuminated by sunlight
and dirty bare feet
and a pocket full of stolen fruit

when he looks at the earth
the sunset goes green
but when he turns his gaze to the sky
it burns red
suddenly frozen

and when he looks at you
you wonder if he sees your face at all
or if his eyes pass straight through
right to the place where your secret wonder hides

you wonder now that he has let the lion out
if you are still are entirely human as you know it
if he was ever entirely human as you know it

and when you look at him
you wonder if you see him at all
or just the concept of him
as he comes to you
he comes to you
and leaves you behind
again
always

House Fire

In my neighborhood,
A house burned down.
I remember looking out my window
And thinking,
How long has that smoke cloud been there?
How long did it take me to notice?

Just a house fire,
They said,
No one was home.
Just routine.
Electrical failure,
No one hurt,
No one's fault.
I didn't really hear them.
I was too busy pressing my face to the fence,
Staring at the skeleton of a building.

The walls that remained were blackened,
And the roof was nothing but a mess of soot and charcoal.
I played a game with myself,
Identifying what each sagging,
Twisted pile of metal used to be:
Washing machine,
Lawn mower,
Card table,
Propane tank (burst open like a flower),

Car.
The front of the house was relatively untouched,
And if you looked from a specific angle and squinted,
It almost seemed like nothing happened.
Except for the front door,
A big X in yellow tape,
nter! Danger! Do not enter! Danger! Do not enter! Dange

While they were talking about homeowners insurance,
I pushed my fingers through the chain link,
Trying to reach out and touch the memories.
So many of them,
All melted,
Scattered among the ash.
It made me wonder where memories go to die;
Do they gather like elephants?
Do they just disappear,
Halls never to be walked again,
Familiar motions forgotten and never repeated?
I wanted to pick up the pieces,
If only to recognize that they used to be something.

While they were mourning the destruction of a house,
I was mourning the death of a home.

AMANDA WILLIAMSEN
THIRD POET LAUREATE OF THE CITY OF CUPERTINO

INTRODUCTION TO CREATIVE WRITING, HALF MOON BAY

Only three students signed up. That's okay. We study
Elizabeth Bishop and Walt Whitman, and I take them
tide pooling. Cold wind blows grit at us, but they open

their notebooks, eyes on their words, and stumble
toward the water. Destiny has brought her camera;
the others want her to photograph a sandpiper, quick

legs skittering through foam, and a kayaker whose green blades
dip and shine on the horizon. I lead them to the mirrors
that pock the bay's broad shelf, and Danielle stops

at the first pool to examine nearly invisible blennies.
Brown and tan zig-zagging fish, she writes,
spotted like cheetahs. Farther out, Katie calls, "Destiny!

There's a purple starfish!" but Destiny is already alone
with her notebook. She hunches on a barnacle-encrusted rock,
scribbling. Gulls cry, not in their usual high keen,

but in sweeter, alto bleats, and pelicans swoop overhead
in a brown squadron. Danielle wants to know
how to spell *sanctuary*. The girls close their eyes, writing blind

about the waves' rise and crash and the jingle of a dog's tags
as it races on the sand. When the jingle changes, they look up
to see the dog digging and digging and digging in animal joy.

They smell the wind—taste the water—write, *flash of brine*.
Danielle tiptoes out to see an anemone but hesitates
just feet from it, fearful of foot on the algae. Bolder Katie,

squatting on the green slick, describes it for her:
"Purple and green, like an iridescent, underwater flower.
Rings of waving, sticky fronds. A body like a potato, or a pig

in a ruffled dress, and a mouth like a wheel. Pretty. But ugly."
Its fronds gently tug on the finger Katie offers. "Maybe it's hungry?"
Danielle writes, *The anemone is ugly with hunger.*

I grin at Katie. She grins back, cocking her head, her black,

blunt-cut hair blowing crazily. "My butt hurts," Destiny calls.
"I've written so many pages my ass is frozen to this rock."

"Language," I say.
"Exactly," says Katie.
"Oh, girls," I say, "it's been a good day."

We pack up. The car is warm. Katie sleeps and Danielle
shares her pretzels with Destiny. Back at school,
we dump sand from our shoes onto the sidewalk.

FLO OY WONG

TWO SISTERS

two sisters
both with white hair
one with glistening strands
reflecting light in the shade
she taps her cane softly
on the cool pavement
the other with thinner strands
layering closely on her scalp
stands to the right
because she wants her
older sibling to be able to hear
with the ear that still functions a bit
sounds for the elder travel as whispers
even when words are shouted loudly
and uttered in peace
for her words are oftentimes
distant or diminished
together
they walk into the restaurant
after they place their orders
at the counter
they scan the dining area
for a section with less diners
in hopes that when they talk
the other can be heard

DANCE WITH TODAY

an old stone
somewhat polished
with jagged edges
clings to my heart
i carry it
feeling sharp jabs
of the edges
of my joy my radiance
i look in the corners of my body
wondering why I was down
i reach for the phone
to call friends and sister
no one answers
i text
no one answers
i wonder
i wander
later a friend calls
our conversation ascends
mirth-filled we share
a void is filled
the next morning
after a fruitful delicious sleep
i check my heart
and discover an epiphany
it's you it said
your expectations
your ego
you wanted
accolades
affirmations
none came
the way you expected
let go
that is your past
dance with today

PLUCKING STARS

plucking stars
don't know if it's the Milky Way
or the Big Dipper that I collect
when I circle my upper body
round and round
first the right hand
with my left hand gripped
in formation of a bird's beak
behind my back
then the left hand repeats
my sweeping of the midnight sky
illumination gently embraces
my head heart and Dan Tian
luminescence reveals my path
towards nirvana or near nirvana
i align with soft healing energy
which gives me insight
to create Five Treasures
first for me
and then for others

EXILE

if i were exiled from webster street
and the hurly burly of rushing cars
the dripping roast ducks dangling in a storefront window
the dried seahorses, twigs and more
in the chinese pharmacy storefront
and the floating odors from great china restaurant and harry's cafe
i would joyously travel to paris
where notre dam sits regally
where the seine feeds life along the quay
where boulevards offer lovers space
to embrace
where boulangeries tantalize taste buds
where the eiffel tower stands tall
where the louvre entices art lovers
where i would say bonjour c'est si bon
while munching on crusty buttered baguettes morning noon and night
ah but this exile comes to life only
in my webster street dreams

TO COMPLETE WHAT I WANTED

at the age of nine
words curled in my ears
tickled my fancy
whispered in my heart
wrapped my wrists
so that i wore bracelets
Of alphabets and words
to keep warm

at the age of eighty
words curled in my ears
tickled my fancy
whispered in my heart
wrapped my wrists
so that I finally gathered courage
to publish my first book of art and poems
it only took me seventy one years
of wearing bracelets of alphabets
and words
to complete what I wanted
when I was nine.

JING JING YANG

WHERE IS MY HOMETOWN

my heart is chasing my hometown
where I was born, raised and moved around
now the skyscrapers planted on the ground
near the magnolia blossom in our courtyard
the neighborhood aunties used to knock at our door
asking grandma if they could have some
the glorious petals & dark green leaves were placed
in the ceramic rice bowls, filled with
crisp, cold water from the community well
the subtle fragrance lingering, my childhood memory
often had these ivory flowers surround

where is my hometown
where is that little wonton shop
grandma used to walk her 3-inch-lotus feet with her cane
the hand-made wonton soup she ordered
was the yummiest treat in my lifetime
where is the "Dongsheng" Photograph Shop mom brought my brother & me
to take pictures for our birthdays and other big events
and where is the theater dad took me in the wicker-baby-seat on his old "Phoenix"
bicycle, which he paddled all the way
through the northern district to the "Silver Palace"
for us to see
Charlie Chaplin's "Modern Time"
many years later
I rode my own bike with him
for "Roman Holiday"
that was the last time
we watched a movie together
in our hometown

where is my hometown
where is my hometown
the old streets and houses are erased by time
my inheritance from mom and dad is my accent
like the enduring magnolia tree, still stands
their roots extended the courage for me to head out
to a foreign land
half of my life divided between the two countries
my hometown seeded my identity &
my homeland sprouted my liberty with a FOREVER stamp

where is my hometown
where is my hometown
where is my hometown
…

H O M E
is where my heart is
I carry it Always
till the end of time

*Jing Jing in a light pink dress,
sitting on a small bamboo stool
under the magnolia tree*

*Jing Jing and younger brother at
the Dongsheng photograph shop
mentioned in the poem*

我的家鄉在哪裡

我的心一直在追蹤著家鄉
我出生，成長和几次搬遷的故园
遍地摩天大樓聳立　离我家咫尺之遠
那是當年街坊唯一玉蘭盛开的地方
隔壁大媽曾敲响我家大门　跟奶奶討要
被绿叶簇拥著潔白的花瓣
浸泡在盛着井水的陶瓷饭碗
幽幽清香环绕著我童年

我的家鄉在哪裡
营盘街口上小小的餛饨店上哪兒去了
奶奶曾拄着拐杖踮著三寸金蓮帶我去逛街
祖孙俩总是兴致勃勃大快朵颐唆完最后一口汤
和她老人家在一起的美滋美味让我终身难忘
那个東昇照相館呢
每逢生日节假日媽媽總帶著我和弟弟去照相
還有那兩間戲院
小時候我坐在爸爸單車前的藤編座椅裡
他踏著那輛老鳳凰載著我　穿梭於大街小巷
去城北銀宮看卓別林的“摩登時代”
十多年後我們興各自蹬車
奔向“羅馬假日”
那是我們父女俩在家
觀看的最後一場電影

我的家鄉在哪裡
我的家鄉在哪裡啊
雖然老街舊房紛紛消逝
但爸媽我留給我的一口鄉音
象那棵純正挺立　不朽的玉蘭 –
他們的根基給我勇氣去陌生國度闖蕩
前半輩子　我分別居住在兩個大國 –
桑梓故土播種了我的血肉
移植家園給我萌芽的自由蓋上了一枚永遠的郵章

我親愛的家鄉
妳在哪裡啊在哪裡
其實　妳一直
住在我心裡
守在我身邊
天荒地老
海枯石爛

LOGOGRAPH
For my Grandfather, Yang, Shuda
First Place Winner of Cupertino's "Celebrate Creativity" Poetry Contest, 2017

grab a handful of Chinese Characters
toss them into heat
erupt them into lava &
cast them into my poetry
black script on white paper
brewing & diffusing the steam
flaming in red hot orange
whilst
our ancestors sharpen the stone
paint their fairy tales
engrave their memory
on turtle shells
in cattle bones
scattered with sparkle splash

scripts started
before time
blistering
as blood and sweat
...
with a stem or pebble
it ***rocks*** dragon skin
'n' ***rolls*** into Human History

Jing Jing in front of my
grandfather, Yang, Shuda's
statue, College of Liberal Arts,
Hunan Normal University

294

中國字
*向祖父**楊樹達**老先生致敬*

抓一把中國字放進熔爐裡
烤成岩漿
把他們鑄進我的詩裡
黑字白底
紅通通的
冒著熱氣
就像
古人磨尖石頭
在龜殼上
在牛骨裡
火星四濺地
畫著她們的童話
刻著他們的記憶

文字
亙古以來
都是熱的 –
鮮血和汗水
一根樹枝
一塊石頭
把歷史
捲進龍骨獸皮

THE WINDOW

dad called downstairs
I heard through the window
my brother and I ran down
dad told us grandma had gone…
years later on a stormy day
mom stood there alone again
shedding tears
gazing after us
through the same window
that morning
my brother and I
walked in the rain
got lost in the country
finally reached the destination
we visited our dad in the prison –

…

he said something he shouldn't have

HEARTACHE

Note from the author: This was written right before the signing of the The Hong Kong Human Rights and Democracy Act of 2019 (HKHRDA)

my heart aches
from what I read -
when I see
the bloody faces
the broken necks
the wounded young minds & death…
three decades ago
the crying mother had prayed
the massacre would never return
yet history repeats itself –
American
British
Chinese
Hong Kongers
everyone is granted
the Right to Speak
why can't let it be
inside the Forbidden City
Forbidden Voice always SING

THANKSGIVING

cold wind
warms up autumn
yellow, orange and red
rolling in the air
it's Thanksgiving -
along the street, walking
I only hear Bailey's* heavy breath &
crispy leaves blown "puff puff"
the puffy clouds look like
babies crawling
on a gigantic blue carpet
while sun dances with moon
celebrating this harvest season

I thank God's creation
no matter
what colors in the sky reflect to our skin -
only one color runs through our bones
it's called human
today is the day
I count stars as well as counting my blessings

I am thankful to my courageous & brave fellow poets
we share lives in the classroom
shedding happy & sad tears
year after year
pearls of wisdom beaded into string of poems
that carries on
the strength & power of writing

Long Live Poetry &
Happy Thanksgiving!

*Bailey is the author's seven-year-old rescue dog

AMELIE YUN

FOUND: THE BATEMAN & THE PRINCE
A found poem created by quotes from **The Little Prince** *and* **American Psycho**

All grown-ups were once children, but only a few remember it.
A rock pile ceases to be a rock pile
The moment a single man contemplates it
There is an idea of a Patrick Bateman
Within him the image of a cathedral
Some kind of abstraction
Where are the people? It's a little lonely in the desert
It is lonely when you are among people too, said the snake
This is not an exit
There is an idea of a Patrick Bateman
Some kind of abstraction
Whomever I touch, I send back to the earth from whence they came,
the snake spoke again
You must come from a star.
Only an entity, something illusory
But the eyes are blind, one must look with the heart
There is an idea of a Patrick Bateman
Although I can hide my cold gaze
There is no real me
A boa constrictor in the act of swallowing an animal
Some kind of abstraction
This confession has meant nothing
This is not an exit.

THE CROCODILE

I ask my son, listen, do you hear the lake?
In this clear water with the humming mist
And the frozen beams of sunlight
Lays a sleeping mother crocodile

A crocodile cares for her young
By carrying them in her smiling jaws, from the nursery to the lake
But the danger lies: are you prey or kin?
As she lures you in like a fisherman and his bait

I ask my son, listen, do you hear the lake?
Sometimes the heavy silence breaks like a hidden knife
And the smoke curls into a shriek of whispers
A thrashing in the water, then a static calmness
Igniting shadows from her rippling steel armor

You wouldn't have seen her until she's close
Except her awakened eye that shines above the water
Those of a glare that reflects the red flags of cain
And as she entrances you with droplets on her scales
that dance like lightning in the rain

I ask my son, listen, do you hear? The mother beast is coming near,
The screeching of metal creates sparks of madness
That hold mortal treasures in her murky lair
And flashes of color in the soft smoke - striking red scales tapering into white silk
Valkyrie emerging like flags that dance on waves of fire

The embrace of her encroaching maw hint at her calculating stare
As in certain tongues, love at first sight means lightning strike
This is the gamble that you must pay
When you see the steel beast with scales
That glisten like city lights in the water

I ask my son, listen, do you not hear my words?
Do not be fooled by her promises
Do not be fooled by her smile
Yet he strains to watch her place her young
Into the lake of their desired destination

I hear her singing, softly, and my son listens to the nursery song of her kin
Red fire dancing to the beat of the drum, as the shadow stirs from the depths
Bristling manes of a jain palette rising, excited
A seafield of poppies biting on their gold coined stamens
Lays a sack of fur and flesh, mangled and swollen red

Its flesh ripping open by a frenzy of little jaws
And how they sing, how they sing, how they sing of rage
Beaks dipping into pockets of blood,
And necks that arch like a flowing stream, and how they sing
Manes quivering, how they sing
Claws tap tap tapping - my restless son, how they sing --

I hear my son, listen, even now I hear his words
She slumbers, dreaming amongst the dark flowers
He pokes her, says,
hey,
take me where they go
She opens one eye
and smiles

PROSE

FLOI BAKER

THE MAGICAL TREE

OCTOBER, and the Privet berries are starting to turn a deep blue purple, their color for winter. These berries hang in airy clusters throughout the branches of the tree, resembling those of grape clusters, and are continuously being transformed by nature's sleight of hand, as if by magic, from one thing to another all the year round.

During the summer, each cluster becomes a lacey bouquet of crème colored fluff, and looks like a bridal bouquet, bursting with tiny flowers, which resemble the tiniest of miniature lilies, and are full of heavy pollen for the bees. So heavy, that one can smell the pollen even at night when the crickets sing. In July, it is the heaviest, almost stifling. If there is a breeze, one can see creamy crystalline powder spilling from the bouquets, making the brick patio under the tree and the nearby fence top, to look as if there's been a summer snow. But instead of snowflakes, this is a snow of tiny flowers.

If I bump my head into one of the lower hanging clusters…at first glance, it looks like my hair has been sprinkled with stars. So I don't brush them out. However, if someone sees me like this, they say, "You have flowers in your hair!"

When the honeybee visits one of these bouquets, it moves among the flowers, gathering pollen, which clings noticeably to its legs, and its head becomes sprinkled with it as it bumps into the stamens, while moving from flower to tiny flower. When it flies off, one can see its iridescent wings, dotted with the pollen, glistening like fairy wings in the sunlight…its flight slower than when it arrived, due to the weight of its golden treasure.

Sometimes a big black wood boring bee will come, and I have seen the Swallowtail butterfly land briefly on one of the lacey bouquets…just long enough for me to admire it, but not long enough for me to get a picture of it. Once, it actually skimmed the very top of my hair before it flew away over the fence. That was better than any picture!

Each morning a squirrel or two will come for the shelled walnuts that I have placed as high up as I can reach in a hollowed-out area above the thick trunk. The birds love feasting on the berries and the seeds which one can hear constantly dropping from the tree onto the patio below.

It is not unusual for various birds to build their nests in the tree, some of which include mourning doves. One spring, a pair of hummingbirds built a low hanging nest near an edge of the tree, where I was able to observe the fascinating process of the nest building, their two beautiful eggs and the baby hummingbirds hatched from those eggs. I watched them grow from birth to flight as young hatchlings when they were ready to leave the nest.

When the tree's flower bouquets have completed their cycle, they turn a rust color, which means their seasonal glory is finished. Then poof, like magic, the bouquets are replaced by clusters of brilliant green berries that perfectly match the jungle green color of the veined leaves. This transformation can happen so quickly that one might almost miss it. In turn, those berries will become a reddish brown to blue purple. The leaves of the tree stay evergreen, and in a certain light, one can see each remarkable vein from the backside of any given leaf.

The tree has given up its many gifts throughout the summer. Now, it is October, and the Privet tree begins its magical performance all over again, with an audience of birds, bees, butterflies and me!

MELODY CHEN

THE STAR SERIES

the downward spiral

the night falls, doesn't it? but, don't we see night rise like a black wallpaper, rising above the horizon. a sheet of black carbon paper. stars dot the areas where the paper is scratched out. i just read a chapter from the handmaid's tale and offred made the same contemplation. daytime rises like anything else. a silver plate filters out the light into random corners of the world. we are so predictable: we ignore what we don't like as if not thinking about it would make it disappear from the universe. we love to build towers, covering up the things we refuse to see. night falls because it's temporary. night is too stiff; night seizes on the stars and planets like toy chandeliers revolving in a baby's nest— circling endlessly in the same way. i want a way to the facts, strip naked from all the unneeded details. yet, how ironic? coming from a girl with too many details.

massacre of stars

the stars have disappeared. just a large blanket of ink is left in the massacre. for humans have sucked out all the light from the most beautiful object in the universe. we take in so much light, without knowing its source. the empty sockets in the wake lay deep and weary.

the edible sky

i want to pick the clouds in the sky and eat them, for they are warm and fluffy, yet wispy when you spread your hands around them.

SURRENDER

There was something beautiful about the words all the same. I'd never really considered all the stars that have fallen with each ring of a syllable. The words let loose—tumbling into my tongues into a heap of bells, ringing ceaselessly and divinely. How could I ever afford to soak into the pages of Kingsolver into a world replete with untimed shooting stars? I have ached through more emotions in a book than I could ever realize in a lifetime. I was born in the wrong era: soon, I will ride through different time zones, chasing the words that I can only savor in my mouth. Sometimes, the only way to catch the truth is to walk through as many stories as you can, tripping over stones of raw truths and fiction. Yet, the truth may only be a fleeting illusion that takes the shape of something learned wrong. I can't collect stones the same way anymore—slipping through the gaps and pockets of my own learned palm. I can't spare to hold on to something that will only escape me. I long for something more permanent—something you could invite all your five senses to. I want to spread my fingers through a constellation of metaphors and symbols—a web of words so pristine that allows me to bask in a sea of vulnerability.

CRACKS AND EDGES

I often describe myself as a human sponge of ideas—soaking inspiration from the stories in The New Yorker to the echoing wisdom bites in TED Talk. Random thoughts that may inspire me in a way take delight in entering my head at odd moments in the day. When these thoughts come flying by, I would find a stray piece of paper or my phone to scribble them down. These ideas may be referenced in my journals or reinforced by random segments of my favorite books and TV shows.

I am also a storyteller. Around the budding age of two or three, I would call for a daily "book assembly" where I would order my parents to sit on the floor as I pick up a book (upright or upside down, doesn't matter) and spin a tale of gibberish folklore. Despite not comprehending even my own fabricated tale, I knew full well that I would be a raconteur at an early age.

Yet, my friends often describe me as shy and observant: I would often lend an ear to anyone who wants to. But, when I do get the opportunity to spill out my ideas and philosophy, I wouldn't hold back. Sometimes, I have to stop myself from saying too much because I would become a bit too passionate. This part of me is something I continue to learn each day.

I am a writer. I have never imagined the level of courage required of me to utter that phrase. Even while I am writing this, I fear that I am putting myself out in the open—out of my writer's shell I've carried along for years. In many cases, I feel like my writing belongs in a different era. My writing is a labyrinth: too much emotion and depth that it soon gets tangled into a heap of dried prunes. There's no room for my words to breathe when it loses the way out of the dense maze. My writing has cracks and rough edges even when I try my best to soften the corners. My writing is perfectly imperfect just as the way it is. I have so many years ahead of me to fill in the empty pages ahead of me.

KATERINE ESCOBAR

PERHAPS ONE DAY

Dedicated to Wally

Perhaps one day, somewhere, we can finally get together again. Every single day in my life you are always on my thoughts. Seeing kids getting out of school It brings back memories, good memories. For many reasons you couldn't pick me up from school like the other kids, but ...one day, when I heard my teacher calling my name, That day I knew I wasn't going to walk home by myself. That day, it was you there outside the room waiting for me ,with your favorite hat on! DADDY, it was you! coming to pick me up, carrying my lunch bag, walking home, holding hands, laughing together. I felt like the luckiest girl in the world! When I think about you, that's the first memory. It comes to my mind right away and tears stream down because I know those days will never come again, Sadly, that's the cycle of life. I can never say that the time we spent together was enough and I'm always wishing I could get a chance to give you a last hug and a big kiss. For those who have the joy of having their parents alive, enjoy them! Love them every single second! Sometimes life is too busy for everyone especially when you already have your own family, but please DO NOT FORGET that our parents were in the same spot as us but still somehow they managed to take care of us, every single detail, most of the time even forgetting about themselves. You were their priority in life. NOW is your time to take care of them. At a certain age the body changes radically and that's when our parents become like a little baby again and that is when they need all of our support! be patient with them! YES they are slow when they walk...but imagine how tired their body is with all those years of hard work to provide you the best. YES, they forget things but don't judge them! Make new fresh memories with them. They are tired and everything hurts, absolutely! Don't hesitate to bring them comfort and a big hug and a "everything will be fine" that helps. It doesn't matter if they repeat the same stories all over again, just laugh like it is the first time you heard them. Oh yes, there will be a lot of complaints...just listen and nod. Spending time together will fulfill your heart more than you can even imagine. We only have one set of parents in life and life is short! Enjoy them now as much as possible, so later you won't be regretting or thinking why you didn't spend more time with them. Sometimes the little things are the big things in our hearts, things that we will have in our memories for the rest of our life.

KELLY A. HARRISON

THE PACKAGE FROM CONGO

When the young man handed me the small brown package wrapped in rough twine, he said, "Doctor Ashby, sorry, Madison wanted you to have this." This meant she was dead.

"Hey Maxi. I'm going to need some shots," she had said the last time we met at my clinic.

"Shots?"

"Yeah, dysentery, yellow fever, the whole kit and caboodle."

"Where are you headed this time?"

"The Congo."

"Good God, why?"

She just smiled. I knew she was going to report on the atrocities, slaughter by machete, genocide, sexual terrorism. Madison loved the rough, going where sane men dared not to go.

"I'm also going to need a bunch of pills."

"Malaria." I nodded.

"And antibiotics and AZT."

I reacted before my mind had a chance to make the connection. "AZT?"

"Hello? Women are raped there all the time and AIDS is epidemic. Put your brain in gear." She laughed the same short laugh she had in college, when my heart first fell for her. She played me like that, her heavy words not matching her light spirit, so I didn't know to which I should respond. The thought of her being raped, well, that was too much to bear.

"Madison, can't you stay here? We could go skiing again or..." A pathetic attempt, I realize that now, but then I looked into her eyes and thought about what I wanted, how I wanted to kiss her again. After nearly ten years neither of us had anyone significant, but I can't be certain. Madison was always careful not to reveal private matters, even to me. I loved that about her, never knowing what she was really doing despite her ability to talk endlessly, to keep me welded to her words.

"I don't know if AZT is the best drug, Maxi. You've got to help me with that. I hear in South Africa they give it to all their rape patients. I'll be too far from hospitals and you just don't know."

She said the word rape like it was nothing more than a glass of water at the dinner table. As I looked at her, I wanted to cry. I wanted to profess my love, to hold her forever, but I couldn't. For her sake, not mine. Madison was leaving again and any serious attempts to dissuade her would make me a rejected fool.

"My sweet, sweet Maxi pad." Only she could get away with calling me that, a moniker she created on our first vacation when she started but had to use mine because she hadn't been prepared. She took my hand. "You're worrying again, so I'll make you a deal. I'll buy the pills and if I don't use them, I'll give them to you when I we have dinner next. That way you'll know and we won't have to discuss it. OK? Then you can give them out at the clinic."

Her head cocked to one side and her bangs covered an eye. I pictured her at our future dinner, telling me her tribal war stories over the security of gentle candlelight and dark wine. I thought of holding her, breathing in her scent all night long. I loved her more at that moment than I ever had, and yet at that instant she was less mine than she ever had been.

"OK." That's all I could muster. To say more would have revealed emotions she needn't be burdened by, and then I let her go.

The top of the package, in her left-slanted writing, she'd written: "Return to Dr. Maxine Ashby," et cetera, no return address.

I looked to the young man who had delivered the package. "How," was all I managed to say from the awkward comfort of my chair.

"The tents were slashed, many killed. Some burned. We can't be sure of her body. There was no one left in the village..."

I clutched the box, traced the black letters of my name, and said, "Yes, yes," but I could hear no more.

TRISHA IYER

I AM ONE HUNDRED AND FORTY YEARS OLD

Note from the author: I picked an object that witnessed 9/11 (I chose St. Patrick's Cathedral) and described 9/11 from its perspective.

I am one hundred and forty years old, born in 1878, and built from wood, nails, and love. The workers hammered all day, wiping their sweaty foreheads, and I took their energy and grew on it. I rose and rose until my gleaming spires touched the sky and passed through it. The priest came, striding up and down with a big head and a booming voice that rose to the heavens. They called me a place of faith, where they who believed came every Sunday to forget their worries and reach out to each other. For 123 years I lived this way; then came September 11th, 2001.

On September 11th, the sun hung in the baby blue sky, forcefully perpetuating the lingering last days of summer. My friends, the Twin Towers, cast me in shadow, as they always did. As proud as I was about my superior architecture, they loomed over me. Each tower had 110 floors and reached up into the heavens, reaching even farther than my spires. They dared to scrape the sky—until 8:46 a.m, when a plane crashed into the North Tower.

The North Tower stood still, tall and erect like a proud lion, for just a half-second. Then heat filled the air. Dirt sprayed everywhere. An immense fireball spewing shards of glass filled the air with noxious, acrid-smelling smoke and blocked my vision (sight and smell). The Tower itself glowed red with flickering flames.

I could not hear anything. I only saw that collision. Rage filled me. How dare one pilot make a mistake and harm my best friend of thirty-one years? The Towers—both of them—had always stood over me and protected me, and my walls quaked with grief that one was gone.

Yelling reached my ears. Shouting as well, as the people of New York City scrambled desperately to save those who were now trapped inside the building. I heard screams of uncertainty and helplessness.

Sirens wailed as firefighters rushed to the scene, intent on helping as many as could be helped (hearing).

The North Tower shook as its foundation crumbled, its walls broke down, beams of steel and windows of glass slowly imploded. As the shrieking grew, I recognized four of the firefighters rushing into the building. They had scribbled through the dust on one of my glass windows only a day before. Although I was a cathedral, I had never prayed before. But now I hoped with all my heart that they would survive to come back to Mass. Would there even be Mass now? Would the priest return only to preach to empty pews?

In the midst of this chaos, I raised my eyes to the sky in helplessness, only to notice another plane. It zoomed right toward the second tower. Horrid realization dawned on me—the first crash had not been accidental, but contrived.

More dust. More dirt. More grime and smoke and heat and hurt. Grit and sand lodged into the cracks in my insides. As the towering buildings quivered and shook uncertainly, people pounded through the streets, toward me, as they fled to a haven (touch). Their lips moved fervently as they whispered prayers into my walls. In the midst of the wreck and chaos, New Yorkers turned to me to provide a place of peace and faith, of reassurance that God would take care of them. I stretched my walls, raised my ceiling, and pushed outward to make space inside for the people who needed it.

On the day that everything changed, twins symbols of peace and humanity fell, never to rise again.

On the day that everything changed, 3,200 children lost their parents, and countless more lost a friend or loved one. But New York's soul did not change that day. New York City, a place of business, technology, fashion, and fame, revealed itself to be at its heart a community. New Yorkers entwined their roots with one another and as a whole grew toward the sunlight—toward the hope. **Like a night-blooming cereus, they blossomed in their darkest hour.** The broken heart of America became something people were determined to fix. Although many were killed, those who survived forged a stronger community than before. My dust-laden pews were cleaned. And once again, my interior became a place of worship and faith. The people came back, in droves. The priest boomed louder than before, and my spires carried his message even higher.

Since I do not have the strength to write today, this piece was written by kiddo, I had to share it here.

Peace and love to everyone affected by 9/11. Years may have flown by, but it feels like it happened yesterday. The void can never ever be filled. Let us sit with the grief for a bit and not push it away.

DEBORAH LeFALLE

THE UNEXPECTED GIFT

The winter sun's warmth kisses my face as I step off the porch to retrieve my morning newspaper. A clear day, the sky is scattered with faint cirrus clouds. My eyes are drawn to the east hills of the Diablo Range, and I still myself to absorb their beauty. My gaze is interrupted, however, by the sound of a yapping dog in the opposite direction and my attention shifts. That's when I see Marva coming.

I had been wondering about Marva, asking neighbors "Have you seen her?" For some reason she had departed from her daily trek down the block. But here she was now, decked out in Mrs. Claus attire. "Hello Ms. Marva," I say, and she returns the greeting. I continue, "Hold on, I have something for you," and I run inside to get a small gift I've wrapped for her. I hand her the gift and query, "How have you been? Look at you... all dressed up in the holiday spirit!" She chuckles. "I've been okay, but I've had problems getting around because the wheels on my cart keep getting stuck," she replies. I look at the damaged wheels and ask her to wait once more while I run back inside. I return with cash for her to buy a new pushcart. Surprised, Marva accepts it and thanks me profusely. She then reaches into her coat pocket and pulls out two small bags of peppermint candy. "This is for you," she says. "That is so sweet of you... are you sure?" I ask. "I'm sure," she replies and adds... "I got them off of a Santa Claus display at the drug store. The clerk there invited me to help myself, so I did. I hope you like them." "I love peppermint," I reply. We wish each other a Merry Christmas, and as always when ending our conversations, she softly voices, "God bless you!" "God bless you too Marva," I say... "God bless you too." I watch her walk off struggling to push her cart on the sidewalk with its rickety wheels, then turn and go back inside holding the two bags of candy close to my heart. All I can think of in this moment is how grateful I am.

ALEXANDRA McCORMICK

THE CATERPILLAR, A TRAGEDY

It was mid-afternoon in the beginning of June, on the east coast, the time where it's hot and humid and nobody really wants to be outside. But despite the heat, Abby, my first older sister, and I were outside. We were playing on our old swing set out back, which probably wasn't safe at all. The swing set wasn't new. It wasn't nice or pretty. It wasn't in any condition to even be sat on, as pieces of the gray wood were falling off left and right. But despite the condition, that old play set was where we spent most of those hot summer days. We were outside on the swing set, minding our own business, when Abby pushed me.

"Hey! Why'd you push me?" I asked her.

"You almost put your foot on that caterpillar!" she said, pointing towards a small, furry, brown and orange worm inching its way across the old wood.

As soon as I saw it, I tried to push it off with my foot. It was ugly and was missing little furs in places. This, of course, upset Abby, so she pushed me again a little harder this time, and then twice more for being, as she put it, "bully to the caterpillar." Looking back on this, she was right.

"Let's name 'em Kady, you know, cause he's a caterpillar" she said as she gently scooped him up. The name was pronounced like the name Caddie but spelled Kady because we thought it suited him nicely.

"I don't think Mom would want us to keep him, plus where is he gonna live?" I asked her, now concerned.

Now at the time we enjoyed playing with what we called pocket dogs. The real name for the small plastic toys was Littlest Pet Shops, they were basically small plastic toy animals. We had so many of them, and we also had small houses and buildings for the animals. These houses would serve as the perfect little home for our new pet, Kady.

We spent hours upon hours on our old PC, researching what caterpillars eat, where they live and other important caterpillar facts. We were acting like serious scientists researching before conducting some massively important experiment. We took the whole situation very seriously, we wanted Kady to live for as long as his lifespan would allow.

Abby and I had Kady for a few weeks, keeping him alive by feeding him the mint leaves from the garden, along with kale and tomato leaves. Kady was thriving, to say the least. We liked to think he enjoyed his life in her dark room, drinking water from a bottle cap, chomping on various leaves that were served to him. But, like all good things, our easy time with Kady was suddenly cut short.

"Have you guys packed for the camping trip in New Germany?" my mother asked us.

"Uh, yeah," Abby and I both said. We had both clearly forgotten about this trip to go and camp for a week.

"Okay, make sure you bring your bag downstairs so your dad can put it in the car."

We panicked. We hadn't told her about the caterpillar we had been housing for the past two weeks. I thought Abby was going to tell her. Abby thought I was going to. The whole situation was a mess. The worst part was we couldn't hire a sitter for a caterpillar, seeing that we were seven and eight years old, and it was a caterpillar. But nevertheless, we persisted. Abby had managed to put together a small plastic bag containing mint leaves, tomato leaves, kale, grass, a stick for Kady to walk around on, and a bottle cap to put water in. This bag seemed like a good idea because we had enough food to last Kady a year, and enough grass for him to sleep on.

The day came. All six of us piled into the old minivan. Abby was sure to take Kady into the car with her. I never thought that we would have to account for a caterpillar while traveling, but there we were with this old caterpillar in the hermit crab cage from Rehoboth Beach, hoping our parents wouldn't notice we had taken it.

The drive over to New Germany wasn't the smoothest drive. It felt like we were constantly going over speed bumps and gravel roads. We were being knocked around quite a bit which wasn't really doing anybody any good. Especially not Kady.

~~~

When we arrived at New Germany State Park for our camping trip it was pretty late and dark and we were driving for what felt like days, so we got into our cabin as soon as we could with our belongings. This included the food for the week, our bags and what we thought was our belovèd pet caterpillar, Kady.

Now, during the drive Abby had removed Kady only a few times from his cage. This probably wasn't a good idea, but she said he probably need to stretch his legs or something along the lines of that.

When we woke up the next morning, Abby and I went to Kady's cage to feed him some kale leaves and grass, the usual for a caterpillar, only to find that he was gone.

"Where is Kady?" Abby asked me. I could tell she was concerned about the small caterpillar. After all, she was basically his mother.

"I don't know," I replied, utterly confused as to where he could have gone.

Kady was a small creature. Light brown and orange like a tiger. Tiger may have a been a better name choice given his appearance. But the issue was that Kady was gone. He couldn't walk very fast at all. In fact, he walked very slow like a snail. He also could not open up latches like the one on the crab cage he was staying in for the trip.

We had absolutely no idea where this little caterpillar could have gone to. So like any mother who had lost track of her child would, Abby and I panicked, and we panicked a lot. We searched everywhere are retraced our steps from the previous night. We looked in the car, in every room, under his grass bed, but still there was no sign of Kady.

My mind was so busy worrying about that caterpillar that the next few hours went by slower than those hot June days we had to spend outside, where we first met Kady. Even though he was a small and seemingly insignificant caterpillar, Kady had me and Abby stressed out so much. At almost perfect timing, perfect timing would have been a few hours earlier, my dad came into the room I was sharing with my sisters.

"Could one of you three explain this to me?" He asked as he held in his hand a small black stick.

"Thats a stick, Dad." Abby responded. it was obvious she was upset.

"No, it is not a stick, it's a worm"

"Oh?" Abby suddenly sounded more enthusiastic.

As we looked closer at the stick, we realized it was our pet caterpillar. Abby snatched it out of my dad's hand as she yelled the poor thing's name over and over. He was in bad condition. His little furs were missing in places, so he looked mostly black, which is why we thought he was a stick. Abby immediately brought him over to his cage and gave him water to drink. There wasn't much hope for Kady, his condition was terrible, and we were surprised he was still alive. But, there was hope nonetheless.

~~~

A day, if even that, after the discovery of Kady was made, he passed away. This was no surprise to us, he barely looked like a caterpillar and was only identifiable by the few remaining hairs on his back. We didn't know what to do with him.

"Do we flush him?" I asked. I had never dealt with this type of delicate situation before.

"No! Of course not! We should bury him," Abby said, it sounded more like a question then a statement, she too had never dealt with a dead caterpillar.

My dad agreed to digging a small hole on the side of the cabin for cady to rest inside of. Abby and I lined the bottom of the hole with leaves and grass, mint leaves and other assorted vegetation. She gently set Kady in the hole and covered him with a leaf, then the dirt. It was quite a sad afternoon for everybody, like in TV dramas when a minor inconvenience occurs to one character. Like that, it affected the rest of the trip for me and Abby.

We spent the rest of the trip doing various Park Quest activities in New Germany. Things such as disc golf, hiking, and other outdoorsy activities. While these did somewhat distract me and Abby from the loss of Kady for a little bit, they didn't fill the small, caterpillar sized hole in me and Abby's hearts. My brother

HUNTER McDIVITT

THE ENDURING SOUL

My brother smiles broadly.

"Hi Lu-lu-lu," he says with a squeak. "How was your day?"

"It was great, Chris," I respond, carefully upbeat.

Sitting down on the couch, I look up at him. He laughs, a joyous, carefree laugh, and puts carrot sticks up his nose, joking and guffawing. I laugh, then, too, and he continues until all his food has been joked and guffawed away.

The first thing I remembered after moving was when my brother's new friends came over. I knew immediately there was something different about them than his old ones: these people were meaner, cruder, and clearly took drugs far more frequently than any of them ever had. My first thought upon seeing them was one of disgust. This seemed like the crowd who not only fit the "delinquent teenager" stereotype--drinking excessive amounts of alcohol, egging houses, doing all sorts of weird and disgusting things--but were the very reason for its existence in the first place.

These new friends of his didn't seem like my brother at all. He had been the best person in his whole old school. Last year, he had straight A grades, and he ran a club, and while he hadn't always been nice to me, he had behaved himself better, much better, towards the end.

But then everything changed.

It all seemed so terrible back then. Without Dad, it had felt the whole world would end. But it didn't; Chris and I had each other, and Mom, and so--together--we had survived. Really, the issues only began in bulk when Chris went back to school the next year. He had begun high school then, and I guess things must be different there from middle school, because they definitely weren't the same for him. He stopped hanging out with his friends, or even playing with me. All he ever did was stare into space all the time. He seemed very sad. So, Mom decided we all needed a fresh start, and we moved to San Diego.

I, for one, didn't think it was a good idea at the time. I didn't want to leave my friends! But Mom said it would help Christopher, and that I should care more about my older brother's well-being than about my own selfish desires, and so we had moved. But I think that might have made it worse, since Christopher didn't get any better. He had just kept on staring, never talking, never playing with me, or even bullying me. That was the first time I ever missed being bullied.

So, Mom had been excited when she learned he had new friends and was more than happy to let them come over. She thought, as did I, that this was the beginning of his recovery--that he was turning back into his good old self again.

So, she plastered on a smile and accommodated these boys' rowdy laughing and their frequent obscenities, and--with considerable effort--managed to avoid trying to move them all away from my brother's computer games. And I stayed in my room and didn't do anything loud that might bother them or embarrass Chris, like a good little sister.

And when that pack of delinquents finally left, I burst from my room like a circus man from a cannon, a mile-wide grin stretching across my face, and waltzed up to my brother, happier than I had been in months.

"Chris," I said, smiling sweetly. "Will you play with me now?"

He didn't say a word; he just looked at me, as though confused about why I might ask him this question.

"Please?" I was beginning to grow desperate now.

"I stayed in my room and I was quiet, and I didn't bother anyone."

"Nah. I'm tired." And with that, he walked away.

Chris's new friends continued to come over, and before long, he would go out and spend time with them away from home.

I quickly grew to hate them all.

It is natural, I think, to hate the fever rather than the virus.

The next time I learned that they would be coming over, I arranged a sleepover with some of my friends the same evening.

"Let's play tag. You're it, Em!"

"What? No fair! I'm gonna get you!"

And thus, began what to me seemed a grand crusade; a protest, of sorts. We proceeded to the yard, where we were sure to be energetic and enthusiastic, but most important of all, we were sure to be *loud*.

We yelled and screamed and giggled with furious intensity, me in anger, and them out of desire to help a friend exact revenge.

When the noise grew to a large enough point, one of them--a particularly skinny, rather weasel-looking character I eventually learned went by the name of Rich, came out and hollered at us to be quiet. I responded by sticking out of my tongue. The other girls--plus Melvin, ever the face of diversity--quickly followed suit.

Then my mother was the one hollering, and we changed tact.

Raiding Emily's fake gun supply, we proceeded to fire our foam projectiles at Chris and his friends. This endeavor proved to be more successful than the last one, and this time, it took us mere minutes to get recognition. The delinquents--plus Chris, whom I refused to label as such--argued amongst themselves for a few moments about who would ultimately come to confront us.

They selected--against his will--my very own brother, and from there cajoled him and pushed him and bullied him until he quit his refusing. It was probably because I was his sister that they made *him* deal with us, but I saw it then mostly as an indication they didn't care about him. This fueled my hatred ever more, even though it was precisely what I had intended to bring about from the beginning.

When Chris walked out, I didn't give him time to talk. Instead, I ran right up, tagged him, and told him he was it.

"Lucy, stop."

"We don't talk to the person who's it."

"Can y--"

"You'll have to tag someone first."

I had meant to force Chris to play with us, after which he would surely realize he enjoyed me more than those bad new friends of his. But it only seemed to frustrate him more. I decided to play my hand in full.

"We'll stop bothering you when you tag one of us."

He looked at me like I had antennae on my head. And it twisted something painful deep inside. But I gave him one last chance.

"Please, Chris. Just one round. You don't even need to be it."

I watched the consideration flash in his eyes for a moment. It was a precious moment, the kind that determines many moments after it. Then I saw him remember the presence of his friends. And then the lack of our Dad's presence. The lack of our Dad's life.

"No."

I don't really remember what happened next. I remember that I was mad--searing, red hot mad, but that I didn't do anything. No, I knew this was the kind of anger that needed to simmer. That needed to marinate a little while. So, I did nothing.

Chris's friends didn't come over for a while after that. In that sense, my crusade had been a success. But then that had never really been the point.

Now I grew to hate Chris himself. I grew to hate not only our current relationship, but the very fact that there was a Chris to relate--or to not relate--to. I had to hate Chris, you see. Because the only other option was to hate myself.

When Chris went out one evening, I followed him. I witnessed as he--surrounded by the other delinquents--smoked pot. But I didn't report him, just then. I was more clever than that now. More patient. More ruthless. For now, I simply waited. I waited as he began to diversify and intensify his palate, first being prodded by others, then eventually doing the prodding. I watched as he began to smoke real cigarettes, then take pills--which I later learned were heroin pills. How he and the others procured these I never knew, beyond that one was in a cast for a while and had apparently encountered them during his time at the hospital. Finally, I watched in triumph, as he brought some of the pills home.

Here, I believed would be my grand reveal. I would show the pills to my parents, and land Chris in a heap of trouble. Enough to show him that what he had been doing was wrong. That his friends were wrong. That he had been wrong. And once they were gone, he would naturally go back to his old self and acknowledge me again.

The morning of my Reveal, I went to class, just as usual. I ate lunch and played at recess, just as usual. I came home and did my homework, just as usual. Then I waited until the evening, just after Chris typically left, and just before my parents would usually get home. I thought everything was under control.

But there was one thing I hadn't noticed. The pills all those boys had been taking, by the end of everything, were no longer heroin. The pills my brother had taken home-- unbeknownst to his friends and myself--were not anything so mild. They were fentanyl.

I opened the door to Chris's room to see something very, very wrong. Firstly, Chris hadn't left.

Secondly, there were no pills to show to my parents. Chris had taken them all.

He lay sprawled in his chair, limp and unmoving. His chest didn't rise or fall. I screamed, then. A scream of fear and pain--reflective of the heart crushing itself to pieces inside of me. And my mom, approaching the driveway, heard and ran in, panic visible on her face. She called the doctor, after which an ambulance came rushing, faster than I thought it was possible for medical people to mobilize, arriving in time to save my brother's life.

Sort of.

They say he has hypoxia. They tell me part of his brain died because it didn't have enough air.

My brother frowns as I get up to do my homework. He shouts, a loud, breathy sound, and stands. "Stay," he says, his voice light and airy and odd.

I nod amiably, gulping as water begins to condense in my eyes. *This new Chris at least wants me around*, I think, trying to console myself. He sits back, content now that I've decided to stay with him a little longer.

"Love you Lu-lu-lu."

At least he's happy now.

"A… re you sad about somet-hing, Lu-lu?"

He's not sad about Dad anymore. I guess that's a good thing, right?

"Do...n't be sad, Lu."

All I think about is how he still doesn't bully me. This is the second time, I think, that I've wished to be bullied.

KIARA PALOMINOS

STRENGTH IN SCALING WALLS

The strongest people are those who fight battles we know nothing about. I like most of you are one of those people. I have not realized this before and only upon reflecting in this piece, I realize that at the time when things were hard and continue to be hard, I will only truly know exactly how strong I was and am, at the end. But so far, so many things have happened to me that make me strong, that make me, me. Yet it is not one event that makes me strong, it is the accumulation of walls placed in front of me that I have had to cross, sometimes leaving behind people and parts of me.

I am strong because I live in this society everyday, I go to school with a bullet vest, I go home with the police radio, and I am strong. I walk fast when someone is behind me, I work hard when there are not enough hours in the day, I create even when my hands cannot keep up with my mind, and I am strong. I fight tsunamis with myself, I fight metaphorical arguments with our president, I carry my burdens, and I am strong. I am strong because I live with fear each day of my life and I am fighting to rid that fear from my family, from my home, and from my head. Everyday I am in fear, some days more than others. After a restless night of cops and ambulances passing outside my window and then seeing ICE parked outside the apartment complex in the morning, as I head to school. I leave behind my parents not knowing if that day I will be taken out of class by a police officer informing me that my parents have been taken into custody by ICE, have been placed in handcuffs, have been deemed criminals, instead of inspirations. That is one of the many things that haunts me everyday of my life, and will continue to haunt me because in this place where the statue of liberty stands a hypocrite, my parents are not welcomed and because I am my parent's I therefore am not welcomed.

Everyone says that I look like my dad and on other days they say I look like my mom. And this means that I am like them because my parents are the strongest people I know. They come home everyday with aching backs and legs, not being able to go to the hospital because the doctors have told my dad that he should just stretch, after they pocket the little money he has. My parents are strong. My mom is strong because when the coyote brought her, she suffered thirst and pain after seeing a girl break her ankle and having to leave her, not knowing if she died in another unmarked grave at the border with her family never knowing if their daughter was safe. My father is strong because he left his mother only to cross an unforgiving border with skulls, baby bags, and empty water jugs scattered on the burning floor, escaping hunger and poverty. Although they never really crossed that river, their backs were still soaked, in sweat and blood and tears of pain, suffering and hope. Thus if I resemble my parents, I have strength in my blood, resilience in my skin, perseverance in my heart and bones that are built on sacrifice. And sure, I am physically strong as well, boxing is a special type of strength. I show strength when my legs are so sore that although they have carried me this far for these many years, they can no longer hold the weight of my body, yet I still I get into that ring, and I still throw another punch, like my father did, ten years ago. My strength is in being able to take my demons and knock them out every round.

My art is my strength, and not because I may be good at it, but because I have fought to get at the skill that I am at, and I still have a lot to improve on. For a while, I stopped painting. My brushes would start to crack, my paper would start to tear and my paints would start to crumble. When I started again I had a breakdown, I did not draw as well as when I stopped, I felt that my hands had given up on me. It felt as if I would forever be condemned to create in my mind but never with my hands, feeling useless. But I have overcome that, little by little I have fought to get back to where I was and although I am never satisfied I am strong because I have gotten this far anyways. I am strong because although something happened to me in seventh grade, I am still me. I am resilient. Although my body is technically healthy and my mind is not due to things that I wish I could have changed, I fight, and I will always fight, because my body, she is mine. My body, she has taken me away from poisonous people to better ones, and I have a love hate relationship with her. My body, she is strong.

Although these are just a few of the bricks that have made up the walls that I have jumped and are only the stories I am comfortable with sharing today, they do not make up the barbed wire or thorn bush on top of each and every one of them. This does not explain the thorns and the scars I continue to have after each wall I manage to overcome. Maybe one day I'll be able to talk about other heart-breaking events that have happened but not today because these pages are not enough for the 17 years I have lived. And although you may say that because I cry and because I am vulnerable I am weak. I am not weak. Crying in front of others and being vulnerable is the strongest thing I have ever learned to do.

MY RAINY RIVER

Note from author: The underlined text is from the novel The Things They Carried *by Tim O'Brien.*

The paralysis took my heart. I could see everything but I could not react, I would feel everything but could not express it, I wanted to scream and shout but nothing came out. I was stuck in a state of hidden chaos inside my head and a ferocious silence outside my body. My whole life seems to spill out into the river, swirling away from me, everything I had ever been or ever wanted to be. Everyone was there, my family, friends, and everyone that has made my life interesting since the beginning. Next to the people I new the most, stood a random boy with platinum blond hair and a skinny tall frame that I am pretty sure I met in science camp who had busted open his teeth after slipping and falling on a rock as we crossed a river. It's a blur now as it was then, and all I remember is that he was my first real friend that I had made on my own. When I met him I was nine, I was innocent, I did not know fear or prejudice, I had not yet met insecurity or pressure. I was only happy to be there in the moment, enjoying how naive I was to the society I called home, full of dilemmas with life shattering outcomes. It's like watching an old home movie. It was the first time I ever picked up boxing gloves, the first time I learned that my hands can create, the first time I drove a car, so many first times. But if I left it would be the last time I would see my parents or hug my family. The last time I would sleep in my bed after working until three in the morning. The last time I would punch the ripped black heavy bag I had hit since I was ten. Now I had a choice, my skin felt tight. As my gaze shifted from the boy to my parents I observe the shiny streaks down their cheeks and how their backs are soaked, their wetback reminding me why it is they cry. They do not want to see me leave. They want to see me fight and prove that their sacrifice was not for nothing. That there was a purpose for crossing a similar river to the one that lay in front of me. But they would understand, because I am their flesh and blood, the embodiment of their hard work and perseverance. They are proud of me and will support me no matter what. As my eyes continue moving on I see myself in a cap and gown with a bachelors in mechanical engineering and a minor in studio art. The only problem is that it is fading as I shake my head in tears and look down. The sleepless nights before AP exams, the enormous amounts of stress before a test that would decide where I would apply to college, and the hard work I put into every day of my life is fading as if to never have existed. I would have to start clean, act as if it never happened, because if I leave that is what I would have to do, because it is too painful to remind myself of everything that I have accomplished and would leave behind. I remember a sudden tightness in my chest as I looked up and watched my sister cross the stage at age 22, with a degree of her own, and a cap that says "I did it, Kiara" and it is painted so beautifully I wonder if I made it for her before I left or if she found someone else to make it for her. I see her, happy, acting and singing on stage. I see her at the entrance of the biggest theatre in the world, in New York, but she is by herself with an extra ticket as she walks in slowly because I was supposed to be there, I was supposed to see it with her, I was supposed to fight to stay. There is a sting in my stomach. I can't get my breath; I can't stay afloat; I can't tell which way to go. I can't do it, I have to fight, I have to be there for my family who has sacrificed everything for me so that I can have the opportunity to fight, to succeed, to be more. I know that they would adapt without me but I want to be there for all of their special moments, when my dad and I finally buy a house together, when I graduate from high school with all of my friends, when my sister and I adopt the dog or cat or ferret that we have always dreamed about. I need to be here in this country to fight for those without a voice, I need to protect my family, I need to be here. So I break free from the <u>moral freeze</u> that has taken over my body, and I finally make a decision, for war. I jump into the freezing water, my back becoming soaked, and I swim with reaching arms, towards my family, towards opportunity and future. Just how my parents did.

NILS PETERSON
FIRST POET LAUREATE OF SANTA CLARA COUNTY

PACKING UP TO MOVE TO SEATTLE

*Living in a house
we live in the body
of our lives....*
      -- "House," Robert Hass

Packing up to leave the house I've lived in for 50 years, deciding what books to take and what to leave behind to create their own fate, I came across Hass's *Field Guide.* It won for him the Yale Younger Poets Prize. I'd already packed his collected poems so I thought to leave it behind with a couple a hundred other poetry books finding their own fates, but I leafed through and eye caught the words above. They seemed so true, I tucked it in the bag I was taking with me in my drive north with my younger daughter and my dog.

For fifty years the house I'm leaving made up the body of my life and the life of my wife and daughters. My daughters tell me they think of it as "Home," even though neither one has lived in it for 30 years and more.

Mostly it was a good body, though like even in the best of bodies, there were aches and pains in it and us. The new owners will have to exercise it some to renew its elegance but it has, as is sometimes said of a face that looks good no matter what its age, good bones.

I found this this morning in *The London Review of Books,* "There is a fine Scots word for the sale of a house, farm or factory: a displenishment." Well yes, that's exactly what the emptying of my house felt like, a displenishment, the "plenish" of 50 years is gone, and one heads towards a minimalist world. Haven't gotten there yet. Dragged a lot of stuff with me. Daughters not yet off the hook.

JULIA SATTERTHWAITE

FEED THE RIGHT WOLF

To my friends and family, colleagues and students, and nameless faceless online stalkers, I think I look pretty put together. And I figure they think I am the person in the photos: Big smile. Successful. Confident. Creative.

And why shouldn't they?

· I hooked myself an amazing husband: Rod – who is also a journalism teacher – totes adorbs!
· I have two beautiful, adventurous boys, Micah and Jonah.
· I advise a national award-winning publication.
· I was named a Columbia Scholastic Press Association Distinguished Adviser in 2019.
· I'm a director-at-large for the national Journalism Education Association Board of Directors.
· I'm Digital Media Chair of the JEA NorCal regional Board of Directors.
· I'm a member of elite faculties teaching summer workshops at Ball State, Stanford, Michigan State and sites in between.
· I'm an avid reader, a pretty good singer, not a bad writer. I'm working on incorporating yoga into my life.

Well, here's the truth: The voice inside my head gazes upon all of my many so-called "successes" and whispers to me, "I don't buy it for a minute. You're not that good. Your life isn't that good. People don't like you. You don't even like yourself. Be afraid. Be very afraid."

You think I'm kidding? You think I'm exaggerating? I'm not. I'm not because the voice is talking:

"Hey, Julia. Be careful. Someone may be hiding under your car in the parking lot, waiting for you. Waiting to hurt you. Maybe even kill you."

"Hey, Julia. None of your new head editors for El Valedor think you know what you're doing. They'll probably never grow to trust you."

"Hey, Julia. All these things, these activities, the obligations you've taken on, you suck at all of them."

"Hey, Julia. You're a fraud. A fake. You know it. Everyone does. Or will soon."

This voice inside my head has been there for a long, long time.

When I was younger, I would arrange my stuffed animals into the figure of a body so it looked like I was sleeping under the covers of my bed, just in case someone decided to break into my house, sneak into my room and try to kill me. Ha! I fooled them. I was sleeping on the floor, where they'd never think to look.

In junior high, I screamed and head-banged along to Nirvana's "Smells Like Teen Spirit," Green Day's "Basket Case" and Sublime's "Wrong Way" with friends – too afraid to admit that I'd prefer James Taylor's "Shed a Little Light." Or the Beatles' "Good Day Sunshine." Or Billy Joel's "Leningrad."

Even more embarrassing, I loved Christian music (still do).

I was afraid they'd think I was a kook, a weirdo. Worse still, *I* was afraid I was too.

So, in high school, I was a joiner: volleyball, soccer, softball, travel choir, NHS, peer counseling, literary magazine … always padding that list of accomplishments … yet still feeling like a fraud, a pretender just going through the motions.

That's why Judith Guest's "Ordinary People" resonated with me so much my junior year. It's about death and guilt and anger and the lies we tell ourselves to suppress the pain. If you haven't read it, you should. It'll help you understand where I'm coming from.

I always thought these fears and insecurities would pass, that I'd grow out of them. I didn't. In fact, it got worse, and I had to devise coping mechanisms, ways to control everything, so I became obsessed with things like:

- LOADING THE DISHWASHER. There's only one way to do it, and I'm the only person who knows how to do it right.

- ORGANIZING MY CLOSET. By color and type. Dresses to the left, then shirts from dark to light: black, gray, blue, green, red, pink, yellow, cream and white. Each subset of shirts by color is organized from sweaters to long-sleeves to short sleeves to sleeveless. The pants are on the lower row and organized in the same color order as the shirts.

- SAYING YES. People-please. People like you more when you say "yes." "Hello, Julia. Whaaaaat's happening? I'm gonna need you to come in tomorrow. I know it's a Saturday, but if you could be here around 8, that would be great. mmmKay? Oh, oh. I almost forgot. I'm also going to need you to come in on three evenings next week too. mmmK? You need to be at the Equity Showcase Monday, pitch your new class to the school board on Tuesday and present your School Site Council funding request in person on Thursday. Thanks."

And I would smile and say, "Yes," even though it obliterated whatever other social or romantic or family plans I had.

I was a mess, so it didn't surprise me when, after taking the Myers-Briggs Type Indicator personality test, I learned that I'm one of the rare 1-2 percent of the population that falls into the INFJ group.

To help you understand what this means, let's go through a quick, rudimentary exercise to determine your own MBTI type, if you haven't already:

- Are you a people person who happily chats with strangers? Or are you a Jane Austen/Emily Dickinson nerd?
- Do you get your information from what you see, smell, feel, hear, taste? Or do you hyper-analyze everything in search of some Rosetta Stone to explain why everybody hates you?
- Do you rely on facts or feelings? Gosh, everyone was nice to me today. That means either they like me or they hate me.
- My best friend doesn't know how to load a dishwasher correctly, and her closet isn't color-coded. This is either OK – to each his own – or it's horrible! Terrible! Criminal!

According to Myers-Briggs.org, I'm an INFJ, which means "I seek meaning and connection in ideas, relationships and material possessions. Want to understand what motivates people and are insightful about others. Conscientious and committed to their firm values. Develop a clear vision about how best to serve the common good. Organized and decisive in implementing their vision."

What does that mean? I think it means, "I want a cool husband and sweet boys and a successful, fulfilling career that gets me appointed to important committees and asked to teach at cool workshops nationwide but still gives me time to sing and do some yoga … and I should feel good about it."

It also means I'm a prime candidate for a nervous breakdown because I'm a control freak who expects perfection from myself and the rest of the world, and occasionally, I am forced to come to grips with the fact that things aren't always perfect, so what do I do?

I blame myself.

I blame myself for my inability to keep 18 plates spinning at one time like a circus act from the Lotus position while singing "I Will Survive" and reading "War and Peace."

I blame myself for not raising 100 percent perfect boys. I mean, they pee on the floor around the toilet. There's nothing in the perfect home care guidebook that allows for that.

And this pressure builds, and the voice whispers in my ear, and soon I'm having a full-blown panic attack that feels like something between a heart attack and lockjaw. These attacks became increasingly frequent when I had my kids, because if there's one thing that messes with control freaks, it's children. There's so much that's beyond our control.

So, what do I do? I cope. How? You really don't want to know, but I'm going to tell you anyway. Around the age of 30, I began picking at my skin. I know it sounds gross. It is. Fortunately, I'm not alone here. Some people pick skin around their nails or on their faces, but I always pick on my scalp so I can hide any scabs under my hair. Some days, I looked like I'd run into a briar patch. I wore hats and gloves, and I kept hair bands and nail files and all sorts of other gimmicks to try to keep my hands busy, but none of them worked.

I knew I had to get help, so I began taking the anti-anxiety medication Zoloft and attending sessions on Cognitive Behavior Therapy, which is a form of psychotherapy that treats problems and boosts happiness by modifying dysfunctional emotions, behaviors and thoughts. For example, the therapist would say, "Why aren't you happy?" And I'd say, "I don't know." And he'd say, "Think happy thoughts! That should help."

Well, it's almost seven years later, and I've long given up on those therapy sessions. At any given point in time, I have between 1-4 scabs on my head. You have no idea how hard this is to admit because I know, from this point on, when you see me, you're going to be looking for scabs.

I know it's weird and gross. But it's like being an insomniac. You can't understand it unless you're living it. And I'm living it ... and I'm embarrassed by it.

This is why I get my hair cut no more than twice a year and never by the same person because I can't stand the shame of letting yet another person in on my secret. Well, I guess it's not a secret any more. But you get the point. Imagine sitting in the salon chair, and your hairdresser says to you, "You been running through a briar patch?"

Revealing these dark secrets is part of my therapy. I struggle with anxiety and occasional bouts of depression. I take Prozac now. I see a therapist. I still pick my skin. But I constantly battle the voice inside my head.

Why am I telling you this? Because I want my friends and family, colleagues and students, and nameless faceless online stalkers to know I am the person in the photos: The smile is real. I am confident in my creativity. I am a success for all the right reasons. I'm not a fraud. I'm not a fake. I have nothing to hide. I want my boys to know that I am the mother — I am the strong person — they believe me to be. Yet, I'll always have my work cut out for me battling that damn voice.

I want to end with a story. It's about an old Cherokee chief teaching his grandson about life:

"A fight is going on inside me," the chief said to the boy. "It's a terrible fight and it is between two wolves. One is evil – he is anger, envy, sorrow, regret, greed, arrogance, self-pity, guilt, resentment, inferiority, lies, false pride, superiority and ego."

"The other is good," the chief continued. "He is joy, peace, love, hope, serenity, humility, kindness, benevolence, empathy, generosity, truth, compassion and faith. The same fight is going on inside you – and inside every other person, too."

The grandson thought about it for a minute and then asked his grandfather, "Which wolf will win?"

The chief gazed into his grandson's eyes and replied, "The one you feed."

So, I just want to say, "Feed the right wolf. And maybe try some yoga."

THE FACE OF HUMANITY

Delays suck

Airports have a funny way of reflecting the face of humanity. If you want to get a sense of how we're doing as a human race, go sit in an airport (or at a youth sports event) and observe interactions between patrons and employees, parents and children, spouses … but especially those of random strangers.

I recently experienced an airport complication not unlike those I suppose I've come to expect anytime I'm at the mercy of airlines. The minute a connection is involved, it seems I have about a 50 percent chance of actually making it to my destination on the day of the flight plan.

On this particular trip, it didn't help that I was traveling from San Francisco to Manhattan … Kansas.

On May 18, I boarded American Airlines flight 2207 from SFO to Dallas (DFW), which took off and landed without complication. Then, I had just under an hour to make American Airlines flight 2787, the last of four daily flights that land at the two-gate Manhattan, Kan. airport, two from Dallas and two from Chicago.

Since I had to ride a snail's-pace transit system to get to the farthest terminal and my connection was short, I booked it to the gate. Muscles burning and short of breath, I was relieved to arrive and see that my connection was delayed. At least I hadn't missed it altogether.

I sat down to catch my breath and noticed a pizza and beer place right next to my gate. I was delayed, but at least I had pizza and beer.

I found a spot at the bar alongside a bunch of overweight, middle-aged men, ordered a personal cheese pizza and a draft wheat beer, then proceeded to have a lengthy conversation with a Republican from Anchorage, Alaska who co-owns Kenai River Brewing Co. I patiently listened to his perspective and his brilliant idea to tax the shit out of the immigrants so they won't even want to come anymore, and he did not patiently listen in return. At least there was pizza and the beer! I got out of there quickly and decided to wait out the rest of my delay at the gate.

As time ticked on, the delay lengthened. One hour and 12 minutes. Two hours. Two and a half hours. Apparently, there were some bad storms including the possibility of tornadoes that airline employees thought we'd better not attempt in our puddle-jumper plane.

Photo Credit: Taichi Takano

When the storms cleared, the gate agent started calling us to board and I thought we might actually make it that night, placing this journey in the 50 percent of flights with connections that made it at least on the same day.

Long after everyone was seated and we were beginning to get antsy, the captain came on the loudspeaker and said they needed to remove 1,000 pounds of fuel to "maximize the payload and exercise extreme safety" and "we have other contingencies that include return to DFW." It wasn't looking good for us.

"I'm just hoping to make it to bed sometime before I turn into a pumpkin," I joked via text to Rod.

FYI, I'm a sleeper. I need a minimum of eight hours of sleep or else I get moody. My editorial board even made a moody day box for me for next year when I get fewer than eight hours of sleep and need a pick-me-up. It's a known phenomenon.

Finally, a fuel truck pulled up and removed the 1,000 extra pounds of fuel and I sent, "Just got the message 'hopefully we will be able to push off soon.' Love you!" to Rod.

I always feel as if my last words to Rod need to say "Love you," I guess because I'm morbidly thinking that any plane I get on might crash and I want my last words to be words of love and not bitching about the flight.

Our plane pushed off and hope surged among the passengers. The captain came on the loudspeaker again and let us know we were fifth in line for takeoff and would likely be waiting only another 10-15 minutes. This was an hour-long flight we were talking about, that we'd officially been sitting on for long over an hour, so this was welcome information.

Then he came back on again about 10 minutes later and said he was really sorry, be he and his co-captain were legally not allowed to fly the plane anymore because they'd be over their hours. We would need to return to the gate where they'd find us a new crew to fly the plane.

9:12 p.m. "Bad news: the captain and first officer are now over their hours, so we have to go back to the gate to get a new crew. FML. My butt is numb and we haven't even taken off," I joked to Rod.

9:19 p.m. "Seriously. What the f***? I'm so sorry. We just should never fly again. I love you!" he replied.

While we waited behind planes that were actually going to take off and taxied back to the gate, the rumblings among passengers intensified. Back at the gate, the captain and the co-captain got off and we waited. And prayed. After 15 minutes, the flight attendant got on the loudspeaker, apologized profusely, and asked us to deplane. Definitely not getting anywhere anytime soon.

"On the bright side, no one dragged me off the plane," I joked to Rod, later thinking I may have preferred that to the on-again, off-again antics that I'd been dealing with for four hours.

Plan B

The mass of exhausted, rumpled passengers huddled in a blob in front of the ticketing desk, hoping for a miracle. The woman behind the counter gathered herself and took a good, deep breath before announcing that the flight was cancelled, American Airlines was tagging this incident as "weather related," so there would be no lodging and food compensation, and could we please form three lines for rebooking our flights.

Photo Credit: Taichi Takano

That's when things turned ugly. A privileged man in a blue polo at the front of the line yelled expletives and pointed into this poor woman's face as we all watched on, some cheering him on, and others like me praying that his teenage daughter would grow up to be different than her dear ole' dad.

There were three gate agents and three lines. I was in the back of the middle line. As each traveler reached the front, they uttered their words of extreme dissatisfaction, some more extreme than others, before moving on to the minutiae of rebooking. They soon found out the next flight from Dallas to Manhattan was not until Saturday, two days away … so by the time I was up in line, any potentially extra spots may be snagged by those ahead of me.

After Rod sent me the American Airlines number, I called and begged the woman on the phone to find me any flight into anywhere in Kansas … Kansas City, Wichita, Salina … anywhere, but it had to be tomorrow. After about 25 minutes of searching (and very little line movement), the woman said that, because of the bad storms in the area, any availability on other flights had been taken by customers from earlier in the day and the earliest she could honestly get me to Manhattan, Kan. was by Saturday afternoon. I thanked her for her time and hung up..

The wheels in my brain started formulating options:
1. Wait it out in Dallas for two days and get on a Saturday flight to Manhattan, only

to turn around and go home to California the next day.

2. Find the next available flight to SFO and just go home, waving my white flag of defeat.

3. Check into a hotel to get some rest, then rent a car early in the morning and drive the 7 ½ hours to Manhattan, Kan.

Meanwhile, people around me were in varying stages of grief. A distraught young lady in the line next to me mentioned that her sister's wedding was on Saturday, she was the maid of honor, and the next flight out wouldn't get her to the wedding in time. She joked that a group should rent a car and drive, but wasn't old enough herself to do so. Beyond her, another lady mentioned she was headed to her cousin's graduation and would be down for car-sharing.

Another young man, who looked no older than the high school students I teach, mentioned that he was on emergency leave from the war in Afghanistan to attend his kid sister's funeral, which was the next day.

I heard a record scratch. I lost my breath. Time stopped. Whatever you want to call it, I felt in this moment that I was the recipient of some perspective and had the unique opportunity to do some paying it forward. These people had places to be, I was old enough to rent a car and I wanted to help.

I thought of my mom when I made the next few choices, which included offering strangers a ride in my car to get to their wedding, graduation, and funeral.

I pulled a Peggy.

While we were hatching the beginning of a plan, a mass of people started to gather at the back of the line, focusing on the hope of the drive instead of the hopelessness of getting a flight in a reasonable time frame.

Everybody wanted in the car. I felt like Oprah. You get a car. You get a car. You get a car. But I couldn't give everybody a ride. We ended up organizing ourselves into two groups, a Manhattan group and a Wichita group.

10 p.m. "I'm going to rent a car and drive with a few other folks from the flight, okay?" I texted Rod (as if he had a choice).

10:01 p.m. "How far is the drive, and do you trust these people?"

10:05 p.m. "Seven hours. I guess. One's a preschool teacher, one raises pork in North Carolina, and one's in the army on emergency leave from Afghanistan to go to his 11-year-old sister's funeral (car wreck)."

A shy Japanese man wanted into my vehicle headed to Manhattan. He was wearing a Trump t-shirt, but he seemed like he needed help and this was no time for politics, so I pulled out some rusty Japanese phrases from my time in Japan, including,

"Hajimemashite." Nice to meet you.

10:06 p.m. "Ok. Seven hours is a lot, but if it's what you want to do, it's fine. How will you stay awake until 3 or 4 a.m. and then do a board meeting?"

I was honestly nervous. I asked for people's names, professions, and home cities so Rod could track down my body parts if needed.

10:32 p.m. "I'm riding with Melanie (a preschool teacher from Panama City), Sydney (a swine fertility specialist from North Carolina), Dayton (on emergency leave from the army in Afghanistan for his 11-year-old sister's funeral – car crash), and Taichi (from Japan and works for the U.S. Coast Guard maybe?)."

We stopped at a Starbucks, where I ordered a venti iced vanilla latte with an extra shot. Then we took a shuttle to the rental car area, where it took us several companies, but eventually National agreed to let us take a car one-way.

11:25 p.m. "Safe travels. It's the best way to see Manhattan!" Rod sent.

The Long Ride

Photo Credit: Julia Satterthwaite

Five strangers get stranded in Dallas. They hatch a plan to drive to Manhattan. Watch next week's episode to see the drama unfold.

It felt like a combination of "Lost" and "Real World."

We were seated as such: me in the driver seat, Melanie in the front passenger seat, Sydney (who let me call her Shelby for most of the ride) behind Melanie, Dayton in the middle, and Taichi behind me.

As I pulled the white Toyota 4Runner to the rental car check out, I said aloud, "This may be the weirdest thing I've ever done." Nervous tension filled the air. I could tell my passengers were aware of my anxiety at this point and were wondering if they had hitched their wagon to a death trap. Taichi was gripping the "oh shit bar" in the back seat with an intensity I hadn't seen before.

When we took off, I needed some guidance to the main freeway, but Melanie was in front, and couldn't look at the Waze app and instead gazed intently at the horizon. Luckily, Dayton had driven this same route on more than one occasion from Fort Riley in Manhattan to visit his mom in Texas. I was getting backseat directions in new territory in the pitch black. If it had been safe, I would've been clutching that "oh shit bar" myself.

Eventually, we made our way to the main route, which involved a lot of driving straight. That meant a lot of time for conversation. This is actually the thing people ask me the most about when I relay this story: "What did you talk about?"

(The second most popular question: What music did you listen to? Answer: a new band Rod and I saw at Freewheel Brewing Company the week before called Pistachio – I wondered why they weren't famous yet!, Guster, Adele, and Kacey Musgraves – all my choices because the driver needs to stay awake.)

The conversations were the best part.

We were from the most different walks of life, which reminded me of Kiefer Sutherland's attempt at rejuvenation after his "24" success in the show "Touch," examining the connectedness among humans. I loved it. Critics and most of America did not. It lasted two seasons. But here I was, living the show in the confines of a sparkly white 4Runner.

Sydney

We heard about Sydney's job as a swine fertility specialist. She examines pig semen in a lab for a living and checks to see if at least 70 percent of the sperm in a specimen are viable. If not, it's off to the slaughter mill. I asked her if her job ever felt boring or repetitive and she said no, it was pretty fun and she got to work with a bunch of great people. I thought her job sounded kind of gross, but she said it could be worse; there were people who had to collect the pig semen.

Sydney also shared how excited she was for her sister, who was marrying the best guy in the world. He was deaf, but Syd's sister learned sign language to communicate with him. She happily shared engagement pictures that clearly captured the couple's love for each other.

Sydney is one class shy of her Bachelor's Degree in animal science and will likely continue in the family business of swine management.

Sydney and I differed on two things, she loves bacon and hates Ford Motor Company. I hold the opposite opinion on both. But we bonded on our love for Adele, so we're all good.

Dayton

Dayton told us about his first seven months of duty in Afghanistan (he still had two months of this nine-month tour to serve after his 10-day emergency leave), spending 8-10 hours each day driving around, combing the streets for bombs. When they find one, his team marks it and has a bomb squad come to retrieve/detonate/remove it.

When I asked if he planned to go back for another tour, he said of course, as this was the only way to make money in the military. It reminded me that the only way to make money in education is through administration. Only much sadder.

Dayton spoke almost catatonically about how his 21-year-old stepsister was driving his 11-year-old sister in a car in Indianapolis when a cyclist crashed in front of them. His stepsister veered, lost control of the car, went into oncoming traffic and Kaitlyn was killed instantly. The stepsister lives on with Kaitlyn and family's haunting memories.

Dayton was required to report in person to Fort Riley in Manhattan, Kan. once he was stateside so the Army knew he made it back safely, so he couldn't just reroute to Indy.

Since he was in a time crunch, we decided to stop at Fort Riley where we could meet up with his wife. Instead of embracing the husband she hasn't seen in person in seven months, she agreed to take a picture of our bedraggled crew before sweeping Dayton away to check in, and then drive him to Indy for the funeral.

Dayton Brumett (22), Julia Satterthwaite (34), Melanie Nguyen (28), Sydney Cox (23), Taichi Takano (44)

We didn't decide to become Facebook official friends until we had dropped off Dayton. And we didn't know his last name. It was awful to have to search 11-year-old car accident and every spelling of Caitlyn/Caitlin/Kaitlyn/Kaitlin possible to find him. But I did.

I still don't have the words to explain what transporting him that felt like, and I love words. There was a point near Oklahoma City where weather-watcher Sydney shared that we'd be hitting a pretty big storm (hence the flight delays), but that it would likely only last for about 20 minutes.

As we drove into the storm and I found the windshield wipers couldn't quite keep up with the amount of water trying to drown our hope, I began to panic. I gripped the steering wheel as tight as I could. I leaned forward. I said outloud, "I don't know what to do."

"Keep going," my passengers said.

In that time, I felt the weight of my passengers' lives on my shoulders. I almost couldn't handle it. I don't know how airline pilots do it. In any case, it was precious Dayton's life that I wanted to sustain above all, as he was headed to a funeral for his sister who was killed in a car crash. I couldn't kill another member of his family in a damn car.

Taichi

After a good hour of holding onto the "oh shit bar," Taichi settled in and was the one who was able to sleep every so often on this crazy train to Kansas. When he was awake, Taichi shared about his wife and 8-year-old son, his host family in Kansas that he started visiting when he was in 6th grade, and his trips to the U.S. every year. He was also planning to practice his driving skills with a trip from Kansas to Illinois for work, though he wasn't planning on the Dallas to Manhattan drive (which was the longest ride he'd ever taken by car!).

When we finally reached the Manhattan, Kan. airport in the morning and sat like zombies who missed the apocalypse, I asked him some questions. Tell me about your family.

He showed me a beautiful photo of his wife Seiko and son Yamato during cherry blossom season. I decided to push it and ask him directly about his Trump t-shirt and "Make America Great Again" hat.

"Do you like him?" I asked.

"Oh no! It's a joke. My host family hates Donald Trump and I just wanted to see their faces when I show up wearing a t-shirt and hat," he replied.

But I'm not so sure. After reviewing his Facebook page, he and his son both seem to wear Trump propaganda. I suppose I don't really care, as long as he knows that not all Americans are selfish and rude. Some Americans will give up their night to drive you where you need to be.

Melanie

My privileged life of access to experiences and education seemed to offset the life that Melanie had lived. Melanie had a lot of sad stories.

She told us about her unstructured childhood, her work at the machine shop, her teenage pregnancy (now 9-year-old Lilian), how things got better when she left the baby's dad, her work as a preschool teacher and then preschool manager, her renewed faith in the church and God, how how she found the love of her life (who also worked at the machine shop) and had another child (now 5-year-old Aubrey), yet this one had every challenge possible: she's autistic, has allergies, developed pica and eats everything in sight … as passengers we kept waiting for the story's conclusion, for a happy ending, for things to get wrapped up with a bow. But none came.

Melanie's stories about her family were just as depressing, including that her brother once took a car with a stranger and he wasn't as lucky. As a lady driving a car full of strangers, it was hard to hear, especially when carrying the weight of Dayton's army stories and sister's death.

But then we bonded on another level – many of us had a sibling or close loved one who was a failure. A fuck-up. A danger to society. Mostly, our stories revolved around the connection between mental illness and addiction. It broke my heart that the same issues my immediate family has dealt with for over a decade and my extended family has been haunted by for generations are part of the American fabric. Three out of five of us.

Americans don't take care of the mentally ill. They see mental illness as weakness. And the mentally ill are predisposed to alcohol and drug addiction. It's no surprise that me, Melanie, Dayton and others have members of the family who are suffering, which has a ripple effect. It feels wholly insurmountable. But we can do little things to make a big impact.

5:51 a.m. "Arrived at the Manhattan airport and returned the car." I sent to Rod.

Photo Credit: Taichi Takano

Closing

So what do you do when faced with life's proverbial problems. Do you swear at other folks who didn't cause your problem or do you put on your big person pants?

You gather strangers, buy yourself a venti iced vanilla latte with an extra shot, stand in rental car lines until you find a company that will allow you to rent a vehicle large enough to fit five people and travel 7 ½ hours one-way from Dallas to Manhattan.

To deliver the soldier to his base. The maid of honor to her sister. The cousin to a graduation. The Japanese traveler to his host family.

Because humans are stronger when we work together.

The aftermath

Dayton Brummett with his sister Kaitlyn Ann Wells

Melanie Nguyen with her cousin at his graduation

Sydney Cox as a bridesmaid at her sister's wedding in her purple lace and chiffon full-length dress

Taichi Takano with his host mother on their trip from Kansas to Illinois

I made it to the JEA Headquarters at K-State for the JEA Board Retreat

P.S. Don't even ask about my American Airlines 2802 MHK-DFW OR the American Airlines 2352 DFW-SFO. I thought karma might have worked in my favor. I was wrong.

FLORENCE SRMEK SCHOROW

CLOSE TO FINAL

Here at the senior residence where I live there is a salvation army "event" scheduled once a month. Days before the collection, a corner of the reception room is given over to the accumulation of contributions. The pile of discarded items might include the oversized skillet a resident foolishly brought with her when she moved in, a frayed neck scarf in the garish colors once considered fashionable, six-inch heels in patent leather looking almost new and never worn. In many ways, the pile becomes a symbol for the process of doing away with the non-essential debris of our earlier lives.

What seems to be true for many of us is that there is a gradual stripping away of layers as we enter the final stages of our life's trajectory. Our children grow up, move away, have their own families, grandchildren become immersed in their own lives. Possessions are disposed of as we move from family home to smaller quarters – at one of our children's homes, perhaps, or an apartment, a senior residence, assisted living. With each move we rid ourselves of more items we once thought were essential.

Some of us move more often and at greater distances. I think of the many places where I've lived during my now long life: several homes in Chicago and its suburbs; then Salt Lake City; New York City; an apartment in Connecticut followed by a move to a condominium there when I became more reconciled to living alone. A summers-only waterside cottage in Maine which, after I retired, became an all-year residence with winters in northern California. Later the birth of a beloved grandson was the compelling reason for moving from my beloved Maine to permanent residence in the Silicon Valley. Although I have believed that a move was *final* more times than I can count over the years, the odds are that the Chateau Cupertino will almost certainly be my last home.

Now I live in a sparse two room apartment without so many of the things which, for one reason or another, I once thought were indispensable The dresses and skirts three and four sizes less than I wear now (Keeping those was misplaced optimism of the first order!), the two hats I hadn't worn in thirty years, the half-slips and the full ones too, white gloves, a ski jacket, fur lined boots, long beads, faux pearls, ankle bracelet. Why in the world did I hang on to all that out-sized and out-of-date stuff? Did I think I would really lose all the weight I had gained over the years? Did I think I'd ever learn to ski when I didn't so in Utah where the conditions and my fortitude were both appropriate? Would I even dream of wearing a hat? White gloves? An ankle bracelet?

Two closets in the apartment are more than enough for my wardrobe now with room to spare for the pared down Christmas ornaments and a couple of boxes of photos I have been intending to organize for the past thirty-five years. The "good" pieces of furniture are distributed in my son's and daughter's homes. The pottery, the pewter I once cherished, the chandelier my husband and I carried on the #4 subway from the lower east side to our apartment at 125th Street. It later graced my dining area in two homes in Connecticut and in Maine before installing it in my California condo. Now it "lives" in my daughter's home in Medford, Mass where it looks as if it's always been there.

More wrenching than the stripping away of material objects, of course, is the loss of friends and family but also the iconic events and role models that existed beyond the small circumferences of our lives. We had our first glimpse of raw sexuality in the personalities of Mae West and Carole Lombard. Our first romantic "crush" was on the screen idol – tall, shy, handsome Gary Cooper. We longed for the curves of Betty Grable who, in a revealing bathing suit, turned her head provocatively towards the camera. The only possible President was FDR, the most notorious crook was Al Capone, the greatest national tragedy was the Depression, and the longest war was World War II.

We outlive most of our families, our dentists, our pets. (Oh, Charlie!) Our primary physician suddenly decides to retire at what we consider the tender age of 65. We are shocked when the name Spiro Agnew draws a blank expression when we compare him to – say , Scott Pruitt or Wilbur Ross. We long to turn a dial on the car radio to find a station rather than push an assortment of weird buttons. We won't even mention the mess we encounter when we need a simple answer to a simple question from our bank or our phone company. Most of the time we give up trying to explain, to catch up, to get answers.

And yet.

And yet there's a kind of freedom when we narrow our lives down to its essentials. I'm not sure this would be true for everyone, but I have found that I like doing just what I feel like doing most of the time. More important, I like what I no longer have to do like shopping for groceries, worrying about the snails in the garden, lugging garbage to the dumpster, sending Christmas cards. I do like having more time for reading, learning to be a better Scrabble player, discussing the dismal state of politics at lunch, watching re-runs of favorite PBS shows, even writing little pieces like this one.

The fly in the ointment (and forgive me for using that tired cliché) is that for many of us, the physical disabilities we encounter as we grow old prevent full enjoyment of the new freedom we treasure. No need to go into the dreary list of ailments common to the elderly except to note that there's no magic to living so long. Many of us do not escape the arthritic fingers, the bad backs, the memory loss. We soldier on, however, cherishing those times free of pain and taking delight in just getting out of bed in the morning, free souls – at least for the moment.

AMELIE YUN

ENTITY

Darkness.

All I ever remembered.

But then there was something.

The light at the end of a tunnel, like the tiny bud on the tip of a stem, blossoming, piercing, pristine. Something beautiful emerged from the night.

She was a tiny thing, born in the blank room of a hospital. Her mind was inert at the time, and peaceful. She had the purest complexion I have ever seen. When she slept, her lips curved upward the slightest, as if she had dreams that she would keep secret.

I watched her grow. Her happiness, in the shape of unfurling wings. And other times, her hardships and pain, her tears falling like crystals. The entire world loved her, as one would love a frail child whose beauty was ageless. When she cried, the soil beneath her feet would take in her tears, softening her sadness, relieving her of her worries. The trees whistled a harmonious melody, those that trickled into her mind and rang like the peal of a bell.

I was the juxtaposition of her existence. Not even the pebbles would stir underneath my feet. I would try to soothe her during unimaginably painful times, but I could not be heard, or seen, or even thought of. My only action was to watch, not to speak, which was the life I was exiled to. Sometimes I clutched at my head, screaming at the gods who condemned me to this, and all I would get is silence.

She grew into a young woman, who was nervous and excited for the wonders of the world. Still, her child-like innocence remained, embedding the hearts of the ones around her.

She met a man at a coffee shop. They talked about little things, little hobbies. I could see she was happy. She gave birth to a girl and a boy, some years later, who had her smile and their father's eyes.

And one day, she walked down the wrong path.

It was dark. And cold, and she was shivering while walking toward her warm home. There was a man. A drunkard, with a broken bottle flashing in his hand. The trees and soil weren't there to protect her. There was only me, and in my vast and tiny prison, I could not do anything but watch.

A sea of flowers, with translucent lenses focusing on an ephemeral, exquisite little blossom among them, whose only purpose was to be loved. And me, with translucent lenses, watching, listening, pathetically transfixed on a dot in the universe, whose only purpose was to love another.

Even as she fell to the ground, me screaming, pounding at my invisible barrier, she still looked as she did all those years ago, when I saw her sleeping as a baby, quiet, calm, content. The mind of a ripple-less pond, not yet filled, not knowing, of the wonderful things it would soon contain.

And then, gone.

I brooded over myself. My failures. What I could've done.

But then, I heard the sound of a door unlocking.

I felt her warmth as she embraced me. I felt her hair brushing my cheeks. She disappeared a split second later, with only the shade of the feel of her lingering on my skin.

Where she once stood, a door loomed, wide open, like a blossoming rose, infused with hope and promise. In her death, she still had a soul that could stir the hearts of gods.

In her death, she freed me.

GRAVEYARD OF DREAMS

Do you know of the Graveyard of Dreams?

It's a secret world. It's a rippling world that pave ways for hope, in wispy phoenixes and magic, those that etch markings of dragons in stone walls. It's a spontaneous world where things move around in ways they shouldn't, where they were here but not here, always busy, sparking in and out of existence.

In here, it's a vibrant illogical place. The lake is all full of wonder where giant creatures rise from the water. Strange birds encased in crystal feathers fly through the forest. If you listen closely, you can hear the monsters at night, ones that live in trees.

This is the place where your most guarded, lost, unfulfilled wishes go as they fade. Those little stars called dreams live their last moments in this place, still replaying over and over in their eternal mantra, fading with each rewind. And as they drift off to sleep, their hosts wake, still desperately grasping at the thread-like strands of their fantastical world, that their own consciousness is pushing out. And then, forgotten. In an instantaneous moment, but a moment nonetheless. How quickly bright embers spark out, only leaving an empty, ashen fireplace behind.

But don't cry for these lost children. The Gravekeeper, the guardian of the dying ones, will watch over them as a mother would tend their child. So as their last wispy breath pierces the cold mist, the Gravekeeper will stay by their side until they evanesce out of existence, still encircling their fate, forever.

THE ASTRONOMER

In my world, there are no stars.

No one really knows how it happened, why, or even when. Because when they disappeared, they didn't just die. They blinked out of existence, as if closing the blinds on their windows, accepting their fate of eternal silence. No one really knows if they would appear again.

I think that this event can't really be explained by us humans, with our limited brains made of little particles and chemicals and neurons and meat. Maybe something called those stars, something of an infinitely immense and vast dream, that united them into one moment of space and time, far away from here.

The universe searched frantically when it happened, wondering why or where they've gone. It's glittering gems and necklaces have disappeared, robbed, by a higher purpose. Stripped of its rank and title, the very essence of what defines it, it now calls for them, represented by the beings rooted to Earth. I hear them everyday, their feeble chants praying to a god akin of a receding wave, their voices small and meaningless in the cold, empty world.

And everyday, or every night, I take my telescope into the everlasting darkness, without light to guide me, and only a nick of artificial food gel and a heated jumper. I recognize the path I take, feeling my way through the imperceptible grass underneath my feet, and make my way up to a ridge of a once green hill, with a beautiful frozen meadow behind me, somber and reminding.

I set my telescope onto the ground and suddenly feel a tremendous giddiness I can only describe as a child waiting on the shore, with their toes tucked into the sand and eyes closed tightly, the moment before a low tide threatens to sweep them away. A peal of laughter escapes my throat, and I suck in an icy breath, the juxtaposition of my warm jacket and the sweet cold air sparking a tingling all the way to my toes.

A spray of a cold breeze slaps my face. Staying rooted at my place on top of the hill, I take off my pitch black glasses. My broken eyes are hit with the blast of wind, and the suffocating feeling in my chest lightens and disappears. My free vision is unable to find the eyepiece, but I feel my way to it with my hands. I close one eye and bring my head towards the piece. My fingers knead the focus knob out of habit, and I stare into the glassy frame, making out nothing but everything, alone and empty and infinite in the world.

GUARDIAN OF LOST THINGS

I am a guardian of lost things.

It's a quaint thing to be, centered around a quaint idea. What many of my customers share is the belief that there is always a way of finding lost regrets and passions. Little things, little memories, little ideas swarm around in my possession, ready to be released, rehomed. As if I was a child blowing bubbles in the wind, all the colors and auroras of solitude dance around me. Tiny clear orbs of existence, encapsulated with iridescence, knowing they're lost, find solace in the fact that there is someone who will not let them fade away.

There are various shades of the personalities saddled onto the persons whom find this place, a wide range of ones with eyes of near boredom to ones bordering on an almost animalistic desperation. When these little bubbles and their makers match, there's always a new flavor made between them. I taste all of them, just to check, as if I was a master chef at a five star restaurant. Little buds of sadness, anger, regret; others hopeful, nostalgic, melancholy.

There arrives a customer.

Now, these things cannot be made for a friend, or an errand for a family member. The ones that manage to set foot in my shop are ones driven by primary human need, in need of something they may have lost, or have regretted. I would've known this person is here for a personal errand, even without my little rule. He has a strange taste, like a sharp sweet bitterness. Once swept with bright colors, he has been shaved off; a dull and weary traveler who has no heart to journey on more. Despite his youth, his core is shaded around with that of an aged soul, with wrinkles carved from regret and the sorrow of a disregarded songbird.

"What do you wish to find?"

For a moment, he doesn't say anything. His eyes, vacant, suddenly blink up and look at me, as if he's in a trance, and he was seeing me for the first time. His voice is like a pencil with a broken lead tip, grating and somber, having lost all of his previous charm and grace. He curves his words as if he's been living like this for a long moment, waiting for a chance of a miracle.

"Time."

A pause. Then, repeated.

"I wish to find time."

A strange answer to a simple question. I fold my hands together.

"Then what are you willing to lose?"

He chokes back a dry throat. His eyes become blank again.

"Anything."

From specific tiny points around him, there comes tiny lights that strand themselves into the shape of an orb, as if a bubble was popped in reverse order. A memory flashes through the room. He was lying in a hospital bed, tubes and machines running out of him, as a woman sobbed by his side.

The man in front of me doubles over, and I feel his melancholy in the aroma of a flute melody. "She keeps on forgetting." he mumbled. "We always met at the park near the bookstore, and she thinks that I'll be there again."

With that little bit of information, I form a solid link. A memory that never passed appears around us, timeless, somewhere where nowhere exists. It shows an elderly woman on a park bench, her hands clasped elegantly over her black purse. She seems patient, but waiting for someone.

A new scent, one of mixed memories and new beginnings, forms around us. First it develops a taste of hopefulness, then mixes with a wistfulness that starts to throb into a dear longing. The incandescence of the realities shine, reflected in his wide, starry eyes. I smile at him.

"She was waiting for you for a long time."

In the new memory, I see the elderly woman, poised and expectant, her frail figure twisting slightly, craning her neck to see someone. An old man walks toward her direction, set with purpose, his colors brightened, core pure and ageless.

She stands up. He grasps her hand. "I'm sorry I'm late."

She just shakes her head.

And they fade away, hands held together, until they're washed away in the glowing sunset.

EHTIOPIAN DRAGON

He was a quiet hunter. He waited until it was dark and the ground glowed from the beams of the moonlight. He preferred this, the quietness of everything. He would stay buried underneath the dirt, in a stasis, dormant, during the hours when the sun shone. Regular ones might've gone mad from all this waiting. Every minute frozen would accentuate an itch, a throbbing, and in the end they would burst from the ground, scaring off a flock of birds that rested on the mound. But he didn't. He didn't just tolerate the calmness, he thrived off it.

As you might know, he was a patient beast.

A vibration. His eye shone above the ground, like a crocodile waiting for its prey. His vision was poor, but it gave a more solid image of what he was seeing now, along with his sensors and exceptional sense of smell.

A lone elephant, seemingly distracted. It must be agitated from being separated from its herd. He felt its footsteps trailing along the ground towards him. This was the moment.

A tusk raked up from the ground, and the sand tumbled off his leathery skin like a waterfall. His jaws shot out toward the little creature. He heard screaming. Then silence.

The sun was already starting to rise, as he had waited a long night for his reward. Slowly, he sunk down into his lair, dozing off into a state of immobility.

In an hour, the sun was blistering down onto the measly earth, and the animals of the land started their own routine. Feeding. Killing. Playing. But what they didn't know, and took for granted, was the sleeping, frozen hunter underneath them.

He was a patient beast. And when night shines again, he will be waiting.

ABOUT THE EDITOR

Kaecey McCormick is an author, artist, and educator on a mission to ignite creativity in everyone. She currently lives in the San Francisco Bay Area and was named the 2018-2020 Poet Laureate for the City of Cupertino where she enjoys bringing her mission to life by celebrating creativity in community with others.

Kaecey holds degrees in Anthropology and Psychology from UCLA and the University of Maryland, and an MFA in Writing from Lindenwood University. Her poetic work has won several awards and has been featured in numerous journals and anthologies including recent editions of *Children's Rights Know No Borders, The Red Earth Review, Levee Magazine,* and *The Linden Avenue Literary Journal.* She has also enjoyed serving as judge to various poetry contests. Kaecey's recent chapbook, *Pixelated Tears* (Prolific Press) is currently available, and her full-length book, *The Creativity Blueprint,* is forthcoming from AAE Press in late 2020.

In addition to working as a creativity coach, Kaecey ghostwrites and freelances on a regular basis. When not creating with words, paint, pencils, or whatever she can get her hands on, she enjoys family time with her husband and their four daughters or curling up in a comfy chair with a good book, hot cup of Earl Grey, and her two cats.

Made in the USA
Columbia, SC
23 February 2020